A Florida Indian in the Chace.

From the *Court Miscellany*, 4 (1768), 433.

The American Indian in English Literature of the Eighteenth Century

By
Benjamin Bissell

ARCHON BOOKS
1968

ORIGINALLY PUBLISHED 1925, BY YALE UNIVERSITY PRESS
REPRINTED 1968 WITH PERMISSION
IN AN UNALTERED AND UNABRIDGED EDITION

———————

[Yale Studies in English, Vol. 68]

SBN: 208 00710 5
LIBRARY OF CONGRESS CATALOG CARD NUMBER: 68-9772
PRINTED IN THE UNITED STATES OF AMERICA

PREFACE

The following study was undertaken as a doctoral disser-
tation under the direction of Professor Chauncey Brewster
Tinker, to whom I am indebted for the subject itself, as well
as for encouragement, careful supervision, and many valuable
criticisms. To Professor Albert Stanburrough Cook I also
wish to express my thanks for training in pure research, and
for much sound advice on this and other problems of scholar-
ship. I have also been aided in my work by the officials of
the Yale Library, the Library of Congress, the John Carter
Brown Library, and the New York Public Library.

Sufficient bibliographical information has in all cases been
included in the footnotes, inasmuch as the varied sources of
material made a formal bibliography out of place. First
editions have been consulted, unless a statement is made to
the contrary, and the original spelling has been preserved.

The accompanying illustrations, only a scanty selection
from many others which might well have been chosen,
indicate, better than could be done by words, the æsthetic
conceptions of the Indian—an important factor in determining the literary idealization with which this work is largely
concerned.

Yale University, July 10, 1924.

CONTENTS

ILLUSTRATIONS

INTRODUCTION

The American Indian, as a subject for literary treatment, does not at first sight appear to have made any very great appeal to English writers: of no really first-rate drama, novel, or long poem has he been made the hero. It is rather on the outskirts of literature proper, or in certain forgotten works of minor writers, that the noble savage plays his chief rôle. The significance of the whole subject, therefore, resides not so much in the strictly literary merits of the writings with which we have to deal, as in their relation to some very important tendencies of eighteenth-century thought.

The Renaissance may perhaps be taken as the beginning of a serious inquiry into the authority of tradition, a problem which was to take various forms, and finally come into violent agitation at the end of the eighteenth century. With this whole question the discovery of America is associated in a very vital way. Tradition, or civilization, which is essentially the same thing, could now be viewed in a new aspect—in relation, that is, to primitive nature or savage life. The growing dissatisfaction with civilization which marks the latter half of the eighteenth century—and still persists under changed names in many phases of modernism—was accompanied by a corresponding increase of interest and satisfaction in all that was uncivilized, finally reaching its height in the romanticist's exalted admiration of children, animals, and savages. Hence the literature of the poor Indian or the noble savage, though it offers us nothing in English to compare with the richly imaginative *Natchez* of Chateaubriand, is worthy of a careful study on account of its philosophic import—its connection with sentimental exoticism, and other romantic tendencies.

In order to treat this subject fully, one should, strictly speaking, begin with the discovery of America, and then

follow the course of exotic interest through the literature
of Europe for the next four centuries. My own study,
needless to say, boasts no such ambitious proportions. For
the most part I have restricted my investigations to the
English literature of the eighteenth century, partly because
to do more than this would extend the work beyond the
possibilities of a single study, partly because certain portions
of the general subject have already been covered,[1] and, finally,
because I find within these limits a definite problem, of
which the earlier accounts furnish only an occasional suggestion. In order to construct the background from which
the figure of the romanticized Indian emerged, I have introduced my more formal account of eighteenth-century literary
works by giving a brief survey of some of the earlier histories, descriptions of voyages and travels, and various
miscellaneous writings, which, though seldom treated as
works of literary importance, are nevertheless highly significant, because of the influence they exerted upon men of
letters. After having thus given in my first chapter a kind
of background for the whole subject—the relation of the real
and the idealized Indian, with an analysis of what aspects of
his character were admired, and why—I then proceed to
discuss in more detail certain limited phases of the exotic
movement. Philosophic theories about primitive life, admiration for the uncorrupted state of nature, social satire from

---

[1] I refer especially to Gilbert Chinard's two works, *L'Exotisme
Américain dans la Littérature Française au XVI Siècle* (Paris, 1911) ;
and *L'Amérique et le Rêve Exotique dans la Littérature Française au
XVII et au XVIII Siècle* (Paris, 1913). The first of these works
shows the relation of the Middle Ages to the early conception of
America, the influence of such writers as Thévet and Léry, and the
importance of Montaigne in establishing the belief in a people good
by nature. The second discusses the effect the *Jesuit Relations* had in
perpetuating this idea, and passing it on to the philosophers of the
eighteenth century, and also includes some account of a large number
of other writers who helped to continue the belief in the noble savage.

the standpoint of the Indian, receive extended treatment in chapters 2 and 3. In my last three chapters, which discuss the appearance of the Indian in fiction, drama, and poetry, my aim has been to show to what extent the Indian is consciously or unconsciously idealized, how far his superficially picturesque qualities are admired, and what, if any, is the philosophic significance of such material—its relation to that current of thought and feeling commonly known as the romantic movement. Such material as I have presented, though by no means all that might be accumulated, seems to me fairly representative of the different kinds of interest in the Indian, and the variety of beliefs regarding his nature, condition, and character.

CHAPTER I.

In the earliest views of America there are strong traces of the influence of the Middle Ages. India and China having long been pictured in the light of the delightful, but highly fanciful, descriptions of Marco Polo and other mediæval travelers, the confusion of America with the Indies made natural a transference to the new land of all the marvels and wonders heretofore attributed to the Orient. Another influence of the Middle Ages springs from the belief in an Earthly Paradise,[1] vaguely located far away in the western ocean, with surrounding peoples good by nature— a notion very readily applied to the American natives.[2] Some traces of these mediæval legends appear in the *Decades* of Peter Martyr, a work very popular all over Europe, published at Seville in 1511, translated into French in 1532, and into English in 1555 (in part; completely in 1612). In general, however, there is very little of this influence in the early English accounts, partly perhaps because they were later than the Spanish and Italian, partly also because the voyagers, and those who described their adventures, were men of little education or literary background.

The great period of English maritime discovery and exploration properly begins with the reign of Elizabeth, and is generally associated with the names of Hawkins, Frobisher, Drake, Gilbert, Cavendish, and Raleigh.[3] The accounts of

---

[1] For a discussion of mediæval views of the Earthly Paradise, cf. the *Elene* (ed. Cook) p. lv.

[2] Cf. Chinard, *L'Exotisme Américain*, Introduction; Paget Toynbee, *Romania* 21. 288, 240.

[3] For a concise collection of the accounts of these voyages, cf. E. J. Payne, *Voyages of Elizabethan Seamen* (London, 1893, first series; 1900, second series). My quotations concerning these voyages are from this work.

their voyages are in general of very little interest for any testimony they supply regarding the Indians, either because their contact with the aborigines was relatively slight in whatever places they touched at, or because, with the exception of Raleigh, they were men of little imagination or literary inclination. They seem to be most impressed with the color of the Indian, his strange dress, his beads, feathers, and other striking adornments. It is not surprising that the element of wonder should have played so important a part in these early accounts, especially when we consider the persistency of this type of interest. Even the eighteenth-century travelers, when telling of their meetings with the Indians, seldom fail to note down color, size, and physical appearance, all with as much care and exactness as though these had never been fully appreciated. We note in passing that Sparke's account of Hawkins' second voyage is said to have been the first account of American natives published in English, written by an English eye-witness.[4] It is also curious to observe the early interest in the Indian's religion. Francis Pretty, in his account of Drake's famous voyage, speaks of the Indians of Brazil sacrificing to devils;[5] and Edward Hayes, describing Gilbert's voyage, also shows concern for their spiritual welfare, urging the importance of converting them to Christianity,[6] and deploring their 'paganish religion.' By far the most interesting of all this material is Raleigh's description of Guiana.[7] Here there is a large admixture of the purely fabulous, such as his account of the Amazons, the Indian king covered with gold, his magnificent palace, and

---

[4] Cf. Payne, 1st ser., p. 4.
[5] *Ibid.*, p. 201.
[6] Cf. Payne, 2d ser., pp. 6 ff.
[7] For a study of the El Dorado legend, cf. a work by Ferd. Abd. Junker von Langegg, *El Dorado, Geschichte der Entdeckungsreisen nach dem Goldlande El Dorado im XVI und XVII Jahrh.* (Leipzig, 1888).

other wonders. This may be explained in part by his reading of French and Spanish authors, and in part also by his desire to create a favorable impression, and thus secure support for his enterprises.

Probably something of this same motive of policy was influential in producing the alluring description of the Virginian explorations of Amidas and Barlow, sent out by Raleigh to view the country preparatory to colonization. Barlow, who wrote the account, describes the natives as 'very handsome and goodly,' and 'in their behavior as mannerly and civil as any in Europe.'[8] When the 'king' visits them, they notice the great respect his subjects show him. 'No people in the world carry more respect to their king, nobility, and governors than these do.'[9] They also visit the Indians, and are 'entertained with all love and kindness, and with as much bounty (after their manner) as they could possibly devise. We found the people most gentle, loving, and faithful, void of all guile and treason, and such as live after the manner of the golden age. . . . A more kind and loving people than these cannot be found in the world, as far as we have had trial.'[10]

The above citations are of significance only in showing the general tendency among many of the early voyagers to regard the Indian as being for the most part a simple, harmless sort of being, and in some cases to let their imaginations carry them much further than this, even to the point where America appeared as a primitive Arcadia, inhabited by a gentle, kind, innocent people, living in a veritable golden world. This was of course relatively easy under the influence of such a climate as that of Virginia, a feat much more difficult when the writer's knowledge was restricted to the bleak coasts of New England. One reason, perhaps, why

[8] Cf. Payne, 2d ser., p. 56.
[9] *Ibid.*, p. 59.
[10] Cf. Payne, 2d ser., pp. 62, 63.

the Arcadian imagination of English writers seldom associated its fancies with the newly discovered regions in
America, was the fact that so many of the early settlements
were in regions where such an Elysium could not be conceived as possible. In other words, a tropical element is
essential to the full realization of the Arcadian dream. This
natural background of beautiful scenery and mild climate
was present, in a measure at least, in most of the Spanish
accounts as well as in the earlier French—Léry and Thévet.
Had the English had more contact with the coasts of Florida
or Brazil, and less with New England, it is possible that
such accounts as this of Barlow's might have become more
numerous and influential. Instead of this, the English and
French during the seventeenth and eighteenth centuries were
for the most part limited to acquaintance with the various
tribes of North America, a circumstance which could not
but tend more and more to prevent what we may perhaps
call the tropical exoticism. Not having the background of
a flowery Eden, they tended to admire the Indian for qualities more in keeping with his environment—his stoical
endurance, and his love of freedom.

Many of these early accounts of America reached their
readers through the collections of travel-literature which
became so popular during the sixteenth century. One of
the first of these was that of Ramusio, published at Venice
in 1550-9. A still more important collection was that of
De Bry published at Frankfort in 1590-1634. Like most of
the others, this compilation did not deal exclusively with
America, but included accounts of Asia, Africa, and other
remote places. The original intention of the publishers was
to collect all the existing literature of travel, and give parallel
texts in English, French, and Latin. This plan was soon
abandoned, however, and most of the works appear only in
German and Latin. This collection was known all over
Europe, and became immensely popular, partly, without

doubt, because of the large plates accompanying it. The father and two sons who compiled this were engravers by trade, and used these fanciful descriptions of far-away places as an opportunity for showing their skill in even more fanciful illustrations. These pictures, and others like them, were used again and again during the next two centuries, and are of importance here chiefly because of the influence they had on the æsthetic conception of the Indian. Although there is no slight element of realism in these earliest representations of American natives, a marked tendency developed in the course of the next two centuries to picture the Indians with all the beauty and grace of classical statuary, and, parallel with this, an impulse to transfer the moral qualities of the Greeks, particularly those of the Spartans, to a people generally supposed to resemble them in external appearance. The English collections of Hakluyt and Purchas are so well known that it is merely necessary to mention them. They are important in showing the strong exotic taste of the time, and were of great value in bringing together, and preserving to English readers of the next two centuries, certain early accounts of America which might otherwise have been lost or forgotten.

The sixteenth-century view of America and the Indian, which I have thus roughly sketched, the seventeenth century was to continue and enlarge, chiefly in the direction of a greater realism. Thus far, as we have seen, contact with the Indian was, for the most part, very slight, and the knowledge of his customs and character correspondingly superficial. With the beginning of permanent settlements, however, the Indian began to play a part in the daily lives of the colonists. In the endless stream of histories and descriptions of America, which now began to pour into England, the Indian still appears as the object of much curiosity and wonder, but along with this there is a large amount of realistic detail; enough was now known of his ways to supply picturesque and striking bits of local color. A great variety of subjects appear in the pages of these early historians. Sometimes they relate stories of thrilling adventures with the Indians, narratives of captivity and escape, with an occasional romantic touch, as in the well known story of John Smith and Pocahontas.[11] There is also an interest in the Indian's government and religion, and a great variety of conflicting opinions, but no very great amount of admiration. The notion of his performing religious rites to the devil, or devils, is continued, and the importance of his conversion discussed. Another question much debated was the Indian's origin[12]— was he a part of the human race, from what branch was he sprung, where had he come from, and how did he get to America?—all questions which were taken seriously, and studied with much display of erudition. Some of the historians, such as Mason, Hubbard, and Church, give long accounts of the Indian wars, filled with tales of horror and cruelty. These, and the stories of captivity among the Indians, of which the later seventeenth and eighteenth centuries furnished many examples, probably show the Indian in the worst light—as savage, cruel, revengeful, and bloody. Besides these histories and the various descriptions of travelers, there were a good many tracts and pamphlets issued

[11] The earliest mention of this story is in Captain John Smith's *Generall Historie of Virginia, New England, and the Summer Isles* (London, 1624), p. 49. There have been a number of modern studies of the life of Pocahontas, with attempts to prove and disprove Smith's story. The *Universal Encyclopedia,* under the article on Pocahontas, gives a bibliography of such works.

[12] The question of the Indian's origin provoked the wildest speculations, and an amazing bulk of pseudo-scientific theorizing. Historians and casual observers record many extraordinary similarities between the Indians and other remote nations. Adair, for example, in his *History of the American Indians* (London, 1775), adduces the most elaborate and far-fetched analogies to prove the Indians descendants of the Jews. Many other equally strange theories are to be found in the histories and periodicals of the time.

by the different land-companies, designed to give the reader a favorable impression, and thus encourage colonization. To the general public, however, these were probably of little interest.

To sum up this mass of seventeenth-century testimony, both as regards the points of view and the general influence, we notice, first of all, that the statements here given concerning the Indian's nature and habits are of a very varied character. Many minute observations are recorded, and there is some attempt at explanation, but the result is so warped by preconceived theories, and the writer's own prejudices, that it proves to be neither scientific nor romantic. On the whole, I am afraid that disapproval of the Indian's impiety, and resentment at his cruelty—of which latter some of the writers, it must be remembered, had been the victims or the witnesses—play a larger part than naïve admiration of savage virtues. The immediate influence of all this literature was not very great. Except in special cases, people of the seventeenth century were not deeply interested in the Indian[13]—either as a romantic or an unromantic figure. Among most men of letters the classical influence was too strong to leave much room for exotic feeling. Whatever significant influence these earlier writers had was largely upon others of the same kind during the next century. The qualities of the real Indian had been by 1700 pretty fully set forth, modified, to be sure, by certain distortions and exaggerations. His metamorphosis into the noble savage was gradually to come about during the next hundred years,

---

[13] This statement refers particularly to the North American Indians, in whom there was of course a certain amount of practical interest, manifested by such persons as the trader, explorer, and prospective settler. Romantic interest, if it may be called such, was generally confined to the Indians of Peru or Mexico, stimulated in large measure by Spanish accounts. This point will be brought out more fully in later chapters.

chiefly under French influence.[14]   Let us follow this mysterious evolution.

The real Indian, or, if not the real Indian, at least the unromanticized and unidealized Indian, is nowhere more repulsively, and at the same time vividly, presented than in the stories of captivity, which appeared in such large number from the latter years of the seventeenth century to the end of the eighteenth.   One of the earliest and most popular of these was the narrative of the captivity of Mary Rowlandson.[15]   Judging from her narrative, Puritan prejudice, as much as anything she actually suffered, forms the basis of her aversion to the Indians.   Here is an extract:[16]

> None can imagine what it is to be captivated and enslaved to such atheistical, proud, wild, cruel, barbarous, bruitish (in one word) diabolical creatures as these, the worst of the heathen; nor what difficulties, hardships, hazzards, sorrows, anxieties, and perplexities do unavoidably wait on such a condition, but those who have tried it.

To strengthen the impression thus given, she proceeds to exhaust her store of abusive epithets, directed, it would appear, less against their inhumanity than against their impiety.   Within the next few pages they are spoken of as murderous wretches, bloody heathen, merciless heathen, infidels, wolves, hell-hounds, ravenous beasts, barbarous creatures, pagans, merciless enemies, some of the epithets being repeated a good many times.   Her sufferings from cold and

---

[14] This may be thought of as beginning with Montaigne, whose essays were translated into English by John Florio in 1603. For a discussion of Montaigne's point of view, cf. Chinard's *L'Exotisme Américain.*

[15] Cambridge, Mass., 1682. For the numerous later editions of this work cf. Rich, *Bibliotheca Americana.*

[16] As the early editions of this work are rare, I have made my citations from the account as printed in Charles H. Lincoln's edition of *Narratives of the Indian Wars* (New York, 1913). The following passage is found in the *Preface*, p. 116.

hunger and grief for the death of her child are also told, as well as the horrible and terrifying behaviour of her captors. Thus we are told:[17]

> This was the dolefullest night that ever my eyes saw. Oh the roaring, and singing, and dancing, and yelling of those black creatures in the night which made the place a lively resemblance of hell.

Of considerable importance also is the *Decennium Luctuo-sum*[18] of Cotton Mather, containing, amid a great mixture of other material, some accounts of Indian captivity, taken from various sources, often at first hand. Most of these are filled with examples of wanton cruelty and bloodshed, described in a pompous style, with sentimental appeals to the reader's sympathy for the sufferers, especially the many children who are scalped or have their brains knocked out. Little James Key, a child of four years old, is perhaps one of the most pathetic of these victims:[19]

> This child, lamenting with tears the want of parents, his master threatened him with death, if he did not refrain his tears; but these threatenings could not extinguish the natural affections of a child. . . . It was not long before the child had a sore eye which his master said, proceeded from his weeping on the forbidden accounts; Whereupon, laying hold on the head of the child with his left hand, with the thumb of his right he forced the ball of his eye quite out, therewithal telling him, that when he heard him cry again, he would serve t'other so too, and leave him never an eye to weep withal. . . . This horrid fellow, being provoked, he buried the blade of his hatchet in the brains of the child, and then chopt the breathless body to pieces before the rest of the country.

In the story of Mehitable Goodwin there is a gruesome touch, when an Indian brains a baby before the eyes of its

---

[17] *Ibid.*, p. 121.
[18] Boston, 1699. This is also included in Lincoln's edition, from which my quotations are taken.
[19] *Decennium Luctuosum*, p. 209.

mother, gives her the bloody clothes to wash so that his
child can have them, and then leaves the baby hanging by its
skull on a tree, saying that she can find it again if they come
that way.[20]   The few children who escape from these atrocities owe their good fortune, not to the Indian's clemency,
but to miraculous recoveries from blows and wounds which
should have proved fatal :[21]

> Here, a little girl about seven years old, . . . fell into their
> barbarous hands; they knock'd her o' th' head, and barbarously
> scalped her, leaving her on the cold ground (and it was then very
> cold, beyond what use to be), where she lay all the night ensuing:
> Yet she was found alive the next morning, and recovering, she is
> to this day alive and well; only the place in her skull will not
> endure to be closed up.

Still more remarkable is the account of how they 'struck
an hatchet into the skull of a boy there, even so deep, that
the boy felt the force of a wrench used by 'em to get it out:
. . . He lay weltering a long time in his blood; . . . considerable quantities of his brain came out from time to time,
when they opened the wound; yet the lad recovered, and is
now a living monument of the power and goodness of God.'[22]

An account of the torture and death of Robert Rogers will
perhaps complete this earlier and darker view of the captives'
adventures :[23]

> They stript him, they beat him, and prickt him, and push'd him
> forward with their swords, . . . bid him take leave of his friends;
> which he did in a doleful manner; no pen, though made of an
> Harpies quill, were able to describe the colour of it. . . . [They]
> went behind the fire, and thrust it forward upon the man, with
> much laughter and shouting, and when the fire had burnt some
> while upon him, even till he was near stifled, they pull'd it again
> from him. They danc'd about him, and at every turn, they did
> with their knives cut collops out of his flesh, from his naked

[20] *Ibid.*, p. 210.
[21] *Ibid.*, p. 254.
[22] *Ibid.*, p. 223.
[23] *Ibid.*, pp. 207-208.

limbs, and throw them with his blood into his face. When he was dead, they set his body down upon the glowing coals, and left him tied with his back to the stake; where the English army soon after found him. He was left for us, to put out the fire with our tears!

Other elements of interest, beside the frightful and pathetic, appear in some of these narratives. Stories like that of Hannah Dustan, for example, doubtless owe their popularity to the thrilling adventures of which they are largely made up: to the sense of horror at the Indian's cruelty, there is an additional element of interest in the captive's danger, courage, and final escape. In some of the later accounts, too, where the Indian's motive in taking the prisoners was not so much the gratification of his revenge as the securing of a reward for their return, the hardships endured by the victims are the result of their new mode of life, rather than of the intentional cruelty of their savage captors. Dark and forbidding as these narratives usually appear, they are not entirely disconnected with the idealized Indian of fiction and romance. Compulsory sojourns among the savages, however distasteful in reality, were occasionally pictured as a delightful escape from all that makes civilized life uninteresting or oppressive. Several of these supposed captives relate the hardships which they first experienced, their gradual adoption of the customs of their new companions, and finally their preference for this life of freedom, simplicity, and ease.[24]

[24] Cf. Drake's *Tragedies of the Wilderness* (Boston, 1846) for the story of Alexander Henry, who was captured by the Indians in 1763, or that of Colonel Smith, also a captive during the French and Indian War. Lord Monboddo, in his *Antient Metaphysics* (London, 1784) 3. 212-5, gives an impressive account of how a young British officer was captured by the Indians, and later became very much attached to their way of life. The same narrative also appeared in the *Westminster Mag.* 95 (1784). 377-8, and in the *Universal Mag.* 76 (1785). 26-7.

For a more extended discussion of the whole subject of white persons' living among the Indians, see chap. 2.

However influential these narratives of captivity may have
been, and their popularity in America was certainly considerable, the chief source of general knowledge regarding the
Indian and his ways was provided by a variety of other
sources, in France the famous *Jesuit Relations,* in England
by such works as the letters and journals of travelers in
America, or by the more formal discourses of the historian.
These seemingly different classes of literature in practice,
however, often tended to overlap, because some of the writers
of these histories, Adair and Colden, for example, had
traveled or lived among the Indians, and some of the supposed narratives of travelers, on the other hand, were really
composed from any and every source except the writer's
personal experience.[25] Taken together, these works constitute a very large bulk of printed matter, a curious mixture
of fact and fiction regarding the Indian's character, customs,
and mode of life: sometimes correct observations exaggerated or misunderstood; sometimes novel theories, showing
the writer's imagination or ingenious fancy; sometimes
outbursts in praise of the savage, indicating little knowledge,
but strong opposition to society, and prejudice against all
existing institutions.

The cruelty of the Indians, described, as we have seen,
by so many of their captives, was associated with their perpetual state of war.   Burke says that 'almost the sole occu-
pation of the American [that is the Indian] is war, or such an
exercise as qualifies him for it.   His whole glory consists
in this; and no man is at all considered until he has increased
the strength of his country with a captive, or adorned his
house with a scalp of one of his enemies.'[26] Shocking and

---

[25] Jonathan Carver's *Travels to the Interior Parts of America*
(London, 1778-9) is now thought to be a work of this kind.   On
this point cf. *The Travels of Jonathan Carver.* by E. G. Bourne, in
the *Amer. Hist. Rev.* 2 (1906). 282.

[26] *Account of European Settlements in America* (London, 1757) 1.

inhuman as these practices seem, they were not without picturesqueness, as appears in many of the narratives we are now to consider. Before war was actually begun, there had to be an elaborate preparation, a series of negotiations, councils, speeches, and finally the terrible war-dance. Of this there were many descriptions, Colden's showing perhaps, as well as any, the impressiveness of the whole performance :[27]

> I have sometimes persuaded some of their young Indians to act these dances, for our diversion, and to shew us the manner of them; and even, on these occasions, they have work'd themselves up to such a pitch, that they have made all present uneasy. Is it not probable, that such designs as these have given the first rise to tragedy?

More striking, however, than anything in the preparation or conduct of the war itself were the return home and the treatment of the prisoners. According to many writers, the chief motive in all their fighting, next to revenge, was to secure prisoners to be incorporated into the nation. Hence, after they had all run the gauntlet, a selection was made, some to be tortured at the stake, others to be adopted by those who had lost relatives. It is in connection with these horrible tortures that the Indian is pictured at his worst and at his best. The sufferer's passive and uncomplaining endurance of the most painful torments is a fact enlarged upon by innumerable writers. Lawson, an early historian of Carolina, commenting on this, says :[28]

188 (my citations are from the second edition, 1758). According to the *Cambridge History of English Literature* 11, 431, Edmund Burke revised and contributed to this work, which was probably written by William Burke.

[27] Cadwalader Colden, *History of the Five Indian Nations* (London, 1747), p. 7.

[28] John Lawson, *The History of Carolina* (London, 1714), p. 83 (edition of 1860, Raleigh, N. C.).

> Most commonly, these wretches behave themselves in the midst of their tortures with a great deal of bravery and resolution; esteeming it satisfaction enough to be assured that the same fate will befall some of their tormentors, when they fall into the hands of their nation.

Later writers became more and more impressed with these acts of heroism. Colden speaks of an Indian who went to the torture 'with as much indifference as ever Martyr died at the stake.'[29]   Burke writes as follows:[30]

> What is most extraordinary, the sufferer himself, in the little intervals of his torments, smoaks too, appears unconcerned, and converses with his torturers about indifferent matters. Indeed during the whole time of his execution there seems a contest between him and them which shall exceed, they in inflicting the most horrid pains, or he in enduring them with a firmness and constancy above human.
>
> The constancy of the sufferers in this terrible scene shews the wonderful power of an early institution, and a ferocious thirst of glory, which makes men imitate and exceed what philosophy, or even religion, can effect.[31]

Carver also, after describing the prisoner's suffering in some detail, praises his heroism:[32]

> It is however certain that these savages are possessed with many heroic qualities, and bear every species of misfortune with a degree of fortitude which has not been outdone by any of the ancient heroes of either Greece or Rome.

It would be possible to multiply such passages from the literature of the time, but I shall only give one more, an example of almost unparalleled endurance, related by Adair.[33]

---

[29] *Op. cit.*, p. 136.

[30] *Op. cit.* I. 198-9.

[31] *Ibid.* I. 200.

[32] *Op. cit.*, pp. 341-342.

[33] *History of the American Indians*, p. 392. This account of the Indian's endurance was also printed in the *London Magazine*, 44 (1775). 234. The other magazines of the time also contain such narratives, in many cases reprinted from histories and books of travel.

The victim he describes

underwent a great deal, without shewing any concern; his countenance and behavior were as if he suffered not the least pain, and was formed beyond the common laws of nature. He told them, with a bold voice, that he was a very noted warrior, and gained most of his martial preferment at the expense of their nation, and was desirous of shewing them in the act of dying, that he was still as much their superior, as when he headed his gallant countrymen against them . . . that although he had fallen into their hands . . . yet he still had as much remaining virtue, as would enable him to punish himself more exquisitely than all their despicable, ignorant crowd could possibly do, if they gave him liberty by untying him, and would hand to him one of the red hot gun-barrels out of the fire. The proposal and his method of address, appeared so exceedingly bold and uncommon that his request was granted. Then he suddenly seized one end of the red barrel, and brandishing it from side to side, he forced his way through the armed and surprised multitude, and leaped down a prodigious steep and high bank of the river, dived through it, ran over a small island, and passed the other branch, amidst a shower of bullets from the commanding ground where Fort Moore or New Windsor-garrison stood; and though numbers of his eager enemies were in close pursuit of him, he got to a bramble swamp, and in that naked, mangled condition, reached his own country. He proved a sharp thorn in their side afterward to the day of his death.

What is the significance of all this in the evolution of the noble savage? The dying Indian, deriding his tormentors by telling of his own former cruelties, and defying them to extort any sign of weakness, if not exactly noble according to the best present-day standards, was at any rate a figure much admired by certain writers of the romantic generation,

---

Another account of an Indian who suffered very bravely under torture appeared in the *Weekly Magazine,* 23 (1774). 365. The translation of a passage from Charlevoix describing such an episode was printed in the *London Magazine,* 33 (1763). 459. The *Jesuit Relations* also contain material of this character, and were doubtless influential in spreading this conception of the Indian's heroism.

and the hero of various minor poems, which I shall discuss
in a later chapter.[34]   Mention of the Indian's death-song,
so-called, is included among many accounts of his character,
and must have made a very great appeal to the popular
imagination.   That the Indian's courage was largely passive,
rather than active, a good many writers have pointed out,
but as such it must have been very great, considering the
number of tributes it has received.   One of the most beautiful examples of this sort of heroism is that attributed to the
Mexican emperor, Guatamozin, who, when the Spaniards
under Cortes were torturing him in order to extort more
gold, saw one of his companions about to succumb, said to
him, 'Do you think I lie on a bed of roses?'[35]

From the time of the white man's first contact with the
Indians, there seems to have been a marked interest in his
government, along with a tendency to admire the perfection
of its workings.   This appears in the early Spanish historians of Mexico and Peru.   Acosta,[36] for example, though
not inclined to idealize the Indian in general, would like to
'refute that false opinion many doe commonly holde of them
that they are a gross and brutish people, or that they have
little understanding' and thinks there is no better way to do
this than 'in relating their order and manner, in which they
lived under their owne laws, in which, although they
had many barbarous things, and without ground, yet they
had many others of great admiration whereby wee may

[34] Cf. chap. 6.
[35] An account of this famous episode is contained in William
Robertson's *History of America* (London, 1777), Bk. 5. It is mentioned by many of the Spanish historians; Robertson cites B. Diaz,
Gomara, Herrera, Torquemada.   Dryden made use of this incident
in his *Indian Emperor,* Act 5, sc. 2.   Cf. chap. 5.
[36] Jose de Acosta, *The Natural and Moral History of the Indies*
(Seville, 1590).   This was translated into English in 1604 by Edward
Grimston.   A reprint of this by the Hakluyt Society (London, 1880)
is the version from which my quotations are made.

understand, that they were by nature capable to receive any good instructions: and besides they did in some things passe many of our commonwealths.'[37]   It is to be noted that the point which he and others admired was not a freedom from all restraint, or a state in which every one did as he pleased, but a paternal monarchy, differing from those of Europe not so much in its form as in the success with which it attained its object—the order of society and the happiness of the subjects:

> And without doubt, the affection and reverence this people bare to their Kings Incas, was very great, for it is never found that any one of their subjects committed treason against him, for that they proceeded in their governments, not only with an absolute power, but also with good order and justice, suffering no man to be oppressed. . . . They punished faults rigorously, and therefore such as have any understanding heerof hold opinion that there can be no better government for the Indians, nor more assured than that of the Incas.[38]

This idealization of the Peruvian government is carried even further by Garcilaso de la Vega, the Inca, in whose *Royal Commentaries of the Incas*[39] the traces of the Utopian

[37] Bk. 6, chap. 1.

[38] Bk. 6, chap. 12.

[39] The first part of this work was published at Lisbon in 1609, the second part at Cordova in 1617. It was translated into French in 1633, 1658, and 1672. There was an English translation, very much abridged, by Sir Paul Rycaut, Kt., in 1688. The first part has been translated by Clements R. Markham, and published by the Hakluyt Society in two volumes, vol. 1 in 1869, vol. 2 in 1871. My quotations are from this version. Chinard gives the *Royal Commentaries* some discussion, but the best comment on Garcilaso's influence that I have found is in *The Extraordinary Voyage in French Literature before 1700*, by Geoffroy Atkinson (Columbia University Press, 1920), pp. 19-21. 'The translations of Plato and Plutarch had brought to France the legend of perfect government, but in a haze of departed glory. The story of the Incas, according to Garcilaso, was an account of a modern and almost perfect state. It was in some measure the defense of regulation of the affairs of men by a wise and paternal government.

dream are everywhere evident. Not only are the rulers loved and obeyed, the people peaceful and happy, but everything is accomplished by an application of the principles of nature and reason. The Incas gradually extend their domains, not in order to gain greater power, but with a view of spreading the beneficent doctrine of the natural law. Fighting is in many cases unnecessary to gain the victory, hostile and barbarous tribes submitting when the advantages of this beautiful system are explained to them. I postpone a fuller consideration of Garcilaso to the section in which I discuss the Indian's religion, where his importance is even greater than here. His whole point of view may, I think, be accounted for, partly on the ground of his Indian origin, which naturally makes him favorable to the institutions of his country, and partly on the basis of his classical education. There is much in his picture of the Peruvian commonwealth which suggests the projection of certain elements in the classical tradition, particularly the ideals of Plato, upon the representation of the earlier accounts—those by Acosta, Blas Valera, and others.

The influence of the whole group of Spanish historians must have been very great in England. A good deal of this, to be sure, came through the French, but the early date at which many of these were translated would seem to indicate considerable direct interest. Selections from some of these appeared in the collections of Hakluyt and Purchas. Without attempting any complete list of these translations (many of them, like Rycaut's of Garcilaso, incomplete and inaccurate), I will mention a few of the more important, in order to give some idea of their popularity. Gomara appeared in English in 1578, Acosta in 1604, Oviedo in 1613, Las Casas in 1656 (an adaptation in a work called *The Tears of the Indians*), Cieza de Leon in 1709, Herrera in 1740. Las

In one sense, the idealized community of the Incas was a reproach against existing evils of government and social affairs in Europe.'

Casas, because of his sympathy with the Indians, and opposition to their enslavement, has generally been supposed to have had the most influence upon the later conception of the noble savage, but a careful study would probably bring out as much or even greater influence by Garcilaso. Robertson, in his *History of America*, was, so far as I can make out, the first in England to have a thorough knowledge of this group of writers at first hand.

In tracing the view of the Indian's government as found in English writers, I shall begin with a citation[40] from Strachey's early seventeenth-century account of Virginia, which may possibly show some traces of the point of view we have found in the Spanish historians. The significance of his statements lies in the absence of any mention of savage freedom and liberty, such as we find common in later writers:

> Although the country people are very barbarous, yet have they amongst them such government as that their magistrates for good commanding, and their people for good subjection and obeying, excell many places that would be counted civil.[41]

This notion of an orderly government with some sort of authority is continued into the eighteenth century, and described with a good many details, from which one gathers, despite the many contradictions, that an aged chieftain held sway, surrounded by councillors and warriors. Lawson pictures such a body, in which 'all affairs are discoursed of and argued pro and con, very deliberately (without making any manner of parties or divisions) for the good of the public; for, as they meet there to treat, they discharge their duty with all the integrity imaginable, never looking toward their own interest, before the public good.'[42]

---

[40] William Strachey, *Historie of Travaile into Virginia Britannia* (exact date of publication not known). My quotations are taken from the reprint published by the Hakluyt Society.

[41] P. 69.

[42] *Op. cit.*, p. 317.

Oldmixon, an early eighteenth-century historian, describing the Indians of Virginia, says that they have no written laws, rather naïvely adding,[43] 'neither can they have any, having no letters.' This absence of laws and letters, here perhaps felt to be somewhat of a limitation, was soon to be viewed as a great advantage, because of its insuring universal liberty, and freedom from restraint. Colden speaks of the Five Nations[44] as having 'such absolute notions of liberty, that they allow no kind of superiority of one over another.' The same idea is developed much more fully by various other writers, particularly by Burke in the following passage:[45]

> Liberty, in its fullest extent, is the darling possession of the Americans. To this they sacrifice everything. This is what makes a life of uncertainty and want supportable to them; and their education is directed in such a manner as to cherish this disposition to the utmost. They are indulged in all manner of liberty; they are never upon any account chastised with blows; they are rarely even chidden. Reason, they say, will guide their children when they come to the use of it; and before that time their faults cannot be very great: but blows might abate the free and martial spirit which makes the glory of their people, and might render the sense of honour duller, by the habit of a slavish motive to action. When they are grown up, they experience nothing like command, dependence, or subordination; even strong persuasion is industriously forborn by those who have influence amongst them, as what may look too like command and appear a sort of violence offered to their will.

A somewhat similar glorification of individual liberty is found in this passage from Long:[46]

> The Iroquois laugh when you talk to them of obedience to kings; for they cannot reconcile the idea of submission with the dignity

[43] John Oldmixon, *The British Empire in America* (London, 1708), p. 288.
[44] *Op. cit.*, p. 10.
[45] *Op. cit.* I. 175.
[46] John Long, *Voyages and Travels of an Indian Trader* (London, 1791), p. 30.

of man. Each individual is a sovereign in his own mind; and as he conceives he derives his freedom from the great Spirit alone, he cannot be induced to acknowledge any other power.

In Adair the naturalistic tendency comes out even stronger, with a strong Rousseauistic coloring :[47]

> The equality among the Indians, and the just rewards they always confer on merit, are the great and leading—the only motives that warm their hearts with a strong and permanent love to their country. Governed by the plain and honest law of nature, their whole constitution breathes nothing but liberty.

> Most of their regulations are derived from the plain law of nature. Natures school contemns all quibbles of art, and teaches them the plain, easy rule 'do to others, as you would be done by.'[48]

The above passage, in thus identifying the principle of the Golden Rule with the plain, simple law of nature, clearly shows the influence, if not of Rousseau, at least of Rousseauism, and is a good example of that tendency of romanticism which Professor Babbitt calls the confusion of the supernatural or super-rational with the natural. In many of these accounts of the latter part of the century, naturalism and Rousseauism are clearly to be perceived in the back of the writer's mind. The institutions of society—private property, law, marriage, etc.—are the objects of a veiled attack, when it is pointed out at great length how well the Indians get along with only the guidance of plain, simple nature. I will not go into all these in great detail here, but will conclude this little outline of the Indian's government by a citation[49] from Bartram, where the naturalistic Utopia appears full-blown :

> The constitution or system of their police is simply natural, and as little complicated as that which is supposed to direct or rule

[47] *Op. cit.*, p. 379.
[48] *Ibid.*, p. 429.
[49] William Bartram, *Travels through North and South Carolina, Georgia, East and West Florida, the Cherokee country* (Philadelphia, 1791), p. 494.

the approved economy of the ant and the bee, and seems to be
nothing more than the simple dictates of natural reason, plain to
every one, yet recommended to them by their wise and virtuous
elders as divine, because necessary for securing mutual happiness:
equally binding and effectual, as being proposed and assented to
in the general combination: every one's conscience being a sufficient conviction (the golden rule, do as you would be done by)
instantly presents to view, and produces a society of peace and
love, which in effect better maintains human happiness, than the
most complicated system of modern politics, or sumptuary laws,
enforced by coercive means: for here the people are all on an
equality, as to the possession and enjoyments of the common
necessaries and conveniences of life, for luxuries and superfluities
they have none.

The tendency to admire the Indian's fortitude and love of
freedom, which we have found so pronounced in Burke and
others, received encouragement from the resemblance, partly
real and partly imaginary, between the virtues of the savage
and those of the ancients, the Greeks and Romans, particularly the Spartans. The question of how this notion arose
I shall not attempt to discuss in any detail; for our present
purpose it may be sufficient to observe that this point of view
is implied in many of the statements in the *Jesuit Relations,*
and put forth as a fully developed theory in Lafitau's *Mœurs
des Sauvages Américains comparées aux mœurs des Premiers
Temps* (Paris, 1724). Here the Indian's government, education, and various social institutions are fully discussed, with
elaborate and ingenious argument given to show his resemblance to the Lacedæmonian. Lafitau's influence in England
was probably not very great, but is of some significance in
relation to Burke, who speaks in praise of Lafitau's theories,
and mentions his own indebtedness to the *Mœurs des Sauvages Américains.* Earlier evidences of a similar point of
view may also be found in Colden, chiefly, however, in
scattered comments, rather than in any formal theory. Their
cruelty to prisoners, for example, he compares to Achilles'

treatment of the body of Hector;[50] their incorporation of subject peoples to a similar practice among the Romans;[51] their notions of hospitality to those described by the ancient poets.[52] When the French burned some of their villages, he says that the old sachems, 'like the old Roman senators chose rather to dye than to desert their houses.'[53] In one of their orators he detects a strong resemblance to the busts of Cicero,[54] and when he sees some of them carrying on their exercises, he says :[55]

> On these occasions, the state of Lacedæmon ever occurs to my mind, which that of the Five Nations, in many respects, resembles; their laws, or customs, being, in both, form'd to render the minds and bodies of the people fit for war.

Burke speaks of the hardihood with which they are trained up from childhood,[56] their gravity of deportment,[57] their self-control, their respect for the aged,[58] and their treatment of the dead, 'the tender piety and affection of these poor people toward their departed friends.'[59] He also speaks of the 'games of all kinds which they celebrate upon the occasion, in the spirit of those which the ancient Greeks and Romans celebrated upon similar occasions.'[60] The effect of their funeral games and strange rites he comments on as follows :[61]

> Though amongst these savage nations this custom is impressed with strong marks of the ferocity of their nature; an honour for the dead, a tender feeling of their absence, and a revival of their memory are some of the most excellent instruments for smoothing our rugged nature into humanity.

Different writers find among them various other classic virtues, such as hospitality to strangers, fidelity in friendship, serenity and composure of mind. Lawson says that

[50] *Op. cit.*, p. 5.
[51] *Ibid.*, p. 5.
[52] *Ibid.*, p. 12.
[53] *Ibid.*, p. 33.
[54] *Ibid.*, p.156.
[55] *Ibid.*, p. 13.
[56] *Op. cit.* 1. 168.
[57] *Ibid.* 1. 170.
[58] *Ibid.* 1. 170.
[59] *Ibid.* 1. 185.
[60] *Ibid.* 1. 185-6.
[61] *Ibid.* 1. 186.

they treat us better than we do them, because they always give shelter and food.[62] Rogers points out that they are 'possessed of a surprising patience and equanimity of mind, and a command of every passion, except revenge, beyond what philosophers and Christians usually attain to. You may see them bearing the most sudden and unexpected misfortunes with calmness and composure of mind, without a word or change of countenance.'[63] Of their remarkable friendships he says:[64]

> Each of them, at a certain age, makes choice of some one near about his own age, to be their most intimate and bosom friend; and these two enter into mutual engagements, and are obliged to brave any danger, and run any risk to assist and support each other; and this attachment is carried so far, as even to overcome the fears of death, as they look upon it to be only a temporary separation, and that they shall meet and be united in friendship in the other world, never to be separated more, and imagine they shall need one another's assistance there as well as here.

Although it was principally as an exemplar of Spartan endurance that the Indian was supposed to resemble the Greeks, he was also, in the eyes of many, endowed with something of the grace and polish of the Athenian, particularly in his supposed oratorical powers.[65] Colden accounts

[62] *Op. cit.*, p. 385.
[63] Robert Rogers, *A Concise Account of North America* (London, 1765), p. 212.
[64] *Ibid.*, p. 214.
[65] Besides the speeches recorded in such works as those of Colden, and other histories and books of travel, the magazines also record many examples of Indian oratory. The *Gentleman's Magazine, 25* (1755). 252, contains some highly metaphorical speeches said to have been made by Indian chiefs to representatives of the American colonies at a conference held at Albany in 1754. The editor thinks these cannot fail to be an agreeable surprise to his readers, 'as they contain not only the sense of the Indians on our state of affairs there, but some strains of native eloquence, which might have done honour to Tully or Demosthenes.' These speeches were reprinted in *The Scots Magazine, 17* (1755). 629.

for this ability as the 'natural consequence of a perfect republican government: Where no single person has a power to compel, the arts of persuasion alone must prevail.'[66] He speaks of the study and exercise by which they attain this skill, and tells of the 'grace and manner' they acquire, finally becoming

> very nice in the turn of their expressions . . . as never to offend the ears of their Indian auditory, by an unpolite expression. They have, it seems, a certain *urbanitas,* or *Atticism,* in their language of which the common ears are ever sensible, though only their great speakers attain it.[67]

The beauty of these speeches was supposed to consist chiefly in the metaphors employed, of which there was not much variety, but a certain quaint picturesqueness, as the following will perhaps make clear. Peace is usually figured as a tree, sometimes as a chain, with certain other variations from time to time. Negotiations with the English are the occasion of a good many of these speeches:

> The covenant must be kept; for the fire of love of Virginia and Maryland burns in this place, as well as ours, and this house of peace must be kept clean. . . . We now plant a tree whose top will reach the sun, and its branches spread far abroad, so that it shall be seen afar off; and we shall shelter ourselves under it, and live in peace without molestation.[68]

> You are welcome to this house, which is appointed for our treaties and public business with the Christians; we thank you for renewing the covenant-chain. It is now no longer of iron and subject to rust, as formerly, but of pure silver, and includes in it all the King's subjects, from the Senekas country eastward, as far as any of the great King's subjects live, and southward, from New England to Virginia.[69]

> Though an angry dog has endeavored to bite the chain in pieces, we are resolved to keep it firm, both in peace and war: We now

---

[66] *Op. cit.,* p. 14.
[67] *Ibid.,* p. 14.
[68] *Ibid.,* p. 50.
[69] *Ibid.,* p. 101.

renew the old chain, so that the tree of peace and prosperity may flourish, and spread its roots through all the country.[70]

Some of the other speeches given by Colden show in a rather pathetic manner the Indian's dawning perception of the advances the white man is making in his territory, and the regret he feels for the loss of his hunting grounds.[71] Long gives a similar speech of an Indian to one who would take his lands away from him:[72]

> You are Sugar, for so you are called in our tongue, but you must not have too much sweetness on your lips. All the Oneida Indians say they have heard that you are come under a pretense to get our lands from us; but this must not be, my young warriors will not suffer any Englishmen to settle here.

One of the most famous of these speeches arising from the Indian's mistreatment by the English is that of Logan,[73] the celebrated Mingo chief. Thomas Jefferson is said to have admired this very greatly, and even to have gone so far as to 'challenge the whole orations of Demosthenes and Cicero, and of any more eminent orators, if Europe has furnished more eminent, to produce a single passage superior to the speech of Logan.' The circumstances of this speech were as follows: Though Logan had 'long been distinguished as a friend of the whites,' his family was cruelly murdered by one Colonel Cresap,' a man infamous for the many murders he had committed on those much-injured people. This led to a war, in which the Indians were

---

[70] *Ibid.,* p. 125.

[71] An interesting example of this type of speech is contained in Johnson's *Idler,* No. 81 (Nov. 3, 1759). The same speech also appeared in the *London Magazine,* 28 (1759). 580. A poetical version of the same was published in the *Gentleman's Magazine,* 35 (1765). 526. Cf. chap. 6. *The Scots Magazine,* 38 (1776). 287, also prints an old Indian's speech of complaint on the treatment of the whites.

[72] *Op. cit.,* p. 173.

[73] Cf. *Universal Mag.* 83 (1778). 181. A poem in which Logan is mentioned I discuss in chap. 6.

defeated, and sued for peace. Logan, however, 'disdained to be seen among the suppliants,' but sent the following speech by a messenger:

> I appeal to any white man to say if ever he entered Logan's cabin hungry, and he gave him not meat; if ever he came cold and naked, and he clothed him not. During the course of the last long and bloody war, Logan remained idle in his cabin, an advocate for peace. Such was my love for the whites, that my countrymen pointed as they passed, and said, *Logan is the friend of white men.* I had even thought to have lived with you, but for the injuries of one man. Colonel Cresap, the last spring, in cold blood, and unprovoked, murdered all the relations of Logan, not sparing even my women and children. There runs not a drop of my blood in the veins of any living creature. This called on me for revenge. I have sought it; I have killed many; I have fully glutted my vengeance. For my country, I rejoice at the beams of peace; but do not harbour a thought that mine is the joy of fear. Logan never felt fear. He will not turn on his heel to save his life. Who is there to mourn for Logan? Not one.

The funeral speeches show in some cases a simple dignity which is quite touching. Carver, describing their manner of burial,[74] says that the relatives stand around the body, and make a speech to the following purport, which in the Indian language is 'extremely poetical and pleasing':

> You still sit among us, Brother, your person retains its usual resemblance, and continues similar to ours, without any visible deficiency, except that it has lost the power of action. But whither is that breath flown, which a few hours ago sent up breath to the Great Spirit? Why are those lips silent, that lately delivered to us expressive and pleasing language? Why are those feet motionless that a short time ago were fleeter than the deer on yonder mountains? Why useless hang those arms that could climb the tallest tree, or draw the toughest bow? Alas! every part of that frame which we lately beheld with admiration and wonder, is now become as inanimate as it was three hundred winters ago. We will not, however, bemoan thee as if thou wast

[74] *Op. cit.,* pp. 399-400.

for ever lost to us, or that thy name would be buried in oblivion; thy soul yet lives in the great country of Spirits, with those of thy nation that are gone before thee; and though we are left behind to perpetuate thy fame, we shall one day join thee. Actuated by the respect we bore thee whilst living, we now come to tender to thee the last act of kindness it is in our power to bestow: that thy body might not lie neglected on the plain, and become a prey to the beasts of the field, or the fowls of the air, we will take care to lay it with those of thy predecessors who are gone before thee; hoping at the same time, that thy spirit will feed with their spirits, and be ready to receive ours, when we also shall arrive at the great Country of Souls.

This speech has a peculiar interest from the fact that Schiller drew on it for his *Nadowessiers Todtenlied,* regarded by Goethe as one of his best poems.[75] Another speech given by Carver, quite as beautiful in some ways, is the lament of an Indian mother for her dead child. He describes how each evening she came to the foot of the tree, 'on a branch of which the bodies of her husband and child were laid, and after cutting off a lock of her hair, and throwing it on the ground, in a plaintive, melancholy song bemoaned its fate:'

If thou hadst continued with us, my dear Son, would she cry, how well would the bow have become thy hand, and how fatal would thy arrows have proved to the enemies of our bands. Thou wouldst often have drank their blood, and eaten their flesh, and numerous slaves would have rewarded thy toils. With a nervous arm wouldst thou have seized the wounded buffalo, or have combated the fury of the enraged bear. Thou wouldst have overtaken the flying elk, and have kept pace on the mountain's brow with the fleetest deer. What feats mightest thou not have performed, hadst thou staid among us till age had given thee strength, and thy father had instructed thee in every Indian accomplishment![76]

[75] For some account of this poem and the various English translations of it, cf. *The Travels of Jonathan Carver,* by E. G. Bourne, *Amer. Hist. Rev.* 2 (1906). 287. Bulwer-Lytton has a poem based on this, called *The Indian Death Dirge.*
[76] *Op. cit.,* p. 406.

The Indian as an orator seems naturally associated with the kindred conception of the Indian as a poet. Without going into this fully here, it seems fitting to mention a few of the songs of love and war found in this group of writers. Timberlake says that they have a 'loose kind of poetry,'[77] and tells of one of the Indians whom he took to England singing a dirge to thank God on his arrival. Long gives an example of a marriage-song, showing some poetic beauty :[78]

> It is true I love him only whose heart is like the sweet sap that runs from the sugar tree, and is brother to the aspin leaf, that always lives and shivers.

The most famous of all this poetry is that attributed to Yariza, 'an Indian maid of the royal line of the Mohawks.' Her *Letter to the Ladies of New York,* together with a group of Indian Songs of Peace,[79] was published at London in 1754, with *The Speech of a Creek Indian, against the Immoderate Use of Spirituous Liquors.* The letter is full of the most flowery figures of speech, as the following paragraph will illustrate:

> May each of you have, in your habitations, a fair shrub, or little tree, as a family tree of peace, to bless your dwellings. May the exhalations from it be, as the sweet odours of incense to gladden your apartments, or as the leaves of the sweetest trees in the forest, when the vernal morn lifts her glistening forehead from the great lake, and darts the splendors of her eyes aslant the dewy earth. Let no rude sounds of discord or disquiet be as a blighting wind, to wither the leaves of, this family-tree; no distress or distrust, like a thick fog, cast an unkindly mildew to taint them; but may the husband's eyes, like the sunbeam, cheer its roots, and the woman's voice, as a gentle breeze, fan its branches and expand its swelling buds. Let her draw deep into her breast the balsam of its effluence, and her lips breathe forth

---

[77] *Memoirs of Lieut. Henry Timberlake* (London, 1765), p. 55.
[78] *Op. cit.,* p. 113.
[79] A selection from this appeared in the *Town and Country Magazine* for 1780, p. 456; also in the *Monthly Review,* 10 (1754). 291.

and improve the fragrance. Thus, with purest flame, the fire of concord shall glow unextinguished upon your hearth, and domestic bliss shall every day add fresh fuel to encrease its strength.

The second of the songs of peace, which Yariza is supposed to sing, is of interest for its elaboration of the familiar metaphor, the tree of peace:

O tree of Paradise, shoot high!
Thy top, ambitious, climb the sky;
Thy vernant boughs still onward spread,
Till all the happy globe they shade.

May ev'ry bird of sweetest note,
Frequent thy shade, and pour its throat;
Rejoice the song of peace to join,
And tune its warbling voice to mine.

Come too, ye deers and tender fawns,
Ye younglings sporting o'er the lawns,
And bounding as you come along,
As sharing in the dance and song.

But hence, far hence, each savage beast,
Whose fell delight is prey and waste,
Monsters of war! No wolf come here,
Nor yet the panther, nor the bear.

O savage war! well may we see,
That rage and death belong to thee;
Like some fell tyger, bath'd in gore,
Eternal fury thou hast swore.

But thou, O Peace, of heav'nly mind,
Art ever gentle, ever kind,
As is the soft ey'd turtle dove,
That cooes in music, breathes in love.

By thee our hearts are eas'd from strife;
And now we'll sooth and polish life:
For why should others us excel,
In softer arts and living well?

What tho' the olive hue be ours?
All virtuous souls boast kindred powers;
As birds of different dye rejoice,
The listening groves with rival voice.

The question of the nature of the Indian's religion was
the subject of a great deal of speculation, much of it so
exceedingly curious and fine-spun that an attempt to give
a concise analysis of it presents many difficulties. Here
again we must begin with the Spanish historians. Acosta,
though in general quite favorable to the Indians, in discussing
their religion naturally shows something of the prejudices
of his age and country. He admits that the Peruvians
acknowledge a 'supreme Lord and Author of all things,'[80]
and that the Mexicans also admit the existence of this being,
but combined with this is a great deal of idolatry. Like the
other pagans (the Greeks), he says, although they acknowledge one supreme God, it is hard to root from their minds
the belief in other gods. The Mexicans, who worship idols,
are viewed in a much worse light than the Peruvians, who
pay their devotion to the works of nature—the sun, the
thunder, the stars, etc. In their worship he finds a greater
excess than in that of the Greeks or other Gentiles, because
'they did worship all things in nature which seemed to them
reasonable and different from the rest, as acknowledging
some particular deitie.'[87]

This notion that the peoples who had not received the
light of the Christian revelation were all in much the same
sort of idolatrous ignorance was characteristic of the age,
and is rather curiously illustrated in a play of Lope de
Vega's:[82] here the Indians are represented as singing hymns
to Phœbus and Diana, Lope's point of view being, like that

---

[80] *Natural and Moral History of the Indies,* Bk. 5, chap. 3.
[81] *Ibid.,* Bk. 5, chap. 5.
[82] *El Nuevo Mundo,* Act 2. This point is mentioned by C. B.
Tinker, *Nature's Simple Plan,* p. 73, note.

of Acosta, that the Mexicans and the Greeks were alike pagan idolaters, and must therefore have had many beliefs and ceremonies in common.   In all this idolatry and human sacrifice, of which he gives very elaborate descriptions, Acosta sees only the hand of the Devil, and therefore does not attribute it to the natural wickedness of the Indians. Most astonishing of all is the number of Christian practices, or imitations of these, which he finds among them.   One might perhaps suppose there would be some expression of approval at the Indian's having such sound Catholic observances as baptism, fasting, penance, confession, and communion, but instead he sees in all this only the machinations of the Devil, who has taken this means—seemingly a rather strange one—of securing honor and glory for himself.

By far the most poetic account of the Indian's religion is that of Garcilaso de la Vega, full of reminiscences of both the classical and Christian traditions, and at the same time surprisingly free from the prejudice of his age.   The origin of the Incas, and hence the foundation of both government and religion, is clothed in a beautiful myth.   In the early days the Peruvians lived in a state of great barbarism, until their Father, the Sun, having compassion on their unfortunate condition, sent his son and daughter to reform their morals, and teach them the laws of nature—a legend which, in Garcilaso's version, seems to me to suggest the influence of the Christian doctrine of the Incarnation.   (Garcilaso appears to have been at all times a firm Catholic.)   'When you have reduced these people to our service,' he says, 'you shall maintain them in habits of reason and justice, by the practice of piety, clemency and meekness, assuming in all things the office of a pious father towards his beloved and tender children.'[83]   He goes on to relate how these children of the Sun were placed in Lake Titicaca, founded the city of Cuzco, and became the first Incas.

[83] *Op. cit.*, Bk. I, chap. 15.

The religion of the Incas was, like their government, founded on the law of nature and reason. Even the existence of God is proved by abstract reason, as is shown in the following argument, ascribed to one of the Incas:[84]

> I tell you then that our father the Sun must have another Lord more powerful than himself, who orders him to make this journey day by day, without resting. If he were supreme Lord he would occasionally go aside from his course, or rest for his pleasure, even though he might have no necessity for doing so.

This belief in a vague, unknown, and unknowable power behind all things in the universe, a point of view having much in common with that of the deist and the pantheist, leads to a very pure form of worship, the worship of the heart:[85]

> Besides adoring the Sun as a visible God, . . . the kings Incas, . . . who were philosophers, sought by the light of nature for the true supreme God our Lord, who created heaven and earth. . . . They called him Pachacamac, . . . He who gives animation to the universe, . . . He who does to the universe what the soul does to the body. . . . They held Pachacamac in much greater inward veneration than the Sun, for they did not even take the name of the former in their mouths. . . . When the Indians were asked who Pachacamac was, they replied that he it was who gave life to the universe and supported it; but that they knew him not, and that for this reason they did not build temples to him, nor offer him sacrifices. But they worshipped him in their hearts (that is mentally) and considered him to be an unknown God.

Such views as these—surprising enough, however they be regarded—readily suggest some connection with the deistic philosophy of the eighteenth century, a fascinating problem for investigation, but obviously outside the limits of this study.

The earlier English writers also at times reflect a point

[84] *Ibid.*, Bk. 9, chap. 10.
[85] *Ibid.*, Bk. 2, chap. 2.

of view toward the Indian's religion similar to that of Acosta, who may, I think, be taken as fairly representative of the Spanish historians. Strachey, for example, thinks that they worship the Devil, but have some knowledge of the true God :[86]

> All things they conceave able to doe them hurt beyond their prevention, they adore with their kind of divine worship, as the fire, water, lightning, thunder, our ordinance pieces, horses, etc.; but their chief God they worship is no other, indeed, than the divell, whome they make presentments of, and shadow under the forms of an idoll, which they entitle Okeus, and whome they worship, as the Romans did their hurtful God Vejovis, more for feare of harme then for hope of any good; . . . the great God (the priests tell them) who governs all the world, and makes the sun to shine, . . . they call Ahone; the good and peaceable God requires no such dutyes nor needes to be sacrificed unto, for he intendeth all good unto them, and will doe noe harme, only the displeased Okeus, looking into all men's accions, and examining the same according to the severe scale of justice, punisheth them with sickness, beats them, etc.

Strachey expatiates on their various idolatries, probably borrowing from Acosta, whom he acknowledges in at least one place.[87] The same notion of the two kinds of spirits, one good and one bad, is found, with various modifications, in numerous other writers, well down into the eighteenth century. Lawson tells how the bad spirit punishes them with evil and sickness, but the good spirit teaches them hunting and fishing, and gives them the fruits of the earth. They do not believe that God punishes any man either in this life, or in that to come; but that he delights 'in doing good.'[88] Oldmixon, speaking of the Indians of New England, says that 'they had no notion of religion or God, they worship'd a certain Devil but not with solemnity or regular rites.'[89]

[86] *Op. cit.*, pp. 82-83.
[87] *Ibid.*. p. 44.
[88] *Op. cit.*, p. 343.
[89] *Op. cit.*, p. 100.

In the later accounts there is, in general, less about idolatry and worship of the devil, and more about the Great Spirit (as he came to be called), who is sometimes pictured in a pantheistic light, with many poetic touches. Colden says that they have no kind of public worship, or any word to express the idea of God, but 'use a compound .word, signifying the preserver, sustainer, or master of the universe.'[90] Burke has a good deal to say about their superstitions, but says that some of them 'entertain better notions; they hold the existence of the Supreme Being, eternal and incorruptible, who has power over all.'[91] Timberlake adds to all this the idea of free thought in all religious matters, showing perhaps the influence of Charlevoix, Lahontan, and other French writers:

> As to their religion, every one is at liberty to think for himself; whence flows a diversity of opinions amongst those that do think, but the major part do not give themselves that trouble. They generally concur, however, in the belief of one superior Being, who made them, and governs all things, and are therefore never discontented at any misfortune, because they say the Man above would have it so.[92]

Robertson, in discussing the religion of the Peruvians and the Mexicans, draws a good deal from the Spanish historians, but in dealing with the North American tribes his point of view is quite different. His criticism of the idea of the Indians worshipping a Great Spirit shows a good deal of penetration and anti-romantic good sense. 'These ideas,' he says, 'are faint and confused, and when they attempt to explain them the word "spirit" has a meaning very different from that in which we employ it.'[93]

In Carver, and other writers of the latter part of the century, there is a great deal about the goodness and beneficence of the Great Spirit, who 'neither wishes nor is able to do

[90] *Op. cit.*, p. 16.
[91] *Op. cit.* I. 173.

[92] *Op. cit.*, p. 63.
[93] *Op. cit.*, p. 384.

any mischief to mankind,'[94] with some picturesque descriptions of their worship. Carver describes meeting a young Indian 'prince' going to the Falls of St. Anthony. Here the prince offers a prayer to the Great Spirit, and as an offering throws pipe, tobacco, bracelets, and other valuables into the falls, upon which Carver makes the following comment:[95]

> I was greatly surprised at beholding an instance of such elevated devotion in so young an Indian, and instead of ridiculing the ceremonies attending it, as I observed my Catholic servant tacitly did, I looked on the prince with a greater degree of respect for these sincere proofs he gave of his piety; and I doubt not but that his offerings and prayers were as acceptable to the Universal Parent of mankind, as if they had been made with greater pomp, or in a consecrated place.

A similar ceremony is described by Long as taking place on a high rock at the entrance to Lake Superior. Their deep humility and entire dependence on a higher power he viewed as even superior to the Christian's attainments in these virtues. Our own good fortune, he says, 'we are too apt to impute to our own wisdom, and to attribute the escape from dangers we have experienced, or the hope of deliverance which we form, entirely to our own sagacity and foresight.' In contrast with our presumption mark the humility of the Indian:[96]

> The Indians, on the contrary, think more properly, they say it is the Master of Life from whom we derive that presence of mind which has extricated or procured us relief. To the Master of Life the Indian addresses himself even for his daily support.— To him he imputes his victories and his successes, and when subdued, and fastened to the stake, he thanks him for giving him courage to open his veins.—It is this confidence which enables him to bear the severest tortures with composure, and in the height of anguish, to defy the utmost malice of his enemies.

[94] *Op. cit.*, p. 382.
[95] *Ibid.*, p. 68.
[96] *Op. cit.*, p. 139.

CHAPTER II.

The impulse to live among the savages, so frequently alluded to by writers in the latter part of the century, will be discussed first of all in connection with such persons, if there were any, who actually made this daring and picturesque social experiment. Convenience, however, rather than sentiment or philosophy, was doubtless the original ground on which this novel mode of existence was adopted. Many instances of traders and others marrying among the Indians, and finding the life there to their taste, could readily be found, proving little more than that the easy indolence of such an existence was sufficient with some to make up for any inconvenience it may have occasioned. Lawson's account of the happiness resulting from these Indian marriages may perhaps be taken as fairly representative. 'We often find,' he says, 'that English men, and other Europeans that have been accustomed to the conversation of these savage women, and their way of living, have been so allured with that careless sort of life, as to be constant to their Indian wife, and her relations, as long as they lived, without ever desiring to return again amongst the English, although they had very fair opportunities of advantages amongst their countrymen; of which sort I have known several.'[1] Somewhat later, 1766, we find an account of eighteen young white women taking young Indian chiefs for husbands,[2] and the year fol-

[1] *Op. cit.,* p. 302.

[2] In the *Scots Magazine,* 28 (1766). 218, appears the following statement: 'London, April 5. By letters from Fort Johnson we learn, that eighteen young white women have lately been married to as many young Indian chiefs; and that Sir William Johnson gives all possible encouragement to intermarriages with the Indians, which has long been practiced by every other nation in America but the English.' For a fuller account of Sir William Johnson and his relations with the Indians, cf. Parkman's *Montcalm and Wolfe* 1. 172-4, 390-3.

lowing forty others making a similar choice, from which circumstances the reader is at liberty to draw his own conclusions as to the part played by sentiment or expedience. The superiority of the savage life seems somehow to receive additional support when it is brought out that although the European frequently prefers to remain among the Indians, the reverse is never the case. Such passages as the following from Pehr Kalm illustrate what many admirers of the Indian had asserted: the white man who has lived in the forest longs to return there, so that neither tears, entreaties, nor material advantages can again bind him to the unwelcome burdens of civilization; the Indian, on the other hand, if he by any chance has lived in a community of Europeans, is by no means satisfied with his condition; he still prefers the freedom of the woods:[3]

> It is likewise remarkable, that a great part of the people they had taken during the war and incorporated with their nations, especially the young people, did not choose to return to their native country, though their parents and nearest relations came to them and endeavoured to persuade them to it, and though it was in their power to do it. The licentious life led by the Indians, pleased them better than that of their European relations; they dressed like the Indians, and regulated all their affairs in their way. It is therefore difficult to distinguish them, except by their colour, which is somewhat whiter than that of the Indians. There are likewise examples of some Frenchmen going amongst the Indians and following their way of life. There is on the contrary scarce one instance of an Indian's adopting the European customs; but those who were taken prisoners in the war, have always endeavoured to come to their own people again, even after several years of captivity, and though they enjoyed all the privileges, that were ever possessed by the Europeans in America.

More significant, however, in connection with the currents of eighteenth-century thought is the experiment of one

---

[3] *Travels into North America* (English translation, London, 1770-71) 3. 153-4. A similar statement is made by Colden, pp. 203-4.

Priber,[4] who tried to establish a Utopia among the Cherokee Indians of South Carolina. Affectation, or the desire for novelty, qualities common among so many of the later admirers of the savage state, appear not to have been the guiding motives in the case of Priber. For many years he had aimed to establish a communistic republic, with complete freedom and equality, even to the abolition of marriage and other social obligations, and, having failed of his purpose in both France and England, he had, in the year 1733, come to the forests of America to make his great experiment. He chose for the scene of his ideal commonwealth the principal Cherokee town, Great Tellico, and there set about forming a confederation of all the southern Indians, which he called the 'Kingdom of Paradise.' Surprising as it may seem, he appears to have made some headway in carrying out this remarkable project. First of all, he tried to gain the Indian's good will by adopting their ways. 'Being a great scholar he soon made himself master of their tongue, and by his insinuating manner indeavoured to gain their hearts, he trimm'd his hair in the Indian manner and painted as they did going generally almost naked except a shirt and a flap.' General Oglethorpe described him as a 'very odd kind of man,' one who, 'ate, drank, slept, danced, dressed and painted himself, with the Indians, so that it was not easy to distinguish him from the natives.'

After having gained the Indians' confidence, he taught them the use of weights and measures, and also tried to show them the importance of preserving their liberties by retaining the possession of their lands. Something of his influence over them may be inferred from the fact that 'he easily formed them into a nominal republican government—

---

[4] In this sketch of Priber and his Utopian venture, I make no claim to originality, having taken all my material from a study by Verner W. Crane, 'A Lost Utopia of the American Frontier,' *Sewanee Review*, 27 (1919). 48-61.

crowned their old Archi-magus, emperor, after a pleasing
new savage form, and invented a variety of high sounding
titles for all the members of his imperial majesty's red court,
and the great officers of state; which the emperor conferred
upon them, in a manner according to their merit. He
himself received the honourable title of his imperial majesty's
principal secretary of state, and as such he subscribed himself,
on all the letters he wrote to our government, and lived in
open defiance of them.'

How far Priber succeeded in realizing this Utopian form
of society, where all was to be according to the law of nature,
would be difficult to determine from any accounts that have
come down to us. At all events, the failure of his scheme
came not, as one would expect, from internal dissensions,
but rather from external interference. The white settlers,
blind to the lofty aims of the social reformer, but keenly
alive to the complications that might arise from a successful
Indian federation—associated in their minds with the
imperial ambitions of the French, and the intrigues of the
Jesuits—set about the capture of the man who was causing
all the mischief. But this proved not so easy, as the man
found who was sent to seize him in the town-house of Great
Tellico. The fidelity of his Indian friends was a factor to
be reckoned with. 'One of the head warriors rose up, and
bade him forbear, as the man he intended to enslave was
become a great beloved man, and become one of their own
people.' Not long after, however, under other circumstances, the English effected his arrest, and he died in prison,
his social experiment frustrated, and the book he was to have
published (then in manuscript) probably destroyed at the
same time.

Although the 'Kingdom of Paradise' was, as Professor
Crane calls it, only a 'lost Utopia' of the American frontier,
it is nevertheless highly significant in its relation to the whole
eighteenth-century current of philosophic exoticism and
social idealism. It is of course impossible to mention social

or political tendencies of the period that preceded the French Revolution without thinking of Jean Jacques Rousseau;[5] and while it is obviously outside my present purpose to give any extended account of Rousseau or Rousseauism, it is necessary to point out briefly his influence in developing the cult of the noble savage.

First of all, it cannot be maintained that Rousseau in any sense invented the noble savage: what he did was rather to popularize and give philosophic explanation to a conception already, as it were, in the air, a notion familiar to the public of his time, and half believed, by some at least, to have its foundation in reality. Rousseau's contribution to the movement was not, indeed, in any new praises of savage virtue (he did not of course pretend to have any first-hand knowledge of them), but rather in the formulation of a plausible, if somewhat striking and paradoxical, philosophic theory to account for phenomena already noted by innumerable writers on America.

Had not Montaigne, the Jesuit fathers, and innumerable poets, philosophers, and romancers, all, amid many contradictions to be sure, sung the praises of the brave and generous Indian, roaming free in his native wilds, uncontaminated by the vices and follies of European society? But how was this to be reconciled with the authority of tradition—the Christian revelation, the doctrine of original sin, and other beliefs essential to virtue and happiness?

The Jesuits[6] had pictured the Indian as endowed with the most splendid 'natural' virtues: had he not the fortitude of the martyr? did he not despise worldly possessions as much

---

[5] For an extended discussion of Rousseau's supposed primitivism, with an attempt at exact analysis of his social theories, the reader is referred to an article by Lovejoy in *Modern Philology* for Nov., 1923, pp. 165-186.

[6] Chinard discusses the Jesuit accounts of the Indians in *L'Amérique et le Rêve Exotique,* particularly pp. 122-150.

as did ever saint or ascetic? All that was needed to complete these natural virtues was the supernatural grace of the Christian religion. But if the Indian already possessed in eminent degree all the virtues of the heroes of antiquity—courage, fidelity, generosity—and was therefore, on the whole, considerably better than the average Christian, the logical inference from such premises was the sufficiency of natural virtue and the relegation of the idea of a supernatural means of grace to a position very much in the background.

At this point the theories of Rousseau come into prominence—not that his connection with American exoticism is quite so obvious or conscious as this brief sketch would seem to imply. Indeed it is doubtful just how far he had the American Indians in mind at all.[7] Chinard holds that his praise of the state of nature was some sort of reflection from his early reading of such writers as Charlevoix, Lafitau, and the Jesuit fathers, but it is difficult to say just how far there is any direct connection between his reading of particular authors and the development of his revolutionary theories. Strictly speaking, the pure state of nature, even in the mind of its great originator, is recognized as little more than a philosophical abstraction—'a state which no longer exists, perhaps never did exist,' but of which, nevertheless, it is necessary to 'have true ideas, in order to form a proper

---

[7] In a footnote in the *Discours sur les Sciences et les Arts* (1750), Rousseau says: 'Je n'ose parler de ces nations heureuses qui ne connaissent pas même du nom les vices que nous avons tant de peine à réprimer, de ces sauvages de l'Amérique dont Montaigne ne balance point à préférer la simple et naturelle police, non seulement aux lois de Platon, mais même à tout ce que la philosophie pourra jamais imaginer de plus parfait pour le gouvernement des peuples. Il en cite quantité d'examples frappants, pour qui les saurait admirer: "Mais quoy! dit il, ils ne portent point de hault de chausses." ' In the development of his social theories, however, Rousseau makes very few direct references to the American Indians. He refers to various peoples remote in time and place, but usually speaks of the savages in a very general way.

judgment of our present state.'[8]   But at this point creeps in what Professor Babbitt would call the fundamental error of the whole romantic school of thought—the confusion of the ideal and the real. The state of nature, which 'perhaps never did and probably never will exist,' is first of all given a kind of shadowy existence in the remote past, the obvious advantage in so vague a location being, of course, the free rein given to the imagination for describing a set of conditions altogether at variance with the observations and experience of every one.   History and common knowledge alike prove man to be a very bad sort of creature; prehistory, however, may, with slight fear of detection, picture a race of beings free from all corruption, in every way good by nature.   Thus, having first confused the ideal and the real in remote antiquity, Rousseau, and, one might add, the Rousseauist, increases the confusion by bringing it down to his own time, locating it in various far-away regions of the earth.   The pure state of nature, to be sure, no longer exists, but an approximation to the ideal may be found among savages.   True, certain generally accepted facts would seem to contradict this—pity has been made the basis of natural goodness, and the savages are notoriously cruel—but this is not, as one might perhaps too hastily conclude, from any defect of natural goodness ('nothing is more gentle than man in his primitive state') ;[9] rather is this, and any other fault the savage may exhibit, to be charged to the general corruption of modern times, the universal defection from

---

[8] Preface to the *Discours sur L'Origine et les Fondements de L'Inégalité parmi les Hommes* (1754) 'car ce n'est pas une légère entreprise de démêler ce qu'il y a d'originaire et d'artificiel dans la nature actuelle de l'homme, et de bien connaître un état qui n'existe plus, qui n'a peut-être point existé, qui probablement n'existera jamais, et dont il est pourtant nécessaire d'avoir des notions justes, pour bien juger de notre état présent.'

[9] *Discours sur L'Origine de L'Inégalité parmi les Hommes*, seconde partie.

primitive innocence, which even the noble savage has not wholly escaped. Describing this primitive society, Rousseau says:[10]

> Thus, though men had become less patient, and their natural compassion had already suffered some diminution, this period of expansion of the human faculties, keeping a just mean between the indolence of the primitive state and the petulant activity of our egoism, must have been the happiest and most stable of epochs. The more we reflect on it, the more we shall find that this state was the least subject to revolutions, and altogether the best that man could experience; so that he can have departed from it only through some fatal accident, which, for the public good, should never have happened. The example of savages, most of whom have been found in this state, seems to prove that men were meant to remain in it, that it is the real youth of the world, and that all subsequent advances have been apparently so many steps towards the perfection of the individual, but in reality towards the decrepitude of the species.

Rousseau, then, by formulating this theory of the goodness of man in a state of nature, associated in a general way with the American savages, gave a very great impulse to the whole movement of philosophic and sentimental exoticism. The Indian was not only to be admired for this or that virtue; his whole mode of life was to be envied as the nearest approach to that ever elusive goal, human happiness. Not only the trader and the adventurer, but the philosopher also, might well consider the advantages of such an existence: if he would escape disappointment, care, ennui, let him fly to the wilderness, make his home the wigwam, the dusky redskin his friend and companion.

Closely parallel in many ways to the teachings of Rousseau are the theories of the Scottish philosopher, Lord Monboddo. With more credulity, and at the same time more confusion and contradiction, he also maintains the superiority of the state of nature. Man in that state, he says, 'is much happier than he is in his civilized life, as it is conducted at present

---

[10] *Ibid.*, seconde partie.

in the nations of Europe. And the reason is plain, that man, as well as other animals in the natural state, is governed by instinct, that is divine intelligence prompting him to do everything that is necessary for the preservation of the individual and the continuation of the kind.'[11] But Monboddo, in trying to picture the ideal state, introduces all sorts of odd fancies, such as the advantages of going without clothing, or the superior health one might enjoy by restricting himself to a diet of raw vegetables.[12] Nor does he entirely reject the arts and sciences or religion: arguing from the benefits the Jesuits had conferred upon the barbarous tribes of Paraguay, he would also include a large part of the results of civilization in his scheme of happiness.[13] Finally he concludes that the 'only men we read of in history, who enjoyed the happiness described by Plato, were the Gymnosophists of India. These alone, of all the men we ever heard of, joined the philosophical with the savage life; for they lived naked in the woods, upon the natural fruits of the earth, and there philosophised.'[14]

Although this perfect union of the philosophical with the savage life is rarely consummated, the North American Indians, he thinks, come very near to what men were 'in the first ages of society, and in countries where a life of toil and labour, and the practice of arts, was of absolute necessity.'[15] Passing over his admiration of their gravity, love of liberty, public spirit, friendship, hospitality, etc., it is worth while to note his explanation of their cruelty in war, which he attributes not to love of revenge, but to a very wise policy:[16]

[11] James Burnett, Lord Monboddo, *Antient Metaphysics* (Edinburgh, 1779-99) 5. 83.
[12] *Ibid.* 3. 171 ff.
[13] *Ibid.* 4. 84 ff. His knowledge of Paraguay he derives from the history of the Jesuit missions by Charlevoix.
[14] *Ibid.* 3. 202.
[15] *Ibid.* 3. 206.
[16] *Ibid.* 3. 211.

War, say they, is the greatest evil that can befall man, and should be prevented by all means possible; therefore, in order to deter our neighbours from attacking us unjustly, we make them suffer the greatest torments when they become our prisoners in war. And I cannot help saying, I so far approve of this reasoning, that, I think, what we call the *humanity* of modern war in Europe, has made war very much more frequent than in ancient times; and we are much readier to take up the *hatchet* (to use the Indian phrase), and do it with much less deliberation, than the Indians do; neither do we let it lie so long *buried* as they do.

A good example of the sentimental longing for the state of nature, reflecting the Rousseauistic theory with a certain melancholy, poetic coloring, is found in Crevècœur's *Letters from an American Farmer*. Here we can see not only the desire for freedom and independence, but the romantic longing for solace in nature, peace in escaping the restlessness of civilized life. He writes of the annoyances and distractions of frontier life, and the advantages of rushing off to the forest with his wife and family, picturing this longed for change as follows:[17]

Thus shall we metamorphose ourselves, from neat, decent, opulent planters, surrounded with every conveniency which our external labour and industry could give, into a still simpler people divested of everything beside hope, food, and the raiment of the woods: abandoning the large framed house, to dwell under the wigwam; and the featherbed, to lie on the mat, or bear's skin. There shall we sleep undisturbed by fruitful dreams and apprehensions; rest and peace of mind will make us the most ample amends for what we shall leave behind. These blessings cannot be purchased too dear; too long have we been deprived of them. I would cheerfully go even to the Mississippi, to find that repose to which we have been so long strangers. My heart sometimes seems tired with beating, it wants rest like my eye-lids, which feel oppressed with so many watchings.

Sentimental exoticism seems to reach its height in William Bartram. His descriptions of the beauties of external

[17] J. Hector St. John Crevècœur, *Letters from an American Farmer* (London, 1782), ed. Trent and Lewisohn, pp. 320-1.

nature, his sense of the divine immanence, his tendency to a vague sort of pantheism, have been much admired, and are of some importance, because of their influence upon Words-worth.[18] But this Arcadian background is also the setting for his picture of a people living in all the perfection of primitive simplicity. The vices of Europe are unknown, natural virtue flourishes, peace and happiness are the endow-ment of all:[19]

> It is astonishing, though a fact, as well as a sharp reproof to the white people, if they will allow themselves time to reflect and form a just estimate, and I must own elevates these people to the first rank amongst mankind, that they have been able to resist the continual efforts of the complicated host of vices, that have for ages overrun the nations of the old world, and so contaminated their morals; yet more so, since such vast armies of these evil spirits have invaded this continent, and closely invested them on all sides. Astonishing indeed! when we behold the idle, immoral conduct of too many white people, who reside amongst them: notwithstanding it seems natural, eligible and even easy for these simple, illiterate people to put in practice those beautiful lectures delivered to us by the ancient sages and philosophers, and recorded for our instructions.

> Thus they enjoy a superabundance of the necessaries and con-veniences of life, with the security of person and property, the two great concerns of mankind. The hides of deer, bear, tigers and wolves, together with honey, wax and other productions of the country, purchase their clothing, equipage and domestic utensils from the whites. They seem to be free from want or desires. No cruel enemy to dread, nothing to give them dis-quietude, but the gradual encroachments of the white people. Thus contented and undisturbed, they appear as blithe and free as the birds of the air, and like them as volatile and active, tuneful and vociferous. This visage, action and deportment of a Siminole being the most striking picture of happiness in this life;

---

[18] For the influence of Bartram on Wordsworth. cf. 'Wordsworth's Sources,' by Lane Cooper, *Athenæum*, Apr. 22, 1905, pp. 498 ff., and 'A Glance at Wordsworth's Reading,' by the same author, in *Mod. Lang. Notes*, March, 1907, pp. 83-9; April, 1907, pp. 110-17.

[19] *Op. cit.*, pp. 491-2; 211-2.

joy, contentment, love and friendship, without guile or affectation, seem inherent in them, or predominant in their vital principle, for it leaves them but with the last breath of life. It even seems imposing a constraint upon their ancient chiefs and senators, to maintain a necessary decorum and solemnity, in their public councils; not even the debility and decrepitude of extreme old age, is sufficient to erase from their visages, this youthful, joyous simplicity; but like the gray eve of a serene and calm day, a gladdening, cheering blush remains on the western horizon after the sun is set.

Such pronounced preferences as these, however, were by no means without exception. Many viewed the matter as an open question, with much to be said on both sides, some giving the balance of preference to life in society, others to the savage state. Anburey, an English army officer, describing his travels through America in a series of letters to a friend in England, discusses this point at some length. The question which interests him is 'whether these untutored nations are more or less happy than us? Whether they, who are in the condition of men left to mere animal instinct, passing their lives in hunting, feeding, producing their species, and reposing themselves, do not pass a life of more felicity than ours, who can enjoy every luxury of life, and vary our indulgences and wants in a thousand ways?'[20] After considering the ease with which the savage supplies his simple needs, and the struggle by which the white man satisfies his more complex desires, he concludes:[21]

> After all, a single word may determine the great question. Let us ask the civilized man if he is happy; and the savage whether he is unhappy? If they both answer in the negative, there is an end to the dispute.

Even among writers who find much to admire in the Indian's character and way of life, civilization is on the whole given the preference. Burke, for example, in describ-

[20] Thomas Anburey, *Travels through the Interior Parts of America* (London, 1789) 1. 76.
[21] *Ibid.* 1. 82.

ing their cruelty, says that this should 'point out to us the advantage of a religion that teaches us a compassion to our enemies,' and should also 'make us more sensible, than some appear to be, of the value of commerce, the art of civilized life, and the lights of literature; which, if they have abated the forces of some of the natural virtues by the luxury which attends them, have taken out likewise the sting of our natural vices, and softened the ferocity of the human race without enervating their courage.'[22] Isaac Weld also, who traveled 'in America near the end of the century, says that before he came he had planned to live among them for some time, but this he gave up when he saw what their manner of life was. 'Few persons,' he says, 'who had ever tasted the pleasures and comforts of civilized life, would feel any inclination to reside among them, on becoming acquainted with their manner of living. The filthiness and wretchedness of their smoky habitations, the nauseousness of their common food to a person not even of a delicate palate, would be sufficient, I think, to deter any one from going to live amongst them.'[23]

By far the most sensible discussion of the respective merits of savage and civilized life comes from the lips of the great moralist, Samuel Johnson. The South Sea voyages of the 'sixties had greatly stimulated among men of letters an interest in far-away places and strange peoples.[24] One of the South Sea islanders had visited England, and Johnson had been very favorably impressed with his genteel manner, which he attributed not at all to natural superiority, but to the good society he had encountered while in England.[25]

---

[22] *Op. cit.* 1. 199-200.

[23] *Travels through the States of America* (London, 1795-97) 2. 295.

[24] For an account of the interest in the South Sea islanders, the visit of Omai, etc. cf. *Nature's Simple Plan*, by C. B. Tinker, chaps. 1-3.

[25] Boswell's *Life of Johnson*, ed. Hill (New York, 1891) 3. 9. My quotations from the *Life of Johnson* and the *Tour of the Hebrides* are from this edition.

When Boswell half seriously defends the superiority of savage life, as such, Johnson speaks with characteristic force and good sense:[26]

> On the 30th of September we dined together at the Mitre. I attempted to argue for the superior happiness of the savage life, upon the usual fanciful topicks. JOHNSON: 'Sir, there can be nothing more false. The savages have no bodily advantages beyond those of civilized men. They have not better health; and as to care or mental uneasiness, they are not above it, but below it, like bears. No, Sir; you are not to talk such paradox: let me have no more on't. It cannot entertain, far less can it instruct. Lord Monboddo, one of your Scotch Judges, talked a great deal of such nonsense. I suffered *him;* but I will not suffer *you.*'

On another occasion, Boswell records the following conversation, which shows that his own longing for the savage life was little more than a passing fancy:[27]

> JOHNSON: 'When we talk of pleasure, we mean sensual pleasure. When a man says, he had pleasure with a woman, he does not mean conversation, but something of a very different nature. Philosophers tell you, that pleasure is *contrary* to happiness. Gross men prefer animal pleasure. So there are men who have preferred living among savages. Now what a wretch must he be, who is content with such conversation as can be had among savages! You may remember an officer at Fort Augustus, who had served in America, told us of a woman they were obliged to *bind,* in order to get her back from savage life.' BOSWELL. 'She must have been an animal, a beast.' JOHNSON: 'Sir, she was a speaking cat.'

Both with those who, like Boswell, affect an inclination for the savage state, and those who actually adopt it, Johnson has very little patience. When Boswell tells him of 'an impudent fellow from Scotland, who affected to be a savage, and railed at all established system,' Johnson replies, 'There is nothing surprising in this, Sir. He wants to make himself conspicuous. He would tumble in a hogstye, as long as

---

[26] *Ibid.* 2. 83.
[27] *Ibid.* 3. 279.

you looked at him and called to him to come out. But let him alone, never mind him, and he'll soon give it over.'[28] His view of the whole subject of living with savages is very well brought out in the following passage :[29]

> The modes of living in different countries, and the various views with which men travel in quest of new scenes, having been talked of, a learned gentleman who holds a considerable office in the law, expatiated on the happiness of a savage life; and mentioned an instance of an officer who had actually lived for some time in the wilds of America, of whom, when in that state, he quoted this reflection with an air of admiration, as if it had been deeply philosophical: 'Here am I, free and unrestrained, amidst the rude magnificence of Nature, with this Indian woman by my side, and this gun with which I can procure food when I want it: what more can be desired for human happiness?' It did not require much sagacity to foresee that such a sentiment would not be permitted to pass without due animadversion. JOHNSON. 'Do not allow yourself, Sir, to be imposed upon by such gross absurdity. It is sad stuff; it is brutish. If a bull could speak, he might as well exclaim,—Here am I with this cow and this grass; what being can enjoy greater felicity?'

Johnson's attitude toward the primitive mode of life may be accounted for partly on the basis of his appreciation of the refinements and amenities of life. A good carriage, for example, is a comfort not to be despised in traveling, furnishing them, as Boswell puts it, 'a pleasing conviction of the commodiousness of civilization,' and the opportunity for a hearty laugh 'at the ravings of those absurd visionaries who have attempted to persuade us of the superior advantages of a *state of nature*.'[30] Similarly, when Boswell tells him how easily the people of Otaheite live on the fruit of the bread-tree, and laugh at the toilsome process by which Europeans procure food, Johnson remains unshaken in his preference for a good loaf :[31]

[28] *Ibid.* 1. 500.
[29] *Ibid.* 2. 262.
[30] *Tour of the Hebrides* 5. 416.
[31] *Life of Johnson* 2. 285.

JOHNSON. 'Why, Sir, all ignorant savages will laugh when they are told of the advantages of civilized life. Were you to tell men who live without houses, how we pile brick upon brick, and rafter upon rafter, and that after a house is raised to a certain height, a man tumbles off a scaffold, and breaks his neck; he would laugh heartily at our folly in building; but it does not follow that men are better without houses. No, Sir, (holding up a slice of a good loaf), this is better than the bread tree.'

Another reason for Johnson's opposition to this repudiation of civilization, and, in fact, to the whole naturalistic movement, was his firm adherence to the humanistic and Christian traditions. In an age when men were beginning to talk about innate goodness, uncorrupted virtue in a state of nature, and to find imaginary examples of this in all the out-of-the-way places of the earth,[32] Johnson held strictly to the belief in original sin, and virtue as the result of rigorous self-discipline. 'Pity,' he says, 'is not natural to man. Children are always cruel. Savages are always cruel. Pity is acquired and improved by the cultivation of the reason.'[33] On another occasion, he brings out this fact by

[32] The method of reasoning on religion, government, or morals by citing the practice of strange peoples in far-away places was a familiar device in the eighteenth century, used extensively by such philosophers as Montesquieu and his imitators. Johnson, however, knew better than to credit any such arguments. When Boswell, in a discussion of women's morals before and after marriage, mentions the supposed custom of some nation in India, Johnson replies, 'Nay, don't give us India. That puts me in mind of Montesquieu, who is really a fellow of genius too in many respects; whenever he wants to support a strange opinion, he quotes you the practice of Japan or of some other distant country of which he knows nothing. To support polygamy, he tells you of the island of Formosa, where there are ten women born for one man. He had but to suppose another island, where there are ten men born for one woman, and so make a marriage between them.' *Tour of the Hebrides* 5. 238.

[33] *Life of Johnson* I. 506. Johnson's statement here stands out in striking contrast to Rousseau's theory of pity as natural to man, the basic virtue in the state of nature, etc. Cf. *Discours sur L'Origine de L'Inégalité parmi les Hommes.*

picturing what his own fate would have been, had he been born among the Indians :[34]

> JOHNSON. 'A great Traveller observes, that it is said there are no weak or deformed people among the Indians; but he with much sagacity assigns the reason to this, which is, that the hardship of their life as hunters and fishers does not allow weak or diseased children to grow up. Now had I been an Indian, I must have died early; my eyes would not have served me to get food. I indeed now could fish, give me English tackle; but had I been an Indian, I must have starved or they would have knocked me on the head, when they saw I could do nothing.' BOSWELL. 'Perhaps they would have taken care of you: we are told they are fond of oratory, you would have talked to them.' JOHNSON. 'Nay, Sir, I should not have lived long enough to be fit to talk; I should have been dead before I was ten years old. Depend upon it, Sir, a savage when he is hungry, will not carry about with him a looby of nine years old, who cannot help himself. They have no affection, Sir.' BOSWELL. 'I believe natural affection, of which we hear so much, is very small.' JOHNSON. 'Sir, natural affection is nothing: but affection from principle and established duty is sometimes wonderfully strong.'

If people no longer seek their happiness in Utopias of the wilderness (and one may surely hope that such is the case), it may perhaps indicate somewhat of a return to the neoclassic good sense, to an increased appreciation of dignity and decorum, and a wise curbing of the romantic imagination in one of its most picturesque, but least wholesome, vagaries. A proposal to live among the savages would doubtless sound not only strange, but very absurd to most persons to-day, a most fantastic solution of the vexing problems of modernism. But whether the twentieth century is so much wiser than the eighteenth will perhaps be most clearly determined by asking how far rational enjoyment is now prized, and how far novelty, in the form of mysterious thrills and sentimental ecstasies, appeals to the popular taste. Lest we condemn the eighteenth century too sweepingly for remoteness from reality in its view of primitive life, let us

[34] *Op. cit.* 4. 242.

remember that the exotic Utopia was only one of many strange social experiments, popular with the many, but consistently opposed by the great philosophers and moralists. Voltaire, it will be recalled, in the concluding pages of *Candide,* makes the performance of homely duty the basis of contentment in this life; and Johnson, besides his treatment of this subject in *Rasselas,* sums up his view of the different degrees and kinds of enjoyment in a passage which Boswell reports as follows :[35]

> I mentioned Hume's notion, that all who are happy are equally happy; a little miss with a new gown at a dancing-school ball, a general at the head of a victorious army, and an orator, after having made an eloquent speech in a great assembly. JOHNSON. 'Sir, that all who are happy, are equally happy, is not true. A peasant and a philosopher may be equally *satisfied,* but not equally *happy.* Happiness consists in the multiplicity of agreeable consciousness. A peasant has not capacity for having equal happiness with a philosopher. . . . A small drinking-glass and a large one may be equally full, but the large one holds more than the small.

[35] *Ibid.* 2. 10.

CHAPTER III.

CIVILIZATION AS SEEN BY THE SAVAGE.

But how did the European and his civilization appear to the Indian? This was a matter of great interest to writers of the eighteenth century; not that any one knew or cared what the Indian really thought, but it was a fascinating subject for speculation, and gave opportunity for much clever satire on the vices of civilization, from the point of view of the uncorrupted man of nature. Although the American travelers and historians gave many accounts of the Indian's detestation of the European and his ways, the alleged superiority of the savage seemed to receive far greater support when he was brought to England, and pictured as looking down on all the splendor of wealth and power, amazed at the vice and hypocrisy of fashionable society, longing only to return to his native wilds. In this connection we should examine the accounts, real and fictitious, of the various Indians who actually visited England, in order to discover the kind of interest they aroused, and the impressions they were supposed to have received.

The early voyagers frequently carried some of the natives back with them, to be shown as objects of curiosity and wonder.[1] Columbus took several back on his first voyage, some of whom died on the trip, while others survived to be presented before the king.[2] Sebastian Cabot also, in 1502, presented to Henry VII three of the natives he had taken in

---

[1] For an account of the conduct of the early voyagers toward the Indians, their carrying them off, etc., cf. Drake, *The Book of the Indians*, Bk. 2, chap. 1. I have taken several references from this work, which gives considerable information, but is not at all clear as to the authorities cited.

[2] Antonio de Herrera gives some account of this in his *Hist. des Indes Occident.*, ed. 1660. 1. 102.

Newfoundland. An early account of these first Indians to come to England is as follows:[3]

> This yere [1502] were brought unto the king three men taken in the new found ilands by Sebastian Gabato, before named, in anno 1498. These men were clothed in beasts skins, and eate raw flesh, but spake such a language, as no man could understand them, of the which three men, two of them were seene in the kings court at Westminster two yeeres after, clothed like English men, and could not be discerned from Englishmen.

Frobisher also brought back some Esquimaux from his first two expeditions, and George Weymouth five Indians from his trip of exploration along the coast of Maine.[4] The strangeness of their appearance must have aroused no little interest, some of which is, I think, reflected in contemporary literature. Shakespeare, for example, appears to refer to one of these Indians in Henry VIII,[5] and still more clearly in *The Tempest,* 'when they will not give a doit to relieve a lame beggar, they will lay out ten to see a dead Indian.'[6] More significant, however, as an indication of

---

[3] John Stow, *Annales of England* (London, 1592), p. 807.

[4] This is mentioned in Rosier's *Relation of Waymouth's Voyage to the Coast of Maine,* 1605. He tells how they captured 'five salvages, two canoas, with all their bowes and arrowes' (ed. Burrage, p. 131). Further information concerning the subsequent careers of these 'salvages' is to be found in Fernando Gorges' *America painted to the Life* (London, 1649). Cf. also Drake, *op. cit.,* Bk. 2, chap. 1.

[5] Act 5, Sc. 4, l. 34.

[6] Act II, Sc. 2, l. 34. There has been much speculation as to whether Shakespeare may have seen a 'dead Indian,' and who the Indian may have been, whether one of the Esquimaux brought over by Frobisher, or some later comer unknown to fame. For a full discussion of the question, the reader is referred to the Variorum edition of the Tempest, p. 128. Halliwell's interesting conjectures are there considered, in which he identifies the Indian in question with one of the Esquimaux brought over by Frobisher (of course the terms Indian and Esquimaux were not clearly distinguished in the time of Shakespeare), and also thinks that drawings of them have been preserved in a manuscript in the library of Canterbury Cathedral.

Shakespeare's interest in America and its native inhabitants is the resemblance of certain passages in the *Tempest* to early accounts of the Indians and their dances.[7]

Pocahontas, the Indian princess whose adventure with Captain John Smith has already been mentioned, claims our attention at this point, because of the fact that she later married a certain John Rolfe, and came with him to England.[8] They arrived June 12, 1616, and, on her finding the smoke of London offensive, Rolfe secured her lodgings at Brentford. She had some time before this embraced the Christian religion, receiving in baptism the name of Rebecca, and had also borne him a son, then a small child. Captain Smith, who was engaged in a voyage to New England, out of gratitude recommended her very strongly to the queen, and she was well received at court. When she found out that Smith had deserted her, instead of being dead as she supposed, she became very angry, and upbraided him for his ingratitude. In the following year she died at Gravesend, just as she was about to embark for America.

Although there can be little doubt that Indians came to England from time to time, there is no evidence of any pronounced interest in their visits till the coming of the four Indian 'kings' in 1710. Boyer, in his *Annals of Queen*

---

[7] This subject is discussed in a paper called 'Indian Dances in The Tempest,' by Rachel Kelsey, in the *Jour. Eng. and Ger. Phil.* 13. 98-103. Miss Kelsey thinks the song, 'Come unto these yellow sands,' reflects early descriptions of Indian dances.

[8] One of the earliest accounts of the marriage of Pocahontas is that of Ralph Hamor in *A True Discourse of the Present State of Virginia* (London, 1615), pp. 3 ff. John Smith also tells the story in his *Generall Historie of Virginia* (London, 1623), pp. 113, 121-3. Many other historians repeat this—Oldmixon, for example, in his *British Empire in America* 1. 361 ff. The account in the *London Magazine*, 24 (1755) 435, which includes many of the same facts as the foregoing, is also of significance as showing a continued interest in the Indian princess and her visit to England.

Anne's Reign,[9] gives us a detailed account of their arrival in England, entertainment at court, and speech addressed to Her Majesty:

> Great Queen!
>
> We have undertaken a long and tedious voyage, which none of our predecessors could ever be prevailed upon to undertake. The motive that induced us was, that we might see our Great Queen, and relate to her those things we thought absolutely necessary, for the good of her, and us, her allies, on the other side of the great water.
>
> We doubt not but our Great Queen has been acquainted with our long and tedious war, in conjunction with her children (meaning subjects), against her enemies the French; and that we have been as a strong wall for their security, even to the loss of our best men. The truth of which our brother Queder, Colonel Schuyler, and Anadagarjaux, Colonel Nicholson, can testify, they having all our proposals in writing. . . .
>
> We need not urge to our Great Queen, more than the necessity we really labour under obliges us, that in case our Great Queen should not be mindful of us, we must, with our families, forsake our country, and seek other habitations, or stand neuter, either of which will be much against our inclinations.
>
> Since we have been in alliance with our Great Queen's children, we have had some knowledge of the Saviour of the world; and have often been importuned by the French, both by the insinuations of their priests, and by presents, to come over to their interest, but have always esteem'd them men of falsehood: but if our Great Queen will be pleas'd to send over some persons to instruct us, they shall find a most hearty welcome.

This speech to the queen was much admired as a specimen of Indian eloquence, and was reprinted or referred to in many of the different magazines. The great interest in the visit of these chiefs is perhaps due not only to their appearance, but to the character of their mission as well. The problem of adjusting political relations with the French and Indians was under consideration all through the century, so that we find in the magazines, even before the period of the French and Indian wars, many discussions as to how the

[9] 9. 189-190.

Indians are to be won to the cause of the English, and especially how they are to be protected from the pernicious influence of the Jesuits. A great deal is made of their supposed duplicity and their zeal in prejudicing the Indians against the English and their religion.

That the visit of these 'kings' was regarded as of more significance than that of any of the other Indians who found their way over before this, is proved by the amount of attention they received during their stay.[10] Besides their audience at court, we learn from an advertisement in No. 165 of the *Tatler* that a concert was also given in their honor. Another advertisement, announcing the sale of their pictures, furnished additional proof of the public curiosity concerning the strange foreigners.[11]

Much of our interest in these four sachems is due to the fanciful descriptions of them by Steele and Addison. In the *Tatler*, No. 171, Steele records a coffee-house conversation on the question, 'whence honour and title had its first original.' Timoleon, a somewhat Rousseauistic young gentlemen, who 'acts against depraved custom, by the rules of nature and reason,' maintains that 'in those ages which first degenerated from simplicity of life, and natural justice, the wise among them thought it necessary to inspire men with the love of virtue, by giving them who adhered to the interests of innocence and truth, some distinguishing name to raise them above the common level of mankind.' Thus on the basis of eminent merit arose the titles and terms of honor. To illustrate this tendency of simple people to give honor where honor is due, Urbanus then tells how the Indian kings did honor to the person where they lodged.

---

[10] A very fanciful poem, picturing a love-affair between one of the Indian kings and a lady of rank was published during their visit. Cf. chap. 6, and appendix.

[11] The edition of the *Tatler* in six volumes, London, 1786, gives some notes about these pictures and other points of interest in connection with the Indians' visit.

They were lodged in a handsome apartment at an upholsterer's in King Street, and, as a result of his kindness in providing a bed for one of the number who fell sick, the other kings consulted how they should honor the merit and services of their host:

> 'It is with these less instructed (I will not say less knowing) people, the manner of doing honour, to impose some name significant of the qualities of the person they distinguish, and the good offices received from him. It was, therefore resolved, to call their landlord Cadaroque, which is the name of the strongest fort in their part of the world. When they had agreed upon the name, they sent for their landlord, and as he entered into their presence, the Emperor of the Mohocks taking him by the hand, called him Cadaroque. After which the other three princes repeated the same word and ceremony.'
>
> Timoleon appeared much satisfied with this account, and having a philosophic turn, began to argue against the modes and manners of those nations which we esteem polite, and express himself with disdain at our usual method of calling such as are strangers to our innovations, barbarous.

In the *Spectator* for the following year (No. 50, April 27, 1711) Addison published what purports to be the observations of one of the Indian kings, contained in a series of letters left by mistake at the upholsterer's, and now for the first time translated, and brought before the public. The magnificent St. Paul's is first of all described from the standpoint of the wondering savage. How, he asks, did this huge house, big enough to contain his whole nation, ever come to be there? E Tow O Koam, king of the Rivers, thinks it was made by the hands of the great God to whom it is consecrated. The other two kings are of the opinion that it was created with the earth, and produced on the same day as the sun and moon. But Sa Ga Yean Qua Rash thinks better: it was at first a huge rock that grew on the top of the hill, which the natives of the country have 'wrought into all those beautiful vaults and caverns,' with 'pillars that stand like the trunks of so many trees bound about the top with garlands of leaves.' While thus admiring the European's skill in the use of tools, the simple Indian also makes some very naïve comments on their devotions:

> It is probable that when this great work was begun, which must have been many hundred years ago, there was some religion among this people; for they give it the name of a temple, and have a tradition that it was designated for men to pay their devotion in. And indeed there are several reasons which make us think that the natives of this country had formerly among them some sort of worship; for they set apart every seventh day as sacred: but upon my going into one of these holy houses on that day, I could not observe any circumstance of devotion in their behavior. There was indeed a man in black, who was mounted above all the rest, and seemed to utter something with a great deal of vehemence; but as for those underneath him, instead of paying their worship to the deity of the place, they were most of them bowing and courtesying to one another, and a considerable number of them fast asleep.

Another source of perplexity for our Indian visitors is the state of hostility existing between the two political parties. One of their guides tells them that the island is 'infested with a monstrous kind of animals, in the shape of men, called Whigs,' who will be apt to knock them down for being kings. Their other guide tells them of another monster called a Tory who would also be likely to treat them ill because they are foreigners. 'These two creatures, it seems, are born with a secret antipathy to one another, and engage when they meet as naturally as the elephant and rhinoceros. But as we saw none of either of these species, we are apt to think that our guides deceived us with misrepresentations and fictions, and amused us with an account of such monsters as are not really in their country.'

They are also surprised by the idleness of the young men, whom they see 'carried up and down the streets in little covered rooms'; and the discomfort of their clothing, contrasting so unfavorably with the beauty and ease of their own, calls forth the following comment:

> Their dress is likewise very barbarous, for they almost strangle
> themselves about the neck, and bind their bodies with many liga-
> tures, that we are apt to think are the occasion of several dis-
> tempers among them which our country is entirely free from.
> Instead of those beautiful feathers with which we adorn our
> heads, they often buy up a monstrous bush of hair, which covers
> their heads, and falls down in a large fleece below the middle of
> their backs; with which they walk up and down the streets, and
> are as proud of it as if it was of their own growth.

In their amusements, too, the Indians are disappointed:
instead of seeing the great men of the country running down
a stag or pitching a bar, they are conveyed into 'an huge
room lighted up with abundance of candles, where this lazy
people sat still above three hours to see several feats of
ingenuity performed by others, who it seems were paid for
it.' In the case of the women of the country they cannot
understand why they cover up their beautiful heads of hair,
while the men make such a parade of what is not their own.
With their beauty, however, they are much impressed:

> The women look like angels, and would be more beautiful than
> the sun, were it not for the little black spots that are apt to
> break out in their faces, and sometimes rise in very odd figures.
> I have observed that those little blemishes wear off very soon;
> but when they disappear in one part of the face, they are very apt
> to break out in another, insomuch that I have seen a spot upon the
> forehead in the afternoon, which was upon the chin in the morning.

Addison concludes this playful little satire by observing
that 'amidst these wild remarks there now and then appears
something very reasonable,' and gently warns his readers
that 'we are all guilty in some measure of the same narrow
way of thinking which we meet with in this abstract of the
Indian journal, when we fancy the customs, dresses, and
manners of other countries are ridiculous and extravagant,
if they do not resemble those of our own.' Apart from its
connection with the visit of the four kings, Addison's essay
is of some interest because of its connection with a large

class of literature of the type commonly known as the Letters of a Foreign Visitor, popular through the eighteenth century. An early example of this is Marana's *Turkish Spy*, similar in many ways to the well known *Lettres Persanes* of Montesquieu, Goldsmith's *Citizen of the World* falling within the same group. Although letters of the Oriental type were more popular, others of the same sort from the standpoint of the American Indian also had a certain vogue, particularly in French. The best example of these is Mme. de Graffigny's *Lettres Péruviennes*, 1747, followed in 1752 by the *Lettres Iroquoises* of Maubert de Gouvet, and in 1769 by the *Lettres Chérokiennes*.[12] Mme. de Graffigny's work was translated into English[13] a number of times, which is sufficient evidence of its widespread popularity. It is interesting, however, as a novel, rather than for any satire or social criticism.

In 1730 another group of kings, seven in all, were brought over under the direction of Sir Alexander Cumming. The real motive in bringing over these Creeks was probably to impress them with the power of the English, so that their visit is of historical rather than literary interest. The signing of their treaties was accompanied by the usual long speeches and exchange of presents.[14]

The next visitors were the famous Tomo Chachi and his companions, who crossed the ocean in 1734 with General Oglethorpe.[15] Among the many interesting memorials of their stay is the account of their visit at court, given in the

[12] Chinard lists this as follows: *Lettres Chérokiennes par Jean—Jacques Russus, Sauvage Européen, Rome* (?), 1769. Neither of the last two works mentioned has been consulted by the writer.

[13] These translations appeared in 1771, 1774, 1782, and 1805. Cf. the *Monthly Review*, 51 (1774), 161, for an account of the second of these.

[14] For an account of their visit, cf. Drake, *op. cit.*, Bk. 4, p. 28.

[15] A full description of this visit is contained in Charles C. Jones' *Historical sketch of Tomo Chi-chi, Mico of the Yamacraws* (Albany, N. Y., 1868), chap. 3.

Gentleman's Magazine.[16]   Tomo Chachi, presenting several
eagle feathers as trophies of his country, then addressed the
following speech to His Majesty:

> This day I see the majesty of your face, the greatness of your
> house, and the number of your people. I am come for the good
> of the whole nation call'd the Creeks, to renew the peace which
> was long ago had with the English. I am come over in my old
> days, tho' I cannot live to see any advantage to myself; I am come
> for the good of the children of all the nations of the Upper and
> of the Lower Creeks, that they may be instructed in the Knowl-
> edge of the English.
>
> These are the feathers of the eagle which is the swiftest of
> birds, and who flieth all around our nations. These feathers are
> a sign of peace in our land, and have been carried from town to
> town there; and we have brought them over to leave with you,
> O great king, as a sign of everlasting peace.
>
> O great king whatsoever words you shall say to me I will tell
> them faithfully to all the kings of the Creek nations.

After recording the king's reply, and Tomo Chachi's
address to the queen, the writer in the *Gentleman's Magazine*
gives the following account of their appearance and dress:

> The war-captain and other attendants of Tomo-cha-chi were
> very importunate to appear at court in the manner they go in
> their own country,—which is only with a proper covering around
> their waist, the rest of their body being naked, but were dissuaded
> from it by Mr. Oglethorpe. But their faces were variously
> painted after their country manner, some half black, others tri-
> angular, and others with bearded arrows instead of whiskers.
> Tomo-Chachi and Senauki his wife, were dressed in scarlet
> trimmed with gold.

A few days later one of them died, and was buried after
the manner of the Indians in St. John's cemetery, Westminster. To console and divert the others after this loss,
they were entertained at various houses, and taken to many
of the principal places of interest. At Canterbury they
visited Lady Dutry, 'where they were entertained in a very

[16] 4. 449, 450, 571.

handsome manner. Tomo Chachi made a compliment to Lady Dutry on his taking leave of her, in which he said, could he but speak English he could tell her the thoughts of his heart, and how sensibly he was touch'd with the noble reception she had given him; and was much more pleased with being able to see and thank her, for having assisted in sending the white people to Georgia.'[17]

On their visit to the Archbishop of Canterbury, his Grace received them very kindly, and expressed hopes for their conversion to Christianity. An instance of Tomo Chachi's politeness here appears in his retiring without making the long speech he had planned, on perceiving that his Grace, though weak, had declined to sit during the interview. After this they visited Eton, Windsor, and Hampton Court, where a great concourse of people gathered to see them.[18] Before leaving for America, Tomo Chachi and his nephew had their pictures painted, and hung in the Georgia rooms. *The Gentleman's Magazine*[19] gives the following account of their departure:

> The Indian king, queen and prince, etc. set out from the Georgia office in the king's coaches for Gravesend, to embark on their way home. During their stay in England, which has been about four months, his majesty allowed them £20 a week for their subsistance, and they have been entertained in the most agreeable manner possible. Whatever is curious and worthy observation in and about the cities of London and Westminster, has been carefully shown them; and nothing has been wanting among all degrees of men to contribute to their diversion and amusement, and to give them a just idea of English politeness and our respect for them. In return they expressed themselves heartily in presents. Prince William presented the young mico John Towanohowi with a gold watch, with an admonition to call upon Jesus Christ every morning when he looked on it: which he promised. They appeared particularly delighted with seeing his

[17] Cf. *Lond. Mag.* 3 (1734). 447 ff.
[18] *Ibid.* 3. 494.
[19] 4. 571.

highness perform his exercises of riding the managed horse,—
the Horse Guards pass in review, and the agreeable appearance
of barges, etc., on the Thames on Lord Mayor's day.

Except for these magazine accounts, and an ode[20]
inscribed to Tomo Chachi, there is little other interest in his
visit reflected in the literature of the time. His coming was
not forgotten, however, for later writers mention this as
an event of some importance.[21] Although Tomo Chachi is
supposed not to have found fault with any of the institutions of civilization, but to have been very properly impressed
with the bigness and grandeur of all he saw, an anecdote
told of his nephew, Toanhowi, attributes to him a preference for his native woods. A writer in the *London Magazine* for 1746 relates:[22]

> I remember to have asked the famous Toanhowi, so caress'd in
> England some years ago, by the royal family, how he liked that
> country? He told me, they were good people, but that it was a
> poor country, and he could not live in it, because they had no
> woods or deer, but what were kept in some gardens; for so he
> stil'd the parks of England.

Mention ought to be made here also of a series of papers
by Philip Freneau, called *Tomo Cheeki, The Creek Indian in
Philadelphia.*[23] Although this has no direct connection with
Tomo Chachi's visit to England, nor, so far as I know, with
any particular visit to Philadelphia, it is interesting as another
example of an Indian writing letters to his friends, relating
his impressions of civilization. As in the case of Addison's

[20] *Georgia, a Poem, Tomo-cha-chi, an Ode* (London, 1736). This
is reprinted in Jones' *Historical Account of Tomo-cha-chi,* pp. 60-63.
[21] Cf. *Gent. Mag.* 18 (1748). 60; *Lond. Mag.* 17 (1748). 81.
[22] 15. 622. The same anecdote is also found in *Gent. Mag.* 15. 621.
[23] This series of sketches was first published in the *Jersey Chronicle,*
May 23, 1795, and following issues, and was reprinted in *The Time
Piece and Literary Companion,* Philadelphia, March 17, 1797, and
following issues. Cf. the *Poems of Philip Freneau,* ed. Pattee, I.
LXVI, LXXIV. My citations are from the *Jersey Chronicle.*

supposed manuscript, this also is given as a translation from an original in an Indian language.

In this series of letters the respective merits of civilization and the state of nature are discussed very fully, usually to the advantage of the latter. The Indian visitor describes his arrival in Philadelphia, the change in the landscape, his longing for his native vales, instead of the paved streets and dark narrow boxes (houses) where the people are shut away from the clear air and sunshine. He paints the peace and happiness of the Indian's wild state, nature supplying him with all the necessities of life, here sold only in 'little niggardly parcels,' and contrasts their contentment with the care and anxiety reflected in the faces of all he meets. He also notices their vanity—how the great men have their likenesses reproduced and hung about in public places, though they can be seen themselves every day; how the women have elaborate paintings made of themeslves, though they have not done anything remarkable. His interpreter reads him history, and he is shocked at the long series of wars, horrors, and crimes—the cruelty of man to man—and speculates on whether the human kind can ever return to its primitive state of happiness. He is taken on board one of their ships, and wonderingly perceives the intricacy of its construction, the skill required in its operation. Then he sees a horseshoe nailed up, and in answer to his inquiry about its use the captain tells him of its power to bring good luck; and the Indian laughs at the superstition of the white man, with all his knowledge and cleverness imagining himself at the mercy of a piece of bent iron. For their superior knowledge he has little respect. Instead of the Indian's understanding of the secrets of nature, the white man's knowledge is of how to gain money. The real mysteries of life they do not understand, any more than the Indian. 'I take the whole of this stupendous system,' he says, 'to be a great machine, answering some prodigious purpose, of which the white men, any more than ourselves, have not the

least idea.' Finally he longs to return home, having decided
that civilization is more of a loss than a gain:

> The more I consider the condition of the white men, the more
> fixed becomes my opinion, that, instead of gaining, they have lost
> much by subjecting themselves to what they call the laws, and
> regulations of civilized societies.

The Indian visitors of the latter part of the century need
not receive extended comment here. None of them aroused
the same enthusiasm as their predecessors, the four Indian
kings, or the great Tomochichi, partly, perhaps, because they
were less of a novelty. The accounts of them in the magazines are confined for the most part to telling of their negotiations about lands and hunting, their complaints about the
encroachments of the English and their own loss of power.
Three Cherokee chiefs came with some such purpose as this
in 1765,[24] and in 1766 Samson Occom,[25] the Indian preacher,
and also a group of Iroquois chiefs with their ladies.[26] An
unfortunate incident attending their departure is thus
described in the *Gentleman's Magazine:*

> The Indian Kings and Queens, having finished the business
> they had in charge, and waiting at Gravesend for the ship that
> was to carry them to North America, to amuse themselves
> repaired to church in the morning, where they were followed by
> a prodigious crowd of people, among whom was a woman out of
> her senses, who, fixing her eyes stedfastly on one of the chiefs,
> struck him three or four blows, and then turning to his consort,
> terribly scratched her face, crying out at the same time, "You
> scalp'd my husband! you scalp'd my husband!" The poor Indian
> woman trembled to think what was to become of her, supposing
> she was brought there to be sacrificed. The whole congregation
> was alarmed; the notion of fire possessed some, and others tho't

[24] Cf. *Gent. Mag.* 25. 95.

[25] For an account of Occom's visit, cf. W. De Loss Love's *Samson
Occom and the Christian Indians of New England* (Boston, 1899),
chap. 8.

[26] Cf. *Gent. Mag.* 36. 387.

[27] 36. 490.

the church was falling; all ran out but the minister, who sat very composedly till the congregation were satisfied of what had happened, and returned again to the service.

Other Indians journeyed to England from time to time,[28] but none of them caused any very great interest, unless it was Colonel Joseph Brant, an Onondaga of the Mohawk tribe, who came over in 1785.[29] An original drawing of Brant is said to have been in the possession of James Boswell.[30]

Although these later Indians came and went without much attention from men of letters, the tendency to discuss and criticize civilization from the standpoint of the savage continued all through the century. Many phases of the urban life of the eighteenth century are thus made the object of more or less cleverly veiled censures—the frivolities of society, the corruption of politics, the injustice of the laws, the hypocrisy of religion. A good example of this kind of satire is found in a paper in the *Scots Magazine* for 1742,[31] which purports to be a continuation of the Indian king's letters given by Addison in the *Spectator*. Here also the savage is pictured as finding everything very strange, the customs of the country so different that he almost fancies himself in another world. 'The very order of nature,' he says, 'is almost inverted here: day and night are not the same as they are with us; the people (whether out of ignorance or perverseness I cannot tell) confounding one with the other. Their day generally begins at noon, and ends at midnight; so that they seldom taste the sweets of the morning: nay, I have been informed, that great numbers in this town have never seen the sun rise. Those indeed who get

[28] Cf. *Gent. Mag.* 40 (1774). 91; *European Mag.* 19 (1791). 268.
[29] Cf. *Gent. Mag.* 55. 1004.
[30] Cf. Drake, *op. cit.*, Bk. 5, p. 21.
[31] 4. 72. The same article also appears in the *London Magazine*, for that year, p. 83.

their livelihood by their labour, are obliged to conform to nature's laws in this respect; but they do it with great unwillingness, and are reckoned miserable, by the better sort, on this account.'

On the whole the people seem to him an 'odd mixture of folly and wisdom.' He hardly knows how to reconcile their ingenious devices for acquiring riches with their ridiculous methods for squandering them away again—i. e. their gambling. His host takes him to a masquerade, a play, and an opera, in all of which he finds something strange and unnatural, especially the Italian singers, with their voices like young girls—'an odd species of creatures, who had an outward human form, but were not *men.*' He observes the audience in the most extraordinary raptures, and concludes that their enjoyment is due to the words, but is later informed that they understood the language no better than he. This leads him to conclude his comments on the English entertainments with the remark that 'they have a strange love of *novelty,* and will prefer whatever is *foreign* to that which is the produce of their own nation, even tho' their own is much more valuable.'

The coffee-houses he also visits, which only the men attend, 'some to do business, some because they have nothing to do.' So many political discussions are here conducted that he concludes every coffee-house to be a cabinet of statesmen, and the whole nation an island of politicians. But, like many another, he finds the mysterious workings of the government and the laws far beyond his powers of comprehension. He cannot but wonder at the great number and variety of these laws, the general ignorance as to their meaning, the shrewd policy of the lawyers in profiting by the popular misunderstanding of what the laws really mean. 'Those very men of law,' he remarks, 'disagree with one another what is or is not law; but however they disagree about it, they live by it, and live the better the more they do disagree; for let which party soever lose, they are sure to gain.'

From all of this he cannot but conclude that the Indian law is far better. 'Ours is summary, and executed immediately; we do justice on the spot: if an Indian steals another's rice, we hang the thief on the first tree we come to.' He then relates an anecdote of a lawyer who came to live among the Indians:

> I remember to have heard my uncle Yow Row Quen Yaden, King of the Six Nations, tell a story, how some British people had a settlement on one of his rivers: they long lived in all peace and quiet, trafficking with our people with all justice and harmony. It so happened, that a law-man at last came among them: they did not long after enjoy their former felicity; there began contention between neighbor and neighbor; they quarrelled about the limits of their plantations, about their rights of inheritance, and the bargains they made. The Indians who dealt with them were defrauded, and the league between our people and the White was scandalously broke; insomuch that Quen Yaden brought down his warriors upon them, not to destroy his old allies, but to inquire into the cause of this change. On inquiry he found that this law-man had been the occasion of all, by setting himself up for a judge of the law, and then fomenting quarrels that he might become a judge of them. Rice and skins he frequently received to give wrong judgment, not only against our Indians, but amongst his own people. On proof of these things Quen Yaden immediately ordered this man of law to be hanged upon an adjacent tree, and restored the people to their ancient peace and felicity.

Satire on the law and various other professions was very popular in all these imaginary Indian observations on the customs of the Europeans. Adair, for example, puts in the mouth of a savage a long discussion of all these occupations, thus bringing out the superiority of the plain simple laws of nature by which the Indian is so happily and peaceably governed. Of the lawyers, and the difficulty of securing justice, he says:[32]

[32] *Op. cit.,* p. 434.

They say, if our laws were honest, or wisely framed, they
would be plain and few, that the poor people might understand
and remember them, as well as the rich—that right and wrong, an
honest man and a rogue, with as many other names as our large
crabbed books could contain, are only two contraries; that simple
nature enables every person to be a proper judge of promoting
good, and preventing evil, either by determinations, rewards or
punishments; and that people cannot in justice be accused of
violating any laws, when it is out of their power to have a proper
knowledge of them. They reckon, that if our legislators were
not moved by some oblique views, instead of acting the part of
mud-fish, they would imitate the skillful bee, and extract the
useful part of their unwieldy, confused, old books, and insert it
in an honest small one, that the poor people might be able to buy,
and read it, to enable them to teach their rising families to avoid
snares, and keep them from falling into the power of our cunning
speakers—who are not ashamed to scold and lie publicly when
they are well paid for it, but if interest no longer tempted them
to inforce hurtful lies for truth, would probably throw away all
their dangerous quibbling books.

As the lawyers and legislators only succeed in obstructing
justice, so, in the eyes of the Indian, do the physicians cause
more illness and suffering than they prevent:[33]

He said, if our physicians used simples in due time to assist
nature, instead of burning corrosive mixtures, they would have
no occasion to dismember poor people, cutting off their limbs in
so horrid a manner, as several were reported to do; and that,
if our law was so weak as not to condemn those to death, who
took away the lives of the low innocent people, yet the strong
feelings of nature ought to incite the surviving relations of the
murdered persons, to revenge their blood on the murderers, by
beating them with long knobbed poles, while they were sensible
of pain, and as soon as they recovered a little, to cut off their
ears and nose with a dull knife, as in the case of adultery, in
order to quench innocent blood, and teach unwary people to avoid
and detest the execrated criminals.

The Indian's scorn is also aroused by the corrupt practices
of the army, according to which weak, incompetent men often

[33] *Ibid.,* p. 438.

secure high places; money, instead of genuine attainment, being made the basis of all promotions :[34]

> They say they are sure, from sundry observations, we sell to the highest bidder, our high titles of' war, which were only due to brave men who had often fought the enemy with success in defence of their country: that they had seen, even in Charlestown several young, lazy, deformed white men, with big bellies, who seemed to require as much help to move them along, as overgrown old women.

Nor does the Indian understand the importance of such institutions as marriage, and the punishments inflicted on those who evade its obligations. He does not see why a couple who do not get along happily should not separate, according to the laws of reason and nature :[35]

> My Indian friend said, as marriage should beget joy and happiness instead of pain and misery, if a couple married blindfold, and could not love each other afterwards, it was a crime to continue together, and a virtue to part, and make a happier choice; and as the white people did not buy their wives after the manner of the Indians, but received value along with them, in proportion to their own possessions, whatsoever the woman brought with her, she ought to be allowed to take back when they separated, that her heart might weigh even, and nothing be spoiled.—That, in his opinion, such determinations belonged to the law, and not to the great beloved men [the bishops and officials of the Church]; and, if he understood me aright, the beloved men threw away the gentleman to the accursed beings of darkness, not for having acted anything against the divine law, but for daring to oppose the words of his mouth, in imitation of the first presumptuous great beloved man, who spoiled the speech of the divine messenger.

Religion is also a popular subject for these supposed criticisms of the savage. The Indian is pictured as listening gravely to the arguments of the missionaries, answering them with better ones of his own, and pointing out the inconsist-

[34] *Op. cit.*, p. 431.
[35] *Op. cit.*, p. 448.

ency of the precepts with the practices of his would-be instructors in morals. Franklin tells of an Indian's curiosity as to why the white people shut up their shops every day in seven, and all assembled in the great house. He is told that they go there to hear *good things,* and not long after he has an opportunity to prove the truth of this statement. He goes to Albany to sell his beaver skins, and receives an offer of four shillings a pound, but is told that he cannot do business on that day, as the people all assemble to hear *good things.* Having nothing to do himself, he decides to go to the meeting, where, he says, 'there stood up a man in black, and began to talk to the people very angrily. I did not understand what he said; but perceiving that he looked much at me, and at Hanson, I imagined he was angry at seeing me there; so I went out, sat down near the house, struck fire, and lit my pipe, waiting till the meeting should break up.'[36] When the meeting is over, he again tries to sell his beaver skins, but now no one will offer him more than three shillings and sixpence. From this he concludes that their purpose could not have been to learn *good things,* but to consult how to cheat Indians in the price of beavers :[37]

> If they met so often to learn *good things,* they would certainly have learned some before this time. But they are still ignorant. You know our practice. If a white man in travelling through our country, enters one of our cabins, we all treat him as I treat you; we dry him if he is wet, we warm him if he is cold, and give him meat and drink, that he may allay his thirst and hunger; and we spread soft furs for him to rest and sleep on: We demand nothing in return. But if I go into a white man's house at Albany, and ask for victuals and drink, they say, get out, you Indian Dog. You see they have not yet learned those little *good things,* that we need no meetings to be instructed in, because our mothers taught them to us when we were children; and there-

[36] *Remarks concerning the Savages of North America,* 3d ed. (London, 1784), p. 37.
[37] *Ibid.,* pp. 38-9.

fore it is impossible their meetings should be, as they say, for any such purpose, or have any such effect; they are only to contrive *the cheating of Indians in the price of beaver.*

Another anecdote showing the Indian's view of Christianity is also related by Franklin.[38] A Swedish minister tries to convert the savages by preaching a sermon on the fall of man by the eating of an apple, the coming of Christ to repair the mischief, and other Christian doctrines. When he had finished the Indian orator replies, 'What you have told us is all very good. It is indeed bad to eat apples. It is better to make them into cyder. We are much obliged by your kindness in coming so far, to tell us those things you have heard from your mothers. In return, I will tell you some of those we have heard from ours.' The Indian then tells him a myth of how at first they had only flesh to eat, till one time a beautiful young woman descended from the clouds, and taught them the cultivation of the ground. 'Where her right hand had touched the ground, they found maize; where her left hand had touched it, they found kidney beans; and where her backside had sat on it, they found tobacco.' To all this the missionary in disgust replies, 'What I delivered to you were sacred truths; but what you tell me is mere fable, fiction and falsehood.' At this the Indian is offended and says, 'My brother, it seems your friends have not instructed you in the rules of common civility. You saw, that we who understand and practice those rules, believed all your stories, why do you refuse to believe ours?'

The tendency to poke fun at the well-meant labors of the missionaries, and the Indian's naïve misunderstanding of the mysteries of the Christian religion, is well illustrated in the following anecdote from Horace Walpole's Letters:[39]

> I have been laughing at another story . . . one of the Methodist apostles who went to America to try to make people believe

[38] *Ibid.,* pp. 31-33.
[39] Ed. Toynbee 1. 245.

what has travelled through all degrees of belief from Jerusalem
to the Lizard Point, was boasting of his success and what great
improvements the poor Indians had made in Christianity; 'You
should only hear me examine the first we meet'—and then stopping
one of his swarthy congregation, he asked him if he had not felt
great comfort last Sunday at the sacrament after receiving the
bread and the wine? 'Yes, indeed,' replied the poor primitive,
'but I wish it had been rum!'

Another example of veiled attack on the principles of
Christian faith is found in the *London Magazine* for 1760,[40]
in what is supposed to be the speech of an Indian chief to
a Swedish missionary. By way of introduction, it is stated
that the missionary on his return to Sweden published his
speech and the Indian's answer, dedicating them to the University of Upsala with the request that they 'furnish him
with arguments to confute such strong reasoning of the
Indian.' The chief argument of the Indian is that his people
have had handed down to them for generations a doctrine of
future rewards and punishments, and therefore do not need
any revelations written in a book. He asks the missionary
the nature of the revelation he has come to teach, and
whether his pious forefathers are all to be damned because
they have not heard of this book. He cannot, however, think
that God would let them remain in fatal ignorance for so
many ages. The doctrine of the Fall of Man and original
sin he replies to as follows:

> Let us suppose that a heinous crime was committed by one of
> our ancestors, like that which we are told happened among
> another race of people: In such a case God would certainly
> punish the criminal; but would never involve us that are innocent
> in his guilt. Those that think otherwise must make the Almighty
> a very whimsical, ill natured being.

[40] 29. 695. Several replies appeared in the same magazine for the
following year on pp. 92, 407, and 636. The original speech also
appeared in the *Philadelphia Magazine* for 1789, p. 273, and in the
Scots Magazine 23 (1761). 12, with replies on pp. 67 and 464.

Finally he asks the missionary to compare the morals of the white people with those of the Indians:

> Once more; are the Christians more virtuous, or rather are they not more vicious than we are? If so, how came it to pass that they are the objects of God's beneficence, while we are neglected? Does the Deity confer his favors without reason, and with so much partiality? In a word, we find the Christians much more depraved in their morals than ourselves; and we judge of their doctrine by the badness of their lives.

In connection with this alleged contempt on the part of the Indian for the white man and his morals, it may of course be urged that such an attitude was not wholly without foundation. Had not the settler defrauded him of his lands? Had not the trader cheated him in the sale of his furs, after first corrupting his morals by the introduction of intoxicating liquors? Be that as it may, the notion of the Indian cleverly ridiculing the follies of civilization, and uttering high-sounding orations in praise of natural goodness, is of course purely fictitious, one of the many projections of the romantic imagination. Such is Bartram's fanciful portrait of a noble savage in this picturesque attitude:[41]

> I saw a young Indian in the nation, who when present, and beholding the scenes of mad intemperance and folly by the white men in the town, clapt his hand to his breast, and with a smile, looking aloft as if struck with astonishment, and wrapt in love and admiration to the Deity, as who should say, O, thou Great and Good Spirit, we are indeed sensible of they benignity and favour to us red men. We did not know before they came amongst us that mankind could become so base, and fall so below the dignity of their nature. Defend us from their manners, laws and power.

[41] *Op. cit.*, p. 492.

CHAPTER IV.

The sentimentalized savage, whether Indian or negro, is not on the whole a conspicuous figure in English fiction, despite the fact that his first appearance was made at a very early date, and that in a work of widespread and enduring fame—I refer to Aphra Behn's well known story of *Oroonoko; or, The Royal Slave.*[1] The publication of this exotic romance in 1688 makes it antedate, by a number of years, not only the writings of Rousseau, but of the various philosophers and poets in whom critics are wont to discern the inception of the whole naturalistic movement. If we have here, as has often been stated, a work which anticipates the fundamental doctrines of romanticism, preaches humanitarianism and natural goodness, besides expressing other ideas and sentiments not current at the time, but destined to flourish about a century later, it is a circumstance indeed remarkable, and worthy of somewhat more than our casual consideration. The hero of the piece is, to be sure, an African, and as such of no particular concern to us here, but the fact that any sort of savage was idealized at that date makes the book a kind of landmark in the history of exotic fiction, and a study of its influence indispensable to our inquiry. Then, too, our friend the Indian is a part of the 'ideal' background, and, in the thought of the time, Indians, negroes, and other primitive peoples were not always clearly differentiated. In the well known story of Inkle and Yarico, for example, we find Yarico now an Indian, now a negro, and in one instance at least the natives of America are described as blacks.

Mrs. Behn gives as the scene of her story a colony in

[1] London, 1688.

America, called Surinam, in the West Indies. She also tells us that she was an eye-witness of much that she has set down, and had the rest from the mouth of her hero, the Royal Slave, statements now regarded as purely fictitious,[2] but long accepted as trustworthy evidence for the genuineness of her much-admired local color. We are first given a pretty complete account of the natives of Surinam, although they play no significant part in the story, and it is in this description of their virtues that the writer gives the fullest and clearest expression to her belief in natural goodness. After telling of their physical beauty, she speaks thus of their moral qualities:[3]

> And these people represented to me an absolute idea of the first state of innocence, before man knew how to sin. And 't is most evident and plain, that simple nature is the most harmless, inoffensive and virtuous mistress, 'T is she alone, if she were permitted, that better instructs the world, than all the inventions of man: Religion would here but destroy that tranquility they possess by ignorance; and laws would but teach 'em to know offences, of which now they have no notion. They once made mourning and fasting for the death of the English governor, who had given his hand to come on such a day to 'em, and neither came nor sent; believing, when a man's word was past, nothing but death could or should prevent his keeping it: And when they saw he was not dead, they ask'd him what name they had for a man who promis'd a thing he did not do? The governor told them such a man was a lyar, which was a word of infamy to a gentleman. Then one of 'em reply'd, Governor, you are a lyar, and guilty of that infamy. They have a native justice, which knows no fraud; and they understand no vice or cunning, but when they are taught by the white men.

The scene now changes to Africa—the country of Cora-mantien, to be exact—which Mrs. Behn pictures with a sort of Oriental coloring still less real than the primitive state

---

[2] On the improbability of Mrs. Behn's having been in Surinam, cf. a study of Ernest Bernbaum's, *Mrs. Behn's Oroonoko,* in the *Kittredge Anniversary Papers* (Boston, 1913).

[3] *The Works of Aphra Behn,* ed. Summers 5. 131-132.

of innocence ascribed to the natives of Surinam. The details of this part of the story may be passed over somewhat hastily; the character of Oroonoko, however, deserves a fuller discussion. Most of the hero's time, we learn, has not been spent at the court, but in the war which the people of Coramantien are always carrying on with their neighbors. The writer therefore says, ' 't was amazing to imagine where it was he learn'd so much humanity; or to give his accomplishments a juster name, where 't was he got that real greatness of soul, those refined notions of true honour, that absolute generosity, and that softness, that was capable of the highest passions of love and gallantry.'[4] Some part of Oroonoko's accomplishments are attributed to the 'care of a Frenchman of wit and learning, who finding it turn to a very good account to be a sort of royal tutor to this young black, and perceiving him very ready, apt, and quick of apprehension, took a great pleasure to teach him morals, language, and science'.[5] Still another reason for his nobility of soul is his contact with the 'English gentlemen that traded thither; . . . the Spaniard also, with whom he traded afterwards for slaves.'[6] Thus Oroonoko, though at all times the most sentimental of heroes, is, by his contact with civilization and his participation in the slave-trade, somewhat removed from the pure state of nature, whose plain, simple laws Mrs. Behn elsewhere extols so highly.

Passing over the amorous intrigues of the court of Coramantien, the love of the royal prince Oroonoko for the beauteous Imoinda, his entrance into the harem of his grandfather, the aged king, his detection there, and the resulting banishment of Imoinda into slavery—omitting this entire harem episode, with its pseudo-Oriental atmosphere of intrigue and exaggerated sentiment, we soon find our

[4] *Ibid.* 5. 135.
[5] *Ibid.* 5. 135.
[6] *Ibid.* 5. 135.

hero and heroine slaves in far-off Surinam. Now the superiority of Oroonoko is disclosed in a variety of novel situations. First of all, the other slaves, most of whom he had sold into these parts, are at his arrival overcome with awe and veneration, so much so, in fact, that 'from the surprize and awe they had at the sight of him, they all cast themselves at his feet, crying out, in their language, Live, O King! Long live, O King! and kissing his feet, paid him even divine homage.'[7] Stranger still, when Oroonoko tells them that he is their fellow-slave, and no better, 'they set up with one accord a most terrible and hideous mourning and condoling, which he and the English had much ado to appease.'[8]

An example of the bravery of Oroonoko, or of Cæsar as he has been renamed, appears in his connection with the Indians. In the first chapter, Mrs. Behn states that the English live with the Indians 'in perfect amity, without daring to command 'em; but, on the contrary, caress 'em with all the brotherly and friendly affection in the world.'[9] At this point in the story, however, disputes arise, making it unsafe for visitors like herself to go to the Indian towns, until one day Cæsar, learning of their desire, tells them they need not fear, he will be their guide. Their visit to the towns of the natives gives opportunity for the introduction of additional local color, more accurate, if less picturesque, than that at the opening of the story. The Indians are here described as ignorant, superstitious, and naïve; they know not what to make of their white visitors, whose clothing in particular contrasts so strikingly with their own nakedness. Their first fear, however, soon passes. 'By degrees they grew more bold, and from gazing upon us round, they touch'd us, laying their hands upon all the features of our faces, feeling our breasts, and arms, taking up one petticoat, then wondering to see

[7] *Ibid.* 5. 170.
[8] *Ibid.* 5. 170.
[9] *Ibid.* 5. 130.

another; admiring our shoes and stockings, but more our
garters, which we gave 'em, and ty'd about their legs, being
lac'd with silver lace at both ends; for they much esteem
any shining things.'[10]

A still more vivid bit of local color may be seen in the
following account of the Indian 'war captains':[11]

> But so frightful a vision it was to see 'em, no fancy can create;
> no sad dreams can represent so dreadful a spectacle. For my
> part, I took 'em for hobgoblins, or fiends, rather than men; But
> however their shapes appear'd, their souls were very humane and
> noble; but some wanted their noses, some their lips, some both
> noses and lips, some their ears, and others cut through each cheek,
> with long slashes, through which their teeth appear'd: They had
> several other formidable wounds and scars, or rather dismem-
> brings. . . . Caesar was marvelling as much at their faces,
> wondring how they should be all so wounded in war; he was
> impatient to know how they all came by those frightful marks
> of rage or malice, rather than wounds got in battle: They told
> us by our interpreter, that when any war was waging, two men,
> chosen out by some old captain whose fighting was past, and who
> could only teach the theory of war, were to stand in competition
> for the generalship, or great war-captain; and being brought
> before the old judges, now past labour, they are ask'd, what
> they dare do, to shew they are worthy to lead an army? When
> he who is first ask'd, making no reply, cuts off his nose, and
> throws it contemptibly on the ground; and the other does some-
> thing to himself that he thinks surpasses him, and perhaps
> deprives himself of lips and an eye: So they slash on 'till one
> gives out, and many have dy'd in this debate. And it's by a
> passive valour they shew and prove their activity; a sort of
> courage too brutal to be applauded by our black hero; neverthe-
> less, he express'd his esteem of 'em.

The further career of Cæsar may be sketched in brief
outline. After enduring his servitude for some time, he
decides to throw off the hateful yoke. He accordingly assem-
bles the other blacks one Sunday when the English are all
drunk, and delivers them a harangue on the miseries and

[10] *Ibid.* 5. 185.
[11] *Ibid.* 5. 187-8.

ignominies of slavery. They all agree to his plan of running away, and forming a separate colony, but in their attempt to carry this out they are overtaken by the soldiers, and all but Cæsar basely yield. Cæsar is now severely whipped—a great blow to his pride—and treated with other indignities. After this, to make a long story short, he flees to the forest with Imoinda, there kills her, that she and the child she is about to bear may not have to live in slavery, is recaptured, and cruelly tortured to death, meeting his fate with great dignity and composure.

In summing up *Oroonoko,* we must be careful not to read into it the characteristics of a later type of romanticism. In many respects, to be sure, it reminds one of Rousseau and his school, as in its praise of primitive virtue, its unfavorable reflections on the religion and morality of civilized peoples, its representation of a 'noble soul' in rebellion against his surroundings. Some of these seeming similarities, however, may, I think, be accounted for on very different grounds. First, it seems fairly clear that Mrs. Behn had no particular social or political theory to demonstrate; her aim was rather to secure striking effects. This she accomplishes, not so much by the originality of her methods as by the novelty of some of her material. For if we analyze her style and manner, we are at once reminded of the heroic romances and dramas of the period, particularly the dramas. The type of play, as is well known, relies for its effects largely on idealized characterization, extravagant and 'elevated' sentiments, and multiplicity of heroic events, which result oftentimes in a grandiose spectacle, but suffer a corresponding lack of dramatic power or intensity.

We may perhaps conclude by saying that Mrs. Behn for the sake of novelty makes a negro—not a common negro, to be sure, but a 'royal prince'—the hero of a very fanciful romance. In order to make him great, or heroic, according to the fashions of the time, she proceeds to exaggerate all his passions; his virtues are highly drawn, so as to stand out in bold relief against the baseness of his companions and captors. In such qualities as these, its lack of restraint, its remoteness from reality, *Oroonoko* possesses a marked resemblance to certain works of the later romantic school. But these same qualities weaken it as an argument against slavery, and tend to differentiate it from the later humanitarian novel, with which it has been more or less associated. For the humanitarian novel, to be convincing, must necessarily be realistic; in *Oroonoko,* on the other hand, the large admixture of the unreal in the hero's character, and the unnatural in his conduct, prevents his receiving very much of the reader's sympathy. We are, I suppose, expected to admire his greatness of soul, but, as in so much writing of that kind, high-flown sentiments and violent actions are likely to impress the modern reader as ridiculous, rather than heroic. Suffice it to say that as a work of fiction *Oroonoko* did not exert any great influence—just why is not so easy to determine. Perhaps it was because the type of romance to which it belonged was already on the decline, while a half century was to elapse before the modern novel really got under way. Or perhaps it was because the drama was a more suitable vehicle for the exotic imagination, and *Oroonoko,* having been made into a play,[12] became more important as a link in the stage-tradition of the noble savage.

In a very different type of story, *The Voyages of Captain Richard Falconer,*[13] the Indian appears, not as an object of more or less slushy sentiment, but rather as a picturesque figure associated with thrilling adventures, imminent dangers, narrow escapes. From the announcement of the title-page, and the torture-scene pictured in the frontispiece, the reader is led to expect the Indian to play an important rôle in the

---

[12] Southerne's tragedy founded upon *Oroonoko* was produced at Drury Lane in 1696. For some account of its career on the stage cf. Introduction to *The Works of Aphra Behn* 5. 128.

[13] London, 1720.

story, but such episodes are introduced largely for the sake of variety, since the book consists of little more than a mixture of exciting adventures, now among the pirates, now on a desert island, now among the Spanish of the Indies.

In the course of the narrative, most of which is related by Captain Falconer, with occasional episodes by some one else, Mr. Randal, a physician, tells of his experience among the Indians of Virginia, which is somewhat as follows: With several of his companions he goes ashore, with the intention of returning to the ship, but instead they unluckily fall into the hands of the Indians, who make them prisoners, and start to burn them at the stake. Just at this point, however, they discover his medical instruments, and are very curious to know their use. He then tells them something of the medical art, whereupon they invite him to demonstrate his skill by curing the king, who then chances to be sick of a fever. When they learn that bleeding is a part of the process, they insist that he try it on one of his companions; this operation proving harmless, they permit him to bleed the king, who, as a result, soon recovers his health. The savages are much impressed by this remarkable cure, in return for which they offer to reward them all with Indian wives. His companions enjoy this experience, but he avoids it by telling them that in his country it is a custom for physicians not to marry. After he has lived with them some time, his captors send him to Jamestown, to make discoveries about the English, with whom they are then at war. This opportunity to escape he is not slow to improve, but comments on his departure from his Indian friends as follows: 'I must confess I went with joy and sorrow; with joy to leave such a cursed place, where death threatened me every day; with sorrow to go without my companions.[14]

Later in the story, Captain Richard Falconer has a similar experience on the island of Dominico. He goes ashore,

[14] *Voyages of Richard Falconer* 2. 24.

misses his way, the ship sails before he can get back, and he is left at the mercy of the savage natives. They are on the point of killing him, but change their minds, and adopt him into their nation. He then chooses a wife from among them, and is united to her after the Indian custom. His married life he pictures as very happy, partly, it would appear, from the amiable character of his wife, whom he describes as endowed with 'a mighty mild nature, very loving and courteous, and nothing like the rest of the savage crew.'[15] After he has lived among them very peacefully for a time, he again gets into trouble, and nearly loses his life. The Indians at the other side of the island are hostile, but, not knowing this, he one day starts to wander over that way, principally from the curiosity his wife had aroused by always holding him back. The Indians, thinking he is trying to escape, decide to put him to death. He is tied to the stake, the fuel is heaped on all sides, the torch is lighted, but, a violent storm coming up, the execution cannot then be carried out. His wife, by trying to save him, only arouses the other Indians' rage, and is cruelly killed before his eyes, the occasion for a very touching description of her death, their love, his grief for her loss.

Now again he is tied to the stake, and everything made ready for the horrid scene; and again he is snatched from death by an attack of the hostile Indians on the other side of the island. In the battle which follows, his companions are all killed, and he is carried off by their enemies. Not much is told of his life here, but something of the customs and beliefs of the savages. Their view of life after death is perhaps the most curious. The dead bodies they throw into the sea, thinking that a large fish will take them to a paradise far out in the ocean, where they eat of a certain kind of leaf, and forget all about this life. When he tells them about his God, and a heaven up in the sky, they are puzzled,

[15] *Ibid.* 3. 132.

and fail to see how any one can get up there. 'Indian Will,'
with whom he discusses this, states their view of the matter
as follows: 'You be de white man, you have soul; when we
die, we fling in water, big fish come carry us to an oder place,
den we live dare and die agen, and fish bring us back to
an oder place.' Finally, an English ship comes to the island,
and he goes back to England, taking 'Indian Will' as his
companion.

During the latter half of the century, novels having their
scene in America become much more common, and in many
of these the Indian plays a conspicuous rôle. *The History
of the Life and Adventures of Mr. Anderson*[16] traces the
fortunes of its hero on land and sea, in Europe and America,
introducing the theme of Indian warfare and captivity as a
source of exciting adventure and picturesque local color.
On one occasion he falls in with a band of hostile Indians.
His companions are killed, he is himself stripped, and the
terrible war-dance begun, in preparation for his death or
a life of captivity. In dividing his clothes, however, the
Indians find his flute, and inquire as to its use. When he
plays to them they are charmed, and, by offering one of them
the flute, he secures his friendship, and thereby kind treatment and freedom.

More impressive in many ways, however, is the story of
Calcathony, a friendly Indian whom Tom falls in with in
the course of his wanderings. Calcathony is distinguished
not only for his swiftness in the chase, his skill with the
bow, his grace in the dance, and other Indian accomplishments, but for 'that greatness of soul which he displayed
either in prosperity or adversity, the justice and honesty of
his actions, the inflexible disposition he displayed to preserve
that jewel liberty, and the strong attachment he had to the
English, which no offers of advantages from the other side

---

[16] London, 1754.

could ever induce him to forsake.'[17] A fitting companion for such a hero is the amiable Talousa, 'all that could appear charming to the eyes of an Indian, nay, of an European; her temper was mild and gentle, her heart soft, and susceptible of the noblest passions, her person beautiful, and her features quite transporting.'[18]

The superior virtue of Calcathony appears most strikingly in his relations with the French. On one occasion, having been made a captive, he is offered his freedom if he will induce his people to take the side of the French against the English. Such a proposal Calcathony indignantly refuses in a speech 'that made all the hearers tremble.'[19] Nothing can induce him to forsake his friends. 'No,' he exclaims, 'I value not your emperor or his substitute, and will sooner submit to all you can inflict, than purchase life at the price of losing my honour.'[20] In the course of his captivity, he is befriended by a gentleman named Marsillac, who, some time after, when Calcathony has regained his freedom, and is again leading his brave warriors, falls into the hands of the Indians, and is about to be sacrificed. Calcathony, recognizing his friend, saves his life, and takes him into his home, with every mark of friendship and esteem. This kindness Marsillac later repays by the basest ingratitude. Having long admired and longed for the beautiful Talousa, he finally seizes her, and carries her off. He is just on the point of violating her virtue when she seizes a sword, stabs him, and then herself, 'without hesitation,' an example, the author remarks, 'of consummate virtue and heroic fortitude.' The loss of Talousa proves a blow from which Calcathony never recovers. 'Poor Calcathony, though happy in his children, has never been seen once to smile since the loss of the

[17] *History of the Life and Adventures of Mr. Anderson*, p. 109.
[18] *Ibid.*, p. 110.
[19] *Ibid.*, p. 114.
[20] *Ibid.*, p. 113.

amiable Talousa, and though alive, but half lives without her inspiring presence.'[21]

In *Lydia*,[22] the noble savage, whom we have already encountered in *Oroonoko*, reappears in an altogether new form, much more fully and consistently developed. The story opens in the forests of North America, and then changes to England, where the corruptions of civilized society furnish a background against which the Indian's innocence and simplicity stand out in bold relief. The tone of the book is quite clearly suggested by the first chapter-heading: 'Strange folks in strange lands. Patriotism, heroism, fainting, dying, loving, sentiment and generosity, all amongst Indians in America.' This is followed, in the first few paragraphs, by a description of these strange folk that should fulfil any reader's expectations, at least in the matter of heroism, sentiment, and generosity:

> On the banks of the great river Catarakui, near the cataracts which fall with foaming thunder from the cloud-capt mountains; deep embosomed in the eternal woods of America, dwell the ancient nations of the Onnondagans and Cayugans.
> No people are equally renowned through all the western world, from the northern bleakest track which human feet have ever trodden, to the most southern point of all this habitable globe.
> Their names pronounced with terror by the nations round; their valour recognized beyond all other people; the tributes annually received from other kingdoms; evince the superiority of their military fame; nor, in the milder parts of legislative knowledge, are their souls deficient. Elocution, reason, truth, and probity, are not less the characteristics of this people's genius.
> In all the oral history of this ancient race, delivered down from sire to son, no instance is to be found of broken faith with other nations; no anecdote of friends betrayed, or allies deserted in the hour of danger and distress; their words are sacredly preserved; their lives offered up in battle are the proof of it.

---

[21] *Ibid.*, p. 124.
[22] John Shebbeare, *Lydia; or Filial Piety* (London, 1755). My citations are from the edition of 1786.

The hero of the piece is next introduced, distinguished even above his noble countrymen for his beauty of form, and his just and virtuous soul:[23]

> No human form was ever seen more graceful than that of Canassatego, his person was as straight as the arrow which his hands directed from his fatal bow, his stature six feet, the most perfect height in human nature. On his large neck his head stood erect and bold; his face was animated with features that spoke sensibility of soul; high and open was his forehead; from his eyes flashed forth the beams of courage and compassion, as each passion at different moments animated his bosom, within which his heart beat with honest throbbing for his country's service. . . . The air, attitude, and expression of the beauteous statue of Apollo, which adorns the Belvidera palace at Rome, were seen animated in this American the instant he had discharged his deadly shaft. And though the fair complexion of the European natives was not to be found in this warrior, yet his face and countenance precluded the perceiving of that deficiency, the perfection of his form and expression of his visage were such that the Grecian sculptors of the famed statue of Laocoon, or the fighting gladiator, might have studied him with instruction and delight.

As a fitting companion for the brave Cannassatego the beautiful Yarico presently enters the story, the model of all that is gentle and lovely in woman:[24]

> No beauty of the five nations was in perfection equal to Yarico. Her eyes vivid as the diamond's ray, and black as ebony, shone like the stars amidst the dusky sky. . . . Her bosom, hard as wax, and formed like the statue of a Grecian sculptor, where no unnatural restraint has spoiled their shape and situation . . . . . Her soul had every tenderness which renders woman the most amiable object and delight of God's creation.

The nobility and elevation of her sentiments are also shown in her protest against 'that pernicious principle of glory, which delights in war and slaughter. She conceived it the most unnatural idea which can enter into a human heart,

[23] *Ibid.*, pp. 1-2.
[24] *Ibid.*, p. 8.

that rage and the destruction of mankind should prevail over the loftier passions of love and friendship, and fame be obtained by what ought to be the horror of humanity.'[25]

No less ideal is the love of Yarico and Cannassatego, in this land where only the laws of nature hold sway over human hearts:[26]

> In this country the primaeval laws of Nature still hold their native sway over human hearts. The intents of Heaven have not yet been violated by the pernicious and impious schemes of corrupted men. The charms which Nature bestowed on the human race to bind with mutual joy the sexes in the wreaths of love, still render lovers happy. Each sympathetic power darting from the soul, is received and fostered by that which is congenial to it. Gold, the bane of European bliss, possesses no esteem among these uncontaminated natives. The perfections which Heaven has given to mortals only influence the virtuous bosoms of the Indian nations.

Against all this background of primitive innocence stand out the wrongs and treacheries of the white men. Cannassatego has heard accounts of former times, before the invaders reached their shores, and now determines to free his nation from the servitude they endure. He sees his people yielding to the vices of the despised European. 'He beheld the Indian Chiefs wrapt in European manufactures, as men bearing the badge of slavery. He detested the day which brought them that intoxicating fluid which had enervated their former strength and ancient valour.'[27] He has heard of the virtues of the English across the water, and thinks he has perhaps thus far seen only their banished criminals. He has therefore learned the language of the English, in order to go to England, and lay before the great king the wrongs endured by his people. This plan he lays before the chiefs in a long speech, of which the following is a fair sample:[28]

[25] *Ibid.*, p. 16.
[26] *Ibid.*, p. 9.
[27] *Ibid.*, p. 6.
[28] *Ibid.*, pp. 7-8.

Fathers and sachems of the Onnondagan nation, hear the voice of youth, and approve me if my counsel finds favour in your hearts. It is my zeal for this sinking people, which prompts me to this undertaking; it is the great Spirit which animates my soul. . . .

Each tufted spring brings forth with it's leaves fresh vows of friendship and alliance: before the naked winter shows it's hoary head, all these have been repeatedly broken, and foregone. . . .

Long have my eyes beheld our situation with afflicted heart. The autumnal blast has not scattered more leaves than I have uttered sighs. The rushing cataracts of Niagara have not poured more drops of water, than I have shed tears in surveying our abject state. Each day treads on the heels of another, loaded with fresh marks of British perfidy and Indian sufferings. . . .

We may pass briefly over Cannassatego's preparations for the trip, his tender parting with Yarico, his voyage across the great water; his only adventure being the rescue of the beautiful young Lydia, whom the wicked captain had attempted to ravish. His landing in England is disappointing. 'Instead of pomp and splendor, vast palaces and magnificent temples, of which he had before heard, he saw little better than the huts of Indians, and a parcel of people with their faces blacker than his own.' He is astonished when he learns that they are colliers just come from the mine, and asks if all the English dig coals. 'Then,' says he, 'I can account for their leaving this country in search of ours.'[29]

Further acquaintance with this people but deepens his aversion. After many adventures he is reunited to Lydia and her husband, the only ones he has found who have 'Indian souls,' miraculous, he thinks, 'among polluted millions.'[30] To them he relates all that has happened, commenting most severely on the faithlessness of the English, and the various other causes of his disappointment. Not the least among these is his meeting with the prime minister:[31]

[29] *Ibid.*, p. 74.   [30] *Ibid.*, p. 204.   [31] *Ibid.*, p. 205.

How different from what my imagination had falsely imaged to itself. Instead of that person of exalted aspect, and august mien, where dignity and wisdom sat expressed, and supremely distinguished, whose every word and action bespoke sagacity and knowledge; there appeared before me that being undignified by nature, ungraceful, whiffling, inconsistent, whose words, hurried out like water from an inverted bottle, included nothing to be understood, ever beginning, never closing one sentence, rambling from man to man, from one half thought to another, the farce and mockery of national prudence. Can it be, I said to myself, that this man can direct the business of a people?

The series of deceptions, rebuffs, and broken promises which mark his attempts to lay his wrongs before the minister, lead him to conclude that the English here are the same as those who have crossed the great water, thirst for gold being their ruling passion:[32]

Alas, we are the scorn of those whose virtues are all venal. Minions of distress, a curled pampered race, who tremble at the northern blasts, the slaves of money; that yellow ore changes the face of nature, the eye sees not, the ear hears not; all human faculties die before it's influence; each liberal motive of the free-born soul is quite erased by that pernicious influence; Oh! bane of every virtue, bane of all our Indian peace and happiness! Oceans roll between, rocks, woods, and mountains, in vain seclude us from the ravenous thirst of gold. Sensation dies, the feelings of humanity expire before it's blasting breath; frozen is the heart; the eye refuses that tear which nature gave to wait upon compassion; we die unpitied like the stricken deer.

In his adventure with a certain Lady Susan Overstay, we have a very entertaining account of his disillusionment concerning the virtue of the English ladies of rank. Lady Susan is described as one who 'considered herself a beauty of the highest rank,' a circumstance which 'had induced her to stay too long at market, by which means, being a little fly-blown, she remained upon hands.'[33] One day she cast her eyes ' a little too waggishly on the person of the Indian

[32] *Ibid.*, p. 206.   [33] *Ibid.*, p. 208.

prince,' and thereupon formed the plan of 'making experiments on the difference of nations in the feats of love.'[34] She thereupon invites him to her house, and begins a very silly conversation. First, she supposes that he speaks French, being a foreigner, and therefore opens a conversation with him in this tongue. Then she inquires if he is not the Prince of Wales in India, being the eldest son of the king, and Cannassatego tells her that no man can be born a prince in his country—courage and wisdom, the love of family and country, virtues of the mind and powers of the body, being the only qualities that give authority and esteem among the Indians. Then she would like to know what are the prevailing fashions at the Indian court, whether the ladies use hard or soft pomatum, and whether grey powder is still in fashion amongst them. On being told that they know only bear's grease, she appears much surprised, as the following conversation brings out:[35]

> 'Bear's grease! O—h hideous!" with a shriek and an air; 'ladies of the court wear bear's-grease! Pray will their gallants come near them when they smell of bear's-grease? But your royal highness rallies me; it is impossible that ladies of quality can go to operas, plays, ridottos, routs, and courts, with their heads daubed with bear's-grease.' Then without stopping for an answer—'Are your father's subjects fond of these entertainments?'
>
> 'No, Madam, we know nothing of them; war and hunting make the study and exercise of our youth; wisdom and virtue those of old age. Our wise men recount the actions and observations of themselves and their forefathers; the young listen, admire, and improve.
>
> 'Our women are busied in domestick affairs, or employed in suckling or sustaining their progeny,' says the Indian.
>
> 'Oh fye, ladies of quality nurse their own children! why does it not absolutely spoil their necks? We never suckle our children in England. And no cards?' says Lady Susan; 'how is it possible to live without cards?' . . . 'Pray, have the Indian ladies fine complexions?' continued Lady Susan to the chief.

---

[34] *Ibid.*, p. 208.
[35] *Ibid.*, pp. 209-210.

Corbould del.

Angus sculp.

LYDIA.

'Indeed,' replied the prince, 'your ladyship approaches the nearest of all the ladies I have seen in England to the complexions of our Indian women. . . .

Thus, in tittle-tattle an hour passed away with Lady Susan Overstay, when being dressed, and her woman withdrawn, she asked if the court of his father was much addicted to gallantry, smiling in the Indian's face with a lascivious leer; throwing herself on the sofa, and desiring the prince to sit near her.

'No, Madam,' answered Cannassatego, 'love being uninfluenced by the pernicious esteem amongst our nations, which is given to gold in this; in this we choose from the pure dictates of nature, where souls correspond to souls, and live happy in each other's arms.'

'That is, your royal highness means the common people do. But your great men and ladies of quality have not such odd ideas, I presume; they surely have intrigues amongst them. I daresay many of the maids of honour of your queen-mother have been happily caressed in those fine arms of yours,' says Lady Susan, 'have they not?' taking him by the hand.

Cannassatego then looking upon her with contempt, told her he had never yet violated his chastity. His whole heart had been, and should be ever reserved for his lovely Yarico—'Absent or present I am her's alone.'

'Poor man?' says Lady Susan, 'I warrant you would not go to bed to a fine lady, lest Yarico should know it! Hah, hah, hah!' squeezing his hand in the laugh, and looking amorously upon him.

'No, Madam, beauty has no powers on me. Adieu.' At which words, drawing away his hand suddenly, he left her in great indignation. When Lady Susan for her soul could not conceive what was come over the man—'Surely,' says she, 'he can be no prince, he knows so little of the manners of the best of company.'

The further career of Cannassatego in England contains little either novel or sensational; no other ladies of rank attempt to corrupt his Indian virtue by their amorous advances. Before he departs, he receives a very affectionate letter from the faithful Yarico, who during his absence has acquired the art of writing; to this he replies with a tenderness of sentiment which I am sure would have made the Lady Susan Overstay very envious of her dark-complexioned rival. Not long after, he returns to America, and there to the assembled chiefs of his nation he delivers a long speech describing his adventures in England, and repeating, with many variations, the familiar theme of Indian virtue and English perfidy. Of course he is happily reunited to Yarico and his faithful dog, in which delightful situation the author leaves the brave Cannassatego, assuming, as I take it must we, that ideal love is to continue to flourish amid these scenes of Arcadian loveliness.

In no other novel of the century does the Indian figure so conspicuously or so heroically as in *Lydia:* elsewhere he appears only as a subordinate character, introduced to add a touch of local color or picturesque adventure. Many examples might be cited of stories located wholly or partly in America, with the Indians moving mysteriously in the background, or perhaps rushing in to carry some one off, such occurrences usually being treated with a mixture of realism, sentiment, and perhaps social satire. The large amount of repetition in the details of all such works precludes any extended account of them here; a few of the more striking situations, however, may be of sufficient interest to merit brief consideration.

Passing over *Virtue Triumphant; or, Elizabeth Canning in America,*[36] in which the appearance of the Indians, and their attempt to scalp the heroine, are decidedly subordinate to the main thread of the story, we come to a novel for which historic truth furnishes at least a slight basis, *Chrysal: or The Adventures of a Guinea.*[37] Sir William Johnson, trader, adventurer, and superintendent of Indian affairs, for many years during the middle of the century played a prominent rôle in negotiations with the restless natives, and so far won the confidence of the savage warriors that they made him a sachem of the Mohawk tribe, and treated him as a

---

[36] London, 1757.
[37] London, 1760-5. Went through many editions quickly. Published anonymously, but generally attributed to Charles Johnstone.

brother chieftain. Of even more interest is the circumstance of his marrying Molly Brant, sister of the celebrated Mohawk war-chief, whose black eyes and laughing face are said to have 'caught his fancy, as, flittering with ribbons, she galloped past him at a muster of the Tryon County militia.'[38] In *Chrysal,* the novelist treats with humorous exaggeration Johnson's relations with the savage women, as well as his influence over the dusky warriors. The coin, which is supposed to relate its adventures in many lands, in the course of long wanderings, falls into the hands of a British general, who soon passes it on to Sir William Johnson. The general and Johnson discuss Indian relations at some length, in the course of which Johnson points out the natives' superiority in war, and at the same time exalts the natural simplicity and integrity of his savage friends. 'All the evils,' he says, 'which have been suffered from them have proceeded from the unhappy error, of thinking ourselves possessed of a superiority over them, which nature, that is Heaven, has not given us. They are our fellow-creatures; and in general above our level, in the virtues which give real preëminence, however despicably we think of, and injuriously we treat them.'[39]

Johnson's hold upon his Indian subjects is evident in the way they receive him, which, the author remarks, was the 'very reverse of what *Sovereigns* usually meet. They welcomed him with sincere joy and respect, which they expressed in the overflowing of their hearts, without ceremony or parade.'[40] A part of this 'Sovereign's' authority rests upon

---

[38] For this statement, and other information about Sir William Johnson, cf. Francis Parkman, *The Conspiracy of Pontiac* (Boston, 1901) I. 95 ff. He is not specifically mentioned in the story, but the similarity is obvious, and has been noted by E. A. Baker in his edition of *Chrysal* (London, 1907), p. 349.

[39] *Chrysal* 3. 143.

[40] *Ibid.* 3. 147.

the fact that he is 'literally the father of his subjects, the king of his own family.'[41]   Believing that restraint among the sexes is detrimental to the public good, he gives liberty to every man to converse with as many females as he pleases, and is himself foremost by example, as well as precept. 'There was scarce a house in any of the tribes around him, from which he had not taken a temporary mate, and added a child to its own number.'[42]   The happiness resulting from these singular domestic arrangements is pictured at some length—the dress, conversation, amusements of these ladies, their friendly rivalry and mutual good will, except when in their games 'emulation and avarice agitated the passions, and set the competitors together by the ears, till they almost clawed out each other's eyes.'[43]

The influence of doctrines akin to those of Rousseau is clearly discernible in the next novel we are to consider, *The Adventures of Emmera; or, The Fair American.*[44]   The story pictures a family living in retirement amid the forests of America, where, as one of them expresses it, they intend to 'form a little society amidst these romantic scenes, where nature reigns in majestic wildness, more consonant to true reason, happiness and virtue, than can ever be met with amidst the pompous glare and polished elegance of your vicious climes.'[45]   In the course of events, the heroine, Emmera, is carried off by a disappointed lover and his accomplices.   Her true lover, learning of her situation, calls on their Indian friends, whose timely aid he thus describes in a letter to a friend in England:[46]

> In about four hours came five Indians:—one of them had a little English: I made him understand my loss—there needed no prayers or entreaties; the worthy creatures felt my sorrows deeply, which, joined to their own affection for my Emmera, made them

[41] *Ibid.* 3. 148.
[42] *Ibid.* 3. 149-150.
[43] *Ibid.* 3. 156.

[44] Dublin, 1767.
[45] *Adventures of Emmera* 1. 8.
[46] *Ibid.* 2. 38.

eager for the pursuit. I shewed them the track taken by my enemy, and told them when he fled. They returned home for arms, and to take a shorter cut across the country, assuring me that I need not fear their rescuing their Queen, so they called my dear, lost angel. . . . Their assurances gave me a little glimmering of hope, . . . for these people are so amazingly expeditious, . . . so wonderfully sagacious, and so indefatigably persevering, that I think there is some chance of their overtaking the villain.

The villain himself, however, manages to escape, while his two companions are cut to pieces by the broad swords of the trusty Indians; after which Emmera is of course restored to her anxious lover, and all ends very happily.

One of the most fanciful and picturesque of the stories having to do with the Indian is *The Female American; or, The Adventures of Unca Eliza Winkfield.*[47] Mr. William Winkfield, the father of Unca Eliza, who is supposed to tell the story, is the son of one of the early settlers of Virginia. When about twenty years old, he, with five of

[47] London, 1767. Reprinted at Newburyport, Mass., about 1790, and at Vergennes, Vt., in 1814. (Cf. O. Wegelin, *Early American Fiction*, New York, 1913, p. 34.) The *Critical Rev.*, 23 (1767) 217, notices the first appearance of the work, with the following comment: 'Mrs. Unca Eliza Winkfield is a most strange adventurer, and her memoirs seem to be calculated only for the wild Indians to whom she is so closely allied. We could therefore have wished, as well for her sake as our own, that this lady had published her adventures at the Fall of Niagara, or upon the banks of Lake Superior, as she would then, probably, have received the most judicious and sincere applause from her enlightened countrymen and princely relations, and have saved us six hours very disagreeable employment.' Cf. also *Monthly Rev.* 36 (1767). 238. For a modern critical discussion and fuller summary of the plot, cf. Loshe, *The Early American Novel* (New York, 1907), pp. 77-79. Some of this writer's comments are interesting, though in one particular incorrect, since she dates the novel by the third edition (nearly fifty years later than the first), and then proceeds to detect 'certain characteristics of several types popular in the fiction of the day,' even finding 'a slight reminiscence of *Atala*.'

his countrymen, is carried off by a party of hostile Indians. Shocking details of cruelty and inhumanity, however, form no part of this writer's representation of Indian captivity. Instead of the usual war-dance and torture, the prisoners are quietly brought before the king, a venerable old man, who 'seemed to address them in a pathetic manner, for tears accompanied his words.'[48]   Most of his speech is devoted to reproving them for having taken the Indians' lands:[49]

> 'Men, for I see you have legs, arms and heads as we have, look to the sun,' here he pointed up to that luminary, 'he is our god, is he yours? he made us, he warms us, he lights us, he makes our corn and grass to grow, we love and praise him; did he make you? did he send you to punish us? if he did we will die, here are our bows and arrows, kill us.' Saying this, they all threw their bows and arrows within the circle, between themselves and the captives. Not then knowing their meaning, they stood silent; the king then continued his speech, 'Our god is not angry; the evil being who made you has sent you into our land to kill us; we know you not and have never offended you; why then have you taken possession of our lands, ate our fruits, and made our countrymen prisoners? had you no lands of your own? Why did you not ask us? we would have given you some. Speak.' It seems they had no idea there are more languages than one; therefore taking their silence for a confession of guilt, their king proceeded, 'You designed to kill us, but we hurt no man who has not first offended us; our god has given you into our hands, and you must die.'

The Indians then proceeded to carry out this sentence. Mr. Winkfield's five companions are beheaded, and he is about to suffer the same fate, when suddenly he is rescued in much the same way as Captain John Smith. One of the king's daughters comes forth, and, by stroking him with a wand, gives the signal for his deliverance. He is unbound from the stake, and led off by the princess to a 'bower composed of the most pleasing greens, delightfully variegated

[48] *The Female American*, p. 11.
[49] *Ibid.*, pp. 11-12.

with the most beautiful flowers; a shady defence from the sun.'[50] Everything is now done for his comfort and convenience: the choicest foods are provided, and slaves are appointed to do his bidding. The princess Unca comes to visit him every day, and as soon as he comes to understand their language, she declares her love for him 'according to the simplicity of the uncorrupted Indians.' Winkfield returns the affection of the young princess, who in person is 'not inferior to the greatest European beauty,' and possesses besides an understanding 'uncommonly great, pleasantly lively, and wonderfully comprehensive, even of subjects unknown to her.'[51]

Only one obstacle presents itself to their union, the jealousy of the king's eldest daughter, Allaca. Finding Winkfield alone one day in the woods, she threatens him with death unless he will accept her love. Rather than prove false to Unca, however, he drinks the poison she and her followers force upon him, and the princess leaves him for dead. Unca, who soon passes that way, discovers the condition of her lover, and restores him by use of an herb known to her people. Not long after, Winkfield and Unca are married, and settle upon his estate in Virginia. Here they live unmolested for six years, during which time she bears him a daughter, Unca Eliza, the heroine and narrator of the story. During this time the old king has died, and the jealous Allaca now reigns in his place. Her continued resentment leads her to plan the murder of Unca and her husband. Winkfield, however, escapes, but his Indian wife is stabbed by her sister's slaves.

After this, Winkfield takes his young daughter to England, where she is brought up with her cousins, his brother's children. As her father has become very rich by the gold received from the Indians, little Unca enjoys the many

---

[50] *Ibid.*, p. 12.
[51] *Ibid.*, p. 15.

advantages of this circumstance. The oddity of her dress, 'neither perfectly in the Indian, nor yet in the European taste,' attracted no little attention yet did not lessen her popularity in polite society:[52]

> My uncommon complexion, singular dress and the grand manner in which I appeared, always attended by two female and two male slaves, could not fail of making me much taken notice of. I was accordingly invited by all the neighboring gentry, who treated me in a degree little inferior to that of a princess, as I was always called; and indeed I might have been a queen, if my father had pleased, for on the death of my aunt, the Indians made a formal tender of the crown to me; but I declined it

The most interesting of Unca's adventures take place upon an uninhabited island. When she is grown up, her father, now somewhat melancholy and restless, takes her to Virginia, and soon after dies there. On her voyage back to England, the Captain tries to force her promise to marry his son, and, when she refuses, places her upon a lonely island, with nothing but her chest of clothes. The circumstances of her life here are in some ways reminiscent of *Robinson Crusoe,* except that her struggle for subsistence is made much simpler and easier. An old hermit, who has lived on the island forty years, dies soon after her arrival, leaving her the food he has gathered, and directions how to procure more. One of the strangest of the many remains she finds upon the island is a huge statue, so contrived that one can enter, and speak from it in a voice much magnified. When the Indians from the surrounding islands come there, according to custom, for their annual worship, she conceals herself in the statue, and addresses them at some length on the Christian religion. The supposedly supernatural utterance is received with great joy by the Indians, and when she discloses herself to them, she is treated as being more than mortal. Some time elapses, during which she continues her efforts towards

[52] *Ibid.,* pp. 30-31.

their conversion. The coming of her cousin Winkfield to her rescue leads the reader to expect a conclusion of the desert-island episode. Instead of their returning to civilization, however, the cousin, after going to England to bid his parents good-bye, joins in her work of converting the Indians.

The element of adventure plays no part in the treatment accorded the Indian in *Emily Montague*,[53] but there appears instead a good deal of philosophizing on the savage state, together with long accounts of primitive customs and beliefs. None of this seems very original, though there is some variety in the views expressed, the letters which make up the story being written by the different characters. Local color and a certain amount of realism also appear in some of these descriptions, as well as long passages discussing the Indian's religion, laws, and mode of life.

Something of the influence of the French philosophers, as well as the opposition their theories aroused in the minds of many, may be perceived in the following letter of an old gentleman, not yet convinced of the superior advantages of the state of nature:[54]

> Rousseau has taken great pains to prove that the most unculti-
> vated nations are the most virtuous: I have all due respect for
> this philosopher, of whose writings I am an enthusiastic admirer;
> but I have a still greater respect for truth, which I believe is not
> in this instance on his side.
>
> From all that I have observed, and heard of these people, it
> appears to me an undoubted fact, that the most civilized Indian
> nations are the most virtuous; a fact which makes directly
> against Rousseau's ideal system. . . .
>
> Père Lafitau has, for this reason, in his very learned com-
> parison of the manners of savages with those of the first ages,
> given a very imperfect account of Indian manners; he is even

---

[53] Mrs. Frances Brooke, *The History of Emily Montague* (London, 1769).

[54] *Ibid.* 3. 107-10.

so candid as to own, he tells you nothing but what makes for the system he is endeavoring to establish. . . .

That the savages have virtues, candor must own; but only a love of paradox can make any man assert they have more than polished nations.

In Smollett's *Humphrey Clinker*[55] we have an example of the Indian captivity-motive, told with a good deal of realistic detail, as well as cleverness and humor. The hero of this episode is a Scotch lieutenant, who, while fighting the French in America, falls into the hands of the Indians. His tortures include having one of his fingers cut, or rather sawed, off with a rusty knife, one of his great toes crushed into a mash between two stones, some of his teeth drawn or dug out with a crooked nail, splintered reeds thrust up his nostrils and other tender parts, and the calves of his legs blown up with mines of gunpowder, dug in the flesh with the sharp point of the tomahawk. His companion, Murphy, who is also put to the torture, becomes so mutilated as to be unfit for matrimony, whereupon they tie him to the stake, and give Lismahago his intended bride. The account of Murphy's death is very lurid:[56]

> The Indians allowed that Murphy died with great heroism, singing, as his death song, in concert with Mr. Lismahago, who was present at the solemnity. After the warriors and matrons had made a hearty meal upon the muscular flesh which they had pared from the victim, and had applied a great variety of tortures, which he bore without flinching, an old lady, with a sharp knife, scooped out one of his eyes, and put a burning coal in the socket. The pain of this operation was so exquisite that he could not help bellowing, upon which the audience raised a shout of exultation, and one of the warriors stealing behind him, gave him the *coup de grace* with a hatchet.

Lismahago, more favored by fortune than his friend Murphy, marries the squaw, and lives with her two years,

---

[55] 1771. My citations are from the edition of Smollett's works by George Saintsbury, New York, 19—.

[56] *Humphrey Clinker* 2. 23-24.

during which time she bears him a son. His happiness with her, however, is suddenly cut short; 'to his unspeakable grief' she dies of a fever, 'occasioned by eating too much raw bear.'[57] At the conclusion of peace he returns to the English.

Mrs. Tabby, to whom these circumstances are related, expresses great interest in all that has happened, and with something of the naïvete of Lady Susan Overstay inquires about the Indian lady's wedding dress—'whether she wore high-breasted stays or bodice, a robe of silk or velvet, and laces of Mechlin or Marionette; she supposed, as they were connected with the French, she used *rouge,* and had her hair dressed in the Parisian fashion!'[58] The lieutenant is finally obliged to tell her that his princess had neither 'shoes, stockings, shift, nor any kind of linen,' but was decorated with variety of ornaments—feathers, colored stones, beads, and wampum, besides having hung about her neck 'the fresh scalp of a Mohawk warrior, whom her deceased lover had lately slain in battle.'[59] In the same way is Mrs. Tabby disillusioned when she inquires about the lady's religion, whether she is High Church or Low Church, Presbyterian or Anabaptist, or favored with the new light of the gospel:[60]

> 'As to religion, madam,' answered the lieutenant, 'it is among these Indians a matter of great simplicity. They never heard of any *Alliance between Church and State.* They, in general, worship two contending principles; one the fountain of all good, the other the source of evil. The common people there, as in other countries, run into absurdities of superstition; but sensible men pay adoration to a Supreme Being, who created and sustains the universe.'

The veiled thrust at Christianity in the above passage is continued in an account of the activities of some Jesuit missionaries, worth reproducing here for the cleverness of the satire:[61]

[57] *Ibid.* 2. 24.
[58] *Ibid.* 2. 25.
[59] *Ibid.* 2. 26.
[60] *Ibid.* 2. 27.
[61] *Ibid.* 2. 27-29.

The lieutenant told her that, while he resided among them two French missionaries arrived, in order to convert them to the Catholic religion; but when they talked of mysteries and revelations which they could neither explain nor authenticate, and called in the evidence of miracles which they believed upon hearsay; when they taught that the Supreme Creator of heaven and earth had allowed his only Son, his own equal in power and glory, to enter the bowels of a woman, to be born as a human creature, to be insulted, flagellated, and even executed as a malefactor; when they pretended to create God himself, to swallow, digest, revive, and multiply him ad infinitum, by the help of a little flour and water, the Indians were shocked at the impiety of their presumption. They were examined by the assembly of sachems, who desired them to prove the divinity of their mission by some miracle. They answered that it was not in their power. 'If you really were sent by Heaven for our conversion,' said one of the sachems, 'you would certainly have some supernatural endowments, at least you would have the gift of tongues, in order to explain your doctrine to the different nations among which you are employed; but you are so ignorant of our language, that you cannot express yourself even upon the most trifling subjects.'

In a word, the assembly were convinced of their being cheats, and even suspected them of being spies. They ordered them a bag of Indian corn apiece, and appointed a guide to conduct them to the frontiers; but the missionaries having more zeal than discretion refused to quit the vineyard. They persisted in saying mass, in preaching, baptizing, and squabbling with the conjurors, or priests of the country, till they had thrown the whole community into confusion. Then the assembly proceeded to try them as impious impostors, who represented the Almighty as a, trifling, weak, capricious being, and pretended to make, unmake, and reproduce him at pleasure; they were, therefore, convicted of blasphemy and sedition, and condemned to the stake, where they died singing *Salve regina*, in a rapture of joy, for the crown of martyrdom which they thus obtained.

The Indian captivity-motive, with a good deal more serious idealization of the Indian, is also contained in a novel published two years after *Humphrey Clinker,* called *The Man of the World.*[62] The misfortunes endured by the victim before

---

[62] Henry Mackenzie, *The Man of the World* (London, 1773).

he goes among the Indians are made to form a sharp contrast with the stern justice he receives at their hands. There is the usual torture-scene, but, having endured his torments without complaint, he is adopted by an old Indian as his son. As the aged warrior puts the wampum around his neck, he speaks thus of the bravery of the Cherokees:[63]

> It is thus that the valiant are tried, and thus they are rewarded; for how should'st thou be as one of us, if thy soul were as the soul of little men; he only is worthy to lift the hatchet with the Cherokees, to whom shame is more intolerable than the stab of a knife or the burning of the fire.

The perfect freedom, and other advantages, he now enjoys among this people are so great that he feels nothing would induce him to return to civilization. When his foster-father dies, however, his thoughts again return to the home and friends he left in England, and he reluctantly prepares to leave his faithful Indian companions. His departure is made impressive by the following speeches of farewell:[64]

> You return to a people, who sell affection to their brethren for money; take therefore with you some of the commodities which their traders value; Strength, agility, and fortitude, are sufficient to us; and he who possesses wealth, having no need of virtue, among the wealthy it will not be found. . . ."
>
> Yonder smoke rises from the dwellings of your countrymen. You now return to a world which I have heard you describe as full of calamity; but the soul you possess is the soul of a man; remember that to fortitude there is no sting in adversity, and in death no evil to the valiant.

The Indian episode in *Sandford and Merton*,[65] though of some length, need not concern us very much here. Again, a Scotchman tells of his adventures, which includes not only his travels among the Indians as a friend, but the dangers

---

[63] *Ibid.*, p. 181.
[64] *Ibid.*, pp. 188-9.
[65] Thomas Day, *The History of Sandford and Merton* (London, 1783-9).

he had encountered during the war, especially at the time of Braddock's famous defeat. The generosity and noble simplicity of the savages are described in a way intended to be very instructive, but the whole account presents little that is striking or picturesque.

A novel called *Euphemia*,[66] by Mrs. Charlotte Lennox, in its introduction of the Indians presents quite a variety of elements. Like *Emily Montague,* and various other stories, this is also made up of a series of letters from an English family in America to their friends across the water. The Indians are discussed by the different correspondents, and a variety of opinions expressed on their virtues and vices.

On one occasion, a large party of them visit an Indian village, and are there entertained with an exhibition of the terrible war-dance. On seeing this, one of the ladies is so frightened that her little boy, born soon afterwards, is marked with a bow and arrow on his left breast. The same little boy, a few years later, in some way strays from his home, is found by the Indians, taken to Canada to be brought up by the Jesuits, and some years later restored to his parents. Although for the most part lazy and drunken, the behavior of the Indians at the death of one of the English officers, Colonel Bellenden, is marked by great delicacy and politeness. Mrs. Neville describes this as follows in one of her letters:[67]

> The request they made, to be permitted to pay their comple- ments of condolence to the widow and daughters of the Great Chief, as they stile him, shew that these untutored savages, have in their minds those natural principles of humanity, which is the foundation of true politeness. I was struck with this piece of politeness [the Indians withdrawing on seeing Mrs. Bellenden's grief]; but more with the tears, which I actually saw standing in the eyes of him who had addressed her. This brought to my recollection, what I once heard Mr. Euston say concerning the

[66] London, 1790.
[67] *Euphemia* 4. 69.

manners of these Indians. . . . 'Let us never believe,' said he, 'that gentleness and humanity are qualities of the earth and air; they are, says a learned friend of mine, neither goods of the East, nor captive virtues of the Greeks; they are wandering and passant. . . . All climates receive them in their turn; and it is not the Cymbrick Chersonesus any longer, it is Athens and Achaia that are at this day barbarous.'

Little, I think, need be said of the Indian's appearance in *The Old Manor House*.[68] Besides the account of his cruel atrocities during the Revolutionary War, now against the Americans at the instigation of the English, now in turn against the English themselves for their treachery and deceit, we have pictured, by way of contrast, the idealized friendship of Orlando, the hero of the story, and a young savage called Wolf-hunter. The younger Indians, Orlando notices, are less inured to blood than the others, and one of these in particular he distinguishes from the rest, 'by remarking his more open countenance—his more gentle manners, and by hearing that he had, at the risk of his own life, saved a woman from the fury of his relation the Bloody Captain, when he was on the point of killing her with a tomahawk.'[69] Wolf-hunter it is who saves Orlando's life when the others would put him to death, washes his wounds, and dresses them with chewed leaves, teaches him the customs of the Indians, and urges him to remain among them, resents Orlando's desire to leave, but by the promises of presents becomes reconciled to the loss.

In the same year as the publication of *The Old Manor House* appeared Gilbert Imlay's *Emigrants*,[70] another novel in the form of letters. The correspondence is supposed to take place between an English family, who have settled near Pittsburgh, and their various friends in England. Enthusiasm for nature and interest in social questions are the out-

---

[68] Mrs. Charlotte Smith, *The Old Manor House* (London, 1793).
[69] *Ibid.*, p. 291.
[70] London, 1793.

standing features of the story. The Indian figures in several ways, sometimes as a friendly, harmless sort of creature, sometimes as a fierce, warlike savage. One day as Caroline, the heroine, is strolling through the woods with her lover, Capt. Arl-ton, she suddenly catches sight of some Indians, whereupon she screams, and falls into her protector's arms. The friendly redskins, however, approach and offer their assistance. They express their good intentions by saying, 'Brother, if we have been your worst foes in war, we will be your best friends in peace,' adding that they were going to Pittsburgh 'for the purpose of burying the hatchet, that white people and Indians might live together like brothers.'[71]

Later in the story, Caroline's uncle relates how his wife and children had been slaughtered by the savages,[72] and finally the heroine herself is seized as she is strolling through the woods. The chief purpose of this incident is to furnish opportunity for a daring and heroic rescue by her lover. In order to draw off the greater part of Caroline's captors, Arl-ton's companions fire several shots in another part of the forest, while he himself rushes in, overcomes the few who are left to guard his mistress, and quickly carries her to a place of safety before the others can return. Commenting on the conduct of the Indians, Caroline says that they 'treated her the whole time with the utmost respect, and scrupulous delicacy.'[73] Such treatment of women captives, the writer of this letter states, 'is corroborated by the testimony of all decent looking women, who have been so unfortunate as to fall into their hands. Indeed, I have been told of instances where women have been treated with such tenderness and attention by them that they have from gratitude become their wives.'[74]

[71] *The Emigrants* 1. 106.
[72] *Ibid.* 2. 84 ff.
[73] *Ibid.* 3. 50.
[74] *Ibid.* 3. 50.

In 1793 there appeared also *The History of Maria Kittle,*[75] a lurid tale of savage atrocities, strongly suggestive of the earlier narratives of Indian captivity. Maria and her husband live on an outlying farm somewhere in the vicinity of Albany. During the French and Indian War they begin to feel alarmed at so exposed a situation, and accordingly make plans to withdraw to a near-by settlement. The Indians, however, with whom they have long had some acquaintance, assure them of continued friendship, a hope which is soon destroyed when Mr. Kittle's brother is shot in the woods. Mr. Kittle then goes for help, but before he can return the savages make a raid, killing his brother, sister-in-law, and children, all except Maria, who is carried off to Canada. The Indians' attack upon the unprotected household is pictured with considerable vividness. First Mr. Kittle's brother is shot, and his body cruelly mangled. Then follows a description of the treatment accorded his wife:[76]

> An Indian, hideously painted, strode ferociously up to Comelia (who sunk at the sight; and fainted on a chair), and cleft her white forehead deeply with his tomahawk. Her fine azure eyes just opened, and then suddenly closing forever, she tumbled lifeless at his feet. His sanguinary soul was not yet satisfied with blood; he deformed her lovely body with deep gashes; and tearing her unborn babe away, dashed it to pieces against the stone wall; with many additional circumstances of infernal cruelty.

A sentimental sort of pathos is also aimed at in the many sanguinary details which describe the murder of Maria's children. The following account of how her youngest babe is torn from her bosom is typical of the writer's style and manner:[77]

---

[75] Published in *The Posthumous Works of Ann Eliza Bleecker* (New York, 1793).
[76] *Works of Ann Eliza Bleecker*, pp. 35-36.
[77] *Ibid.*, p. 37.

So saying he seized her laughing babe by the wrists, and forcibly endeavoured to draw him from her arms. At this, terrified beyond conception, she exclaimed, 'Oh God! leave me, leave me my child! he shall not go, though a legion of devils should try to separate us!' Holding him still fast, while the Indian applied his strength to tear him away, gnashing his teeth at her opposition; 'Help! God of heaven!' screamed she, 'help! have pity, have mercy on this infant! O God! O Christ! can you bear to see this? O mercy! mercy! mercy! let a little spark of compassion save this unoffending, this lovely angel!' By this time the breathless babe dropt its head on its bosom; the wrists were nigh pinched off, and seeing him expiring, with a dreadful shriek she resigned him to the merciless hands of the savage, who instantly dashed his little forehead against the stones, and casting his bleeding body at some distance from the house left him to make his exit in feeble and unheard groans.

Little Anna in the meantime has fled, and hid herself in a closet. When the Indians now fire the house, and all hope of escape is cut off for her second child, Maria again breaks forth into lamentations and reproaches. Her journey to Canada is marked by all manner of sufferings and hardships. On one occasion she nearly loses her life, when her captor, hearing the approach of a deer, thinks it the sound of his prisoner trying to escape. Another time they are obliged to wait two days, because of Maria's inability to travel, 'her feet being greatly swoln and lacerated by the flinty path.'[78] When they encamp by night in a dismal hollow, Maria is overcome with depression. 'The confines of hell could not have given Maria more dismal ideas than her present situation: The horrid gloom of the place, the scowling looks of her murderous companions, the shrill shrieks of owls, the loud cries of the wolf, and mournful screams of panthers, which were redoubled by distant echoes as the terrible sounds seemed dying away, shook her frame with cold tremors.'[79]

Finally they approach the Indian settlement, and Maria

[78] *Ibid.*, p. 59.
[79] *Ibid.*, p. 54.

looks for sympathy in her own sex, to whom, she thinks, 'simple nature, no doubt, has taught humanity.'[80] Instead of consideration, however, the usual amount of cruelty and abuse is meted out to the new arrivals:[81]

> The tawny villagers, perceiving their approach, rushed promiscuously from their huts with an execrable din, and fell upon the weary captives with clubs and a shower of stones, accompanying their strokes with the most virulent language; amongst the rest an old deformed squaw, with the rage of a Tisiphone, flew to Maria, aiming a pine-knot at her head, and would certainly have given the wretched mourner her quietus had she not been opposed by the savage that guarded Mrs. Kittle: he at first mildly expostulated with his passionate countrywoman; but finding the old hag frantic, and insatiable of blood, he twisted the pine-knot from her hands and whirled it away to some distance, then seizing her arm roughly and tripping up her heels, he laid her prostrate, leaving her to howl and yell at leisure, which she performed without a prompter.

At last, after a long and wearisome journey, Maria reaches Montreal, where she is kindly received by the French and other English refugees like herself. The story concludes by recounting her happy reunion with her husband.

In the next novel we are to consider, Robert Bage's *Man as he is not: or, Hermsprong*,[82] we may clearly perceive the influence of the social philosophy of the time. The principal character in the story is a very crude sort of person called Hermsprong, who speaks of himself as a savage, and takes not a little pleasure and pride in the fact that he was brought up among the Indians. In the many discussions of current philosophical questions he always proclaims his admiration of the uncorrupted state of nature, and speaks of the savages of America as making the nearest approach to ideal human happiness. Hermsprong's father, it seems, to

---

[80] *Ibid.*, p. 59.
[81] *Ibid.*, p. 60.
[82] London, 1796. My citations are from the reprint in the *British Novelists* (London, 1810), Vol. 48.

escape a variety of misfortunes, had fled from society, and found a safe asylum among the Indians. Receiving a cordial welcome there, he later brings his wife and young son, and, in addition, as Hermsprong relates, 'our European servants, our books, our music, our instruments of drawing and everything that could be supposed to alleviate the solitude my mother had pictured to herself.'[83] Being a devout Catholic, she soon sets about trying to convert the savages, but instead of accepting her accounts of the Christian mysteries, Lontac, the Indian chief, tells her a long story of a white bear, inspired by the Great Spirit, rising out of the lake, and other legends she can only view as preposterous. Lontac then tells her that 'many things are far removed from the course of nature. . . . It is better to believe than contradict.'[84] Her husband tries to remove the prejudice she has conceived for the Indian's understanding:[85]

> Do, my dear, my father replied, as much as you can with civility for people who are always doing you services, and showing their regard. I despised them myself, till I found them my equals in knowledge of many things of which I believed them ignorant; and my superiors in the virtues of friendship, hospitality, and integrity.

Hermsprong's education, we should note in conclusion, included not only participation in the sports of the other young Indians, but a good many languages and sciences as well, so that we are not altogether unprepared for his deciding to return to society, and content himself with describing to others the advantages of the mode of life he has left.

At the close of the century, we find the Indian given a somewhat striking prominence in a novel of mysterious adventure and Gothic horror—Charles Brockden Brown's *Edgar Huntley; or, Memoirs of a Sleep Walker*.[86] The early part of the story is largely concerned with the strange

[83] *Ibid.*, p. 235.   [84] *Ibid.*, p. 236.   [85] *Ibid.*, p. 236.
[86] Philadelphia, 1799. For a discussion of Brown's treatment of the Indian, and position as a novelist, cf. Loshe, *op. cit.*, pp. 69-73.

behavior of Clithero, a sleepwalker, suspected of murdering Waldegrave, the friend of Huntley. Then Huntley himself becomes a victim of these nocturnal wanderings, and one day wakes up in the depths of a cavern, with no idea of how he came there. In trying to escape from his prison, he comes to an outlet of the cave, where four Indians lie asleep, with a fifth standing guard over a young woman captive. After a time the Indian sentry goes out of the cavern, where-upon Huntley, taking advantage of the opportunity thus offered for escape, makes his way noiselessly past the sleeping savages, and emerges from the cave, only to find his other antagonist seated on a ledge of rock outside. As the only path of escape is thus cut off, his only chance of escape is to strike the Indian with the tomahawk. But Huntley has never shed human blood, and so, after hesitating a long time, decides to return to his former position within the cave. Just at this moment the Indian detects his presence, and leaves him no choice but to kill or be killed. He therefore aims the fatal blow before the savage has a chance to call his companions. 'The stroke was as quick as lightning, and the wound mortal and deep. He had not time to destroy the author of his fate; but sinking on the path, expired without a groan. The hatchet buried itself in his breast, and rolled with him to the bottom of the precipice.'[87]

He now returns to the cave, rescues the fair prisoner from her sleeping captors, and carries her to the hut of Old Deb, a venerable squaw, who, as it later proves, is largely responsible for the Indian massacres. Her wild solitary life is pictured with a certain romantic fancy which has been compared to Scott's treatment of the old hag, Meg Mer-rilies.[88] She is not exactly a real or an idealized Indian, but more like a witch or a gypsy, a creature of darkness and weird mystery:[89]

[87] *Edgar Huntley* 2. 173-174. [89] *Op. cit.* 2. 245.
[88] Cf. Loshe, p. 73.

> The wildness of her aspect and garb, her shrivelled and
> diminutive form, a constitution that seemed to defy the ravages
> of time and the influence of the element; her age, which some
> did not scruple to affirm exceeded an hundred years, her romantic
> solitude and mountainous haunts suggested to my fancy the appel-
> lation of *Queen Mab.*

The rest of the story is made up of other sensational
adventures and hairbreadth escapes, frequently without much
probability or connection.   The Indians whom Edgar has
tricked follow him to Deb's cottage, where, with the usual
complication of dangers, surprises, and mishaps, the hero
succeeds in killing several more of his enemies.   Edgar's
friends now come to his rescue, but this is frustrated when
they mistake his swoon for death, and go off, leaving his
body with those of the dead Indians.   The young lady whom
he had rescued with such heroism also vanishes, to reappear
no more in the story, and Edgar is left alone, to make his
way back as best he can.   His adventures on the way home
include killing another Indian, 'a bloody and disastrous tale,'[90]
and jumping from a high precipice into the river, when he
and his friends meet and mutually mistake each other for
Indians.   By such a novel variety of incidents the reader's
interest is sustained through a number of pages, but at many
points disappointed by so much suspense which seems to
result in no very natural or logical conclusion.

It seems necessary to repeat, perhaps with some modifica-
tion, the statement made at the outset of this chapter, that
the sentimentalized or idealized Indian occupies no very
important place in English fiction before 1800.   In *Lydia,*
which begins with such a glorification of Indian virtue, the
noble-savage motive tends to become subordinate as the story
proceeds, while the realistic elements, the activities of Mrs.
Rachel Stiffrump and her associates, become more and more
prominent.   Yet the American Indian, somewhat less ideal

[90] 2. 207.

than Cannassatego, made no little appeal to the eighteenth-century imagination, and was the occasion of many interesting and even novel literary effects. As the century wore on, the customs of the Indians, the dangers of the wilderness, the hardships of the frontier, more and more found their way into fiction, oftentimes as subordinate threads, to be sure, yet significant as an indication of the universal fondness for spectacular adventure, picturesque local color, veiled social satire, and thrills of mystery and horror.

CHAPTER V.

THE INDIAN IN DRAMA.

To the Elizabethan dramatist America and its strange inhabitants made slight appeal. With the possible exception of Shakespeare's *Tempest*,[1] the first half of the seventeenth century shows little or no trace of American exoticism. In the year 1658, however, the Indians made their appearance on the stage in Sir William Davenant's opera, *The Cruelty of the Spaniards in Peru*. That the performance of such a work was permitted at this time is usually explained by assuming that the exposure of Spanish cruelty was pleasing to Cromwell. *The British Theatre* comments on this circumstance as follows: 'We are told that Cromwell not only allowed this piece to be performed, but actually read and approved of it; and the reason given was, that it reflected on the Spaniards, against whom he was supposed to have formed great designs.'[2]

There is not much plot to the piece, but the most important events attending the Spanish conquest of Peru are shown in a series of tableaux and songs. The general plan of the work is thus summed up in the argument:

> The design is first to represent the happy condition of the people of Peru anciently, when their inclinations were govern'd by Nature; and then it makes some discov'ry of their establishment under the twelve Incas, and of the dissensions of the two sons of the last Inca. Then proceeds to the discov'ry of that new western world by the Spaniard, which happen'd to be during the dissention of the two royal brethren. It likewise proceeds to the Spaniards' conquest of that Incan Empire, and then discovers the cruelty of the Spaniards over the Indians, and over all Christians, excepting those of their own nation, who landing in those parts, came unhappily into their power. And towards

[1] Cf. chap. 3.
[2] William Rufus Chetwood, *The British Theatre* (Dublin, 1750), p. 70.

the conclusion, it infers the voyages of the English thither, and the amity of the natives towards them, under whose ensigns— encourag'd by a prophecy of their Chief Priest—they hope to be made victorious, and to be freed from the yoke of the Spaniard.

One of the things to be noticed in this performance is the attempt to secure a realistic Peruvian atmosphere. The early pictures of the Indians had commonly shown them decked out in feathers; hence the priest of the sun who makes the first speech is described as 'cloth'd in a garment of feathers, longer than any of those that are worn by other natives, with a bonnet whose ornament of plumes does likewise give him a distinction from the rest, and carries in his hand a gilded verge.' His speech and the first song describe the early state of the Indians before the time of the first Incas:

> Whilst yet our world was new
>   When not discover'd by the old;
> Ere beggar'd slaves we grew,
>   For having silver hills, and strands of gold.
>   *Chorus.* We danc'd and we sung,
>   And lookt ever young,
>   And from restraints were free,
>   As waves and winds at sea.

After this the scene changes to a sea-coast, with the Spanish fleet shown in the distance. The second speech describes the peaceful rule of the Incas, and their subjects' alarm at the coming of the Spaniards, the bearded race, who, according to an ancient prophecy, were to spring out of the sea and conquer them:

> In all the soft delights of sleep and ease,
> Secure from war, in peaceful palaces,
> Our Incas liv'd: but now I see their doom:
> Guided by winds, the bearded people come!
> And that dire prophecy must be fulfill'd,
> When two shall ruin what our twelve did build.
> 'Tis long since first the sun's Chief Priest foretold
> That cruel men, idolaters of gold,
> Should pass vast seas to seek their harbour here.
> Behold, in floating castles they appear!

The rest of the play shows the quarrel between the two brother Incas, rival claimants to the throne; the skill of the Spaniards in taking advantage of this to secure control of the country; their subsequent thirst for gold, and cruelty in making the Indians dig this for them; and, finally—the wildest departure from anything really historic, explained by the author as a sort of prophetic vision—the coming of the English and the emancipation of the oppressed Peruvians.

Sympathy for Indian sufferings, the principal theme of the play, is probably due largely to the influence of Las Casas, a partial translation of whose work had appeared two years before (1656), under the title *The Tears of the Indians.* Most of the lofty sentiments attributed to the Indians may therefore be accounted for as springing from English hatred of Spain, rather than from any serious desire to idealize the oppressed Peruvians. One of the scenes, indeed, represents the Spaniards as torturing not only the natives, but some English mariners who had recently landed on the coast. Two Spaniards are described as 'sitting in their cloaks, and appearing more solemn in ruffs, with rapiers and daggers by their sides; the one turning a spit, whilst the other is basting an Indian prince, which is roasted at an artificial fire.' The mildness of the Indian stands in sharp contrast to such inhumanity. On first seeing the arms of the Spaniards, their comment is:

> But how they reason's laws in life fulfill
>   We know not! yet we know,
>   That scorn of life is low.
> Compar'd to the disdain of living ill;
>   And we may judge that all they do
>   In life's whole scene is bad,
>   Since they with arms are clad
>   Defensive and offensive too.
> In nature it is fear that makes us arm:
>   And fear by guilt is bred:
>   The guiltless nothing dread,
> Defence not seeking, nor designing harm.

Furthermore, the notion of the Indian's natural goodness, and the superiority of the state of nature, though not carried very far, are clearly implied in such passages as the following:

> Twelve Incas have successively
> Our spacious empire sway'd;
> Whose power whilst we obey'd,
> We liv'd so happy and so free,
> As if we were not kept in awe
> By any law,
> Which martial kings aloud proclaim.
> Soft conscience, Nature's whisp'ring orator,
> Did teach us what to love or to abhor;
> And all our punishment was shame.

Davenant's *History of Sir Francis Drake,* which appeared in the following year, 1659, also has its scene in America, but makes only slight mention of the Indians. This, and *The Cruelty of the Spaniards in Peru,* are little more than one-act plays, and were therefore later included as separate scenes in a five-act opera, called *The Play-House to be Let,* first published in 1673. That Davenant's attempt to introduce American exoticism on the stage was not very successful is perhaps shown by the fact that, although the other parts of *The Play-House to be Let* were acted in 1706, the second and third acts, *The History of Sir Francis Drake,* and *The Cruelty of the Spaniards in Peru,* were for some reason omitted.[3]

In *The Indian Queen,*[4] first performed in 1664, we have

---

[3] Cf. Genest, *Some Account of the English Stage* (Bath, 1832) 2. 352.

[4] *The Indian Queen* was first published in 1665, in a group of four plays by Sir Robert Howard. As Dryden had some part in it, however, it is now included among his works. For a discussion of the date, authorship, and other such matters, cf. *The Works of John Dryden,* ed. Scott and Saintsbury (Edinburgh, 1882) 2. 225-226.

Genest (2. 558) lists a performance of *The Indian Queen* at Drury Lane, July 19, 1715. It had not been acted for ten years, he says, and was then performed three times.

another attempt to secure novel effect on the stage by the introduction of strange peoples in far away lands. Yet, so far as the characters or situations of the plays are concerned, it might as well be located anywhere else as in Mexico. Except for incidental references to a few of the better known customs of the Mexicans and Peruvians, there is little genuine local color; the principal sources of dramatic effect lie rather in the high-flown sentiments, and the long series of striking situations, such as we find in all the other heroic plays of the time. The plot—too long and complicated to reproduce here—is based on a supposed war between Peru and Mexico, the geography as well as the customs of the two countries being more or less confused in the writer's mind. The hero of the piece, Montezuma, goes from one side to the other, always by his heroic valor carrying victory with him. The Indian Queen, Zempoalla, is drawn in equally bold colors—ready to go to any lengths to gratify her pride or her passion. After the Inca and his daughter have been captured and brought to Mexico, the plot turns largely upon the intrigues of several pairs of lovers, chief among them the Indian Queen and her paramour, Traxalla (also murderer of the former emperor). Finally, after many plots and counterplots, the usurpers are exposed, and the rightful queen, Amexia, and her son, Montezuma, are restored to the throne.

Certain details, to be sure, show a connection with the accounts of the Spanish historians. The Inca, for example, refuses his daughter to Montezuma because it is a custom for the Incas, descendants of the sun, to marry only among themselves. When the request is made he exclaims:[5]

> Thou deserv'st to die.
> O thou great author of our progeny,
> Thou glorious sun, dost thou not blush to shine,
> While such base blood attempts to mix with thine!

[5] Act. I, sc. I.

There are also allusions to human sacrifice, then regarded as a common practice among the Mexicans,[6] and in the opening of the fifth act the scene shows 'the Temple of the Sun, all of gold, and four Priests, in habits of white and red feathers, attending by a bloody altar, as ready for sacrifice.'

Here the idealization of the Indian appears, if at all, in the strained and fanciful sentiments of honor attributed to him, rather than in any praise of natural virtue as such. Acacis, for example, the young Mexican prince taken prisoner for the Inca by Montezuma, refuses to flee with his captor when he decides to go over to the Mexicans. ' 'T were baseness,' he says, 'to accept such liberty.' More intelligible—at least, to a modern reader—is Acacis' protest against the sacrifices planned by his mother Zempoalla :[7]

> Hold, hold! such sacrifices cannot be
> Devotions, but a solemn cruelty:
> How can the gods delight in human blood?
> Think them not cruel, if you think them good.
> In vain we ask that mercy, which they want,
> And hope that pity, which they hate to grant.

In Dryden's *Indian Emperor,* first produced in 1665, we have a sequel to *The Indian Queen,* the action supposed to take place about twenty years later, when the Spaniards have just landed in Mexico. The plot is even more bewildering and confused than that of *The Indian Queen,* and the sentiments equally extravagant. Scott, however, considered it a model of heroic drama, and commented very favorably on the lofty tone of such plays.[8]

The attempt to secure local color consists, as in *The Indian Queen,* chiefly in the feathered adornments of the Mexicans, and in allusions to the large number of human sacrifices. In Act 1, sc. 2, the High Priest says:

[6] Act. 1, sc. 2.
[7] Act. 5, sc. 1.
[8] Scott's view of this play is brought out in his and Saintsbury's edition of Dryden, 2. 317-20.

The incense is upon the altar placed,
The bloody sacrifice already past;
Five hundred captives saw the rising sun,
Who lost their light ere half his race was run.

Although much of the plot is purely fictitious, particularly the complicated love-intrigues which form so much of the story, certain historical events are seized upon for fanciful elaboration. Montezuma's awe, for example, on first seeing the Spaniards, almost makes him doubt whether they are men or Gods, but when he learns more about their real intentions—their desire to secure gold, and extend the authority of Spain—he asks by what right they make such demands. When Pizarro states that this empire has been given them by the Pope, 'who represents on earth the power of heaven,' Montezuma replies:[9]

Ill does he represent the powers above
Who nourishes debate, not preaches love;
Besides what greater folly can be shown?
He gives another what is not his own.

One of the other Spaniards then tells him that the Pope's power must not be questioned on earth, since 'he in heaven an empire can bestow,' and Montezuma answers:

Empires in heaven he with more ease may give,
And you, perhaps, would with less thanks receive:
But heaven has need of no such viceroy here,
Itself bestows the crowns that monarchs wear.

It would of course be going too far to say that Dryden was intentionally glorifying the state of nature, or the virtues of the savage, although he places in a very favorable light their simplicity and endurance. His sympathy with the Mexicans appears most pronounced in his picture of their religion—not in its bloody, sacrificial aspects, but rather in its opposing priestly tyranny with reason and courage. In his introduction he says:

[9] Act. I, sc. 2.

The difference of their religion from ours, I have taken from the story itself; and that which you find of it in the first and fifth acts, touching the sufferings and constancy of Montezuma in his opinions, I have only illustrated, not altered, from those who have written it.

As this play was written a good many years before Dryden entered the Roman Church, it is not surprising that the methods of the inquisition are presented in a not altogether favorable light. In Act 5, sc. 2, Montezuma is shown on the rack, Pizarro trying to make him disclose his hidden store of gold, the Christian priest trying to convert him to the Catholic religion. The following dialogue takes place:

> *Christian Priest.* Those pains, O prince, thou sufferest now,
>   are light
> Compared to those, which, when thy soul takes flight,
> Immortal, endless, thou must then endure,
> Which death begins, and time can never cure.
> *Montezuma.* Thou art deceived; for whenso'er I die,
> The Sun, my father, bears my soul on high:
> He lets me down a beam, and mounted there,
> He draws it back, and pulls me through the air:
> I in the eastern parts, and rising sky,
> You in heaven's downfall, and the west must lie.
> *Christian Priest.* Fond man, by heathen ignorance misled,
> Thy soul destroying when thy body's dead:
> Change yet thy faith, and buy eternal rest.
> *Indian High Priest.* Die in your own, for our belief is best.
> *Montezuma.* In seeking happiness you both agree;
> But in the search, the paths so different be,
> That all religions with each other fight,
> While only one can lead us in the right.
> But till that one hath some more certain mark,
> Poor human-kind must wander in the dark;
> And suffer pain eternally below,
> For that, which here we cannot come to know.
> *Christian Priest.* That, which we worship, and which you
>   believe,
> From nature's common hand we both receive:
> All, under various names, adore and love
> One Power immense, which ever rules above.

Vice to abhor, and virtue to pursue,
Is both believed and taught by us and you:
But here our worship takes another way—
    Montezuma. Where both agree, 't is there most safe to stay:
But what's more vain than public light to shun,
And set up tapers, while we see the sun?
    Christian Priest. Though nature teaches whom we should
    adore,
By heavenly beams we still discover more.
    Montezuma. Or this must be enough, or to mankind
One equal way to bliss is not designed;
For though some more may know, and some know less,
Yet all must know enough for happiness.
    Christian Priest. If in this middle way you still pretend
To stay, your journey never will have end.
    Montezuma. Howe'er, 't is better in the midst to stay,
Than wander farther in uncertain way.
    Christian Priest. But we by martyrdom our faith avow.
    Montezuma. You do no more than I for ours do now.
To prove religion true—
If either wit or sufferings would suffice,
All faiths afford the constant and the wise:
And yet even they, by education swayed,
In age defend what infancy obeyed.
    Christian Priest. Since age by erring childhood is misled,
Refer yourself to our unerring head.
    Montezuma. Man, and not err! what reason can you give?
    Christian Priest. Renounce that carnal reason, and believe.
    Montezuma. The light of nature should I thus betray.
'T were to wink hard, that I might see the day.
    Christian Priest. Condemn not yet the way you do not know;
I'll make your reason judge what way to go.
    Montezuma. 'T is much too late for me new ways to take,
Who have but one short step of life to make.
    Pizarro. Increase their pains, the cords are yet too slack.
    Christian Priest. I must by force convert him on the rack.
    Indian High Priest. I faint away, and find I can no more;
Give leave, O king, I may reveal thy store,
And free myself from pains, I cannot bear.
    Montezuma. Think'st thou I lie on beds of roses here,
Or in a wanton bath stretched at my ease?
Die, slave, and with thee die such thoughts as these.
        (High Priest turns aside, and dies.)

The Indian Emperor continued to enjoy a moderate degree of popularity well on into the eighteenth century, and was doubtless of considerable influence in keeping alive the tradition of a drama founded on events in America. Genest records scattered performances up to 1734; and, later in the century, when Peruvian plays were again becoming popular, *The Indian Emperor* was closely imitated by Henry Brooke, in a play called *Montezuma*.[10]

After Dryden's, no Indian dramas appeared until 1728. In that year Francis Hawling's tragedy called *The Indian Emperor*[11] was acted, but not published, and *Polly,* a continuation of Gay's *Beggar's Opera,* was written, but suppressed by the Lord Chamberlain before it could be produced. Although *Polly* was not actually seen on the stage till 1777,[12] it seems desirable to discuss it here, as an early eighteenth-century attempt to show the noble Indian in drama.

The opera opens showing Polly just arrived in the West Indies in search of her lover, Macheath, who, instead of reforming, has turned pirate, and now threatens the colonists with an armed force. The Indians enter in to help the settlers, and it is in this situation we see their bravery and honor contrasted with the baseness of Macheath (or Morano as he is now known) and his followers. In the course of the struggle, Cawwawkee, son of the Indian chief, falls into their hands, but steadfastly refuses to disclose the hiding-place of their treasures. Morano threatens him with torture, but his courage remains unshaken:

> *Morano.* Do you know me, Prince?
> *Cawwawkee.* As a man of injustice I know you.
> *Morano.* Do you know my power?

[10] Cf. Genest 6. 67-68; *Biog. Dram.* 3. 58.
[11] Cf. *Biog. Dram.* 2. 323.
[12] Genest lists performances of *Polly* in 1777, 1782, and 1813. The opera has also been revived during the last year (1922-23) at the Kingsway Theatre, London. For an account of this production, cf. the *Living Age,* Dec., 1922, p. 787.

Cawwawkee. I fear it not.

Morano. Do you know your danger?

Cawwawkee. I am prepar'd to meet it.

Morano. Stubborn prince, mark me well. Your life is in my power.

Cawwawkee. My virtue is in my own.

Morano. Can you feel pain?

Cawwawkee. I can bear it.

Morano. In what condition are your troops? What numbers have you? How are they disposed? Act reasonably and openly, and you shall find protection.

Cawwawkee. What, betray my friends! I am no coward, European.

Morano. Torture shall make you squeak.

Cawwawkee. Pain shall neither make me lie or betray.

Vanderbluff. What, neither cheat nor be cheated! There is no having either commerce or correspondence with these creatures.

Polly. How happy are these savages! Who would not wish to be in such ignorance?

[ASIDE.

Morano. You have treasures, you have gold and silver among you, I suppose.

Cawwawkee. But out of benevolence we ought to hide it from you. For, as we have heard, 't is so rank a poison to you Europeans, that the very touch of it makes you mad.

Morano. Discover your treasures, your hoards, for I will have the ransacking of 'em. I will have immediate compliance, or you shall undergo the torture.

Cawwawkee. With dishonour life is nothing worth.

Morano. Furies! I'll trifle no longer. Torture him leisurely, but severely. I shall stagger your revolution, Indian.

Cawwawkee. Your menaces do but move my contempt, European.[13]

The Indian talks of honor and virtue all through the play, and, in the latter part, when Morano has been captured, Pohetohee, the father of Cawwawkee, addresses him as follows on his injustice:

[13] Act 2.

Pohetohee. Trifle not with justice, impious man. Your barbarities, your rapin, your murthers are now at an end. Would not your honest industry have been sufficient to have supported you?

Morano. Honest industry! All great geniusses are above it.

Pohetohee. Have you no respect for virtue?

Morano. The practicers of it are seldom found in the best company.

Pohetohee. Is not wisdom esteemed among you?

Morano. Yes, Sir; as a step to riches and power; a step that raises ourselves, and trips up our neighbours.

Pohetohee. Honour, and honesty, are not those distinguish'd?

Morano. Honour is of some use; it serves to swear upon.

Pohetohee. Let justice take her course. Immediate death shall put a stop to your further mischiefs.[14]

Still more ideal does the Indian appear in his relation with Polly, who, in the course of her adventures, dresses herself as a boy, and rescues Cawwawkee from the hands of the pirates. An intimate friendship follows between the two, and Cawwawkee takes his rescuer to the Indians' settlement, to receive the thanks of the chieftain Pohetohee:

Cawwawkee. Let this youth then receive your thanks. To him are owing my life and liberty. And the love of virtue alone gain'd me his friendship.

Pohetohee. This hath convinc'd me that an European can be generous and honest.[15]

At the end of the play, Macheath is killed, and Polly, through grieving much, is almost willing to accept the Indian in his place. The extent to which the brave Cawwawkee has won her respect and affection may be inferred from this closing scene:[16]

Polly. He's dead, he's dead! Their looks confess it. Support me! O Macheath!

Cawwawkee. Justice hath reliev'd you from the society of a

[14] Act 3.
[15] Act 3.
[16] Act 3.

wicked man. If an honest heart can recompence your loss, you would make me happy in accepting mine. What, no reply?

Polly. Abandon me to my sorrows. For in indulging them is my only relief.

Cawwawkee. By your consent you might at the same time give me happiness, and procure your own. My titles, my treasures, are all at your command.

Polly. I am charm'd, Prince, with your generosity and virtues. Those that know and feel virtue in themselves, must love it in others. Allow me to give some time to my sorrows.

Cawwawkee. Fair princess, for so I hope shortly to make you, permit me to attend you, either to divide your griefs, or, by conversation, to soften your sorrows.

Polly. 'T is a pleasure to me by this alliance to recompence your merits. Let the sports and dances then celebrate our victory!

Although the Indian Cawwawkee makes a very fine stage-hero, and a striking contrast to the rascally Macheath, the light playful tone of the whole opera forbids us to regard the idealization of the savage as having any serious purpose. So also in *Art and Nature*,[17] the next play we are to consider, the treatment of the Indian is only half serious. Like the French *Arlequin Sauvage*,[18] which it imitates, the play contains a great deal of wit and cleverness, its main purpose being a light satire on the artificiality of polite society. This is accomplished by exhibiting the surprise and displeasure of an Indian who comes to Europe, and having him denounce, in the name of Nature and Reason, all the petty follies of fashionable life, and injustice of civilized society. This contrast between nature and civilization is well brought out in Truemore's account of the young savage whom he has brought with him from America. 'The pure natural wit, strong good sense and integrity of soul, which appear'd in everything he said, induc'd me to bring him into Europe.

[17] First performed Feb. 16, 1738. Cf. Genest 3. 531.

[18] This play, by Louis Francois de la Drevetière Delisle, was first performed June 17, 1721. For an account of this, and other plays of the same type cf. Chinard, *L'Amérique et le Rêve Exotique*, pp. 221 ff.

I take great pleasure in seeing pure simple Nature in him oppos'd to Laws, Arts and Sciences amongst us.'[19]

Julio's observations soon lead him to form very strange conclusions concerning his new surroundings, for we next find him relating to Violetta, the maid, his first impressions of the country.[20] 'What a strange ridiculous country this is,' he exclaims. 'Some are carry'd about in cages, others are help'd to their very victuals and drink, and a great many don't know how to put on their own clothes; one would think they had neither arms nor legs to help themselves; This is a mighty villainous country indeed, I wish myself in my own habitation again, I'm sure.' So also when Violetta tries to explain to him the nature of the laws, the various classes of society, and all the other advantages of civilized life, the untutored savage can only wonder more and more at the ways of this strange people. Their singular notions of happiness, so contrary to the dictates of reason and nature, he cleverly ridicules in many conversations with his new friends, while their elaborate arrangements for securing comfort and health appear to him altogether superfluous:[21]

> Is this then the only happiness of the great, to have more dishes to gaze upon, more hours to do nothing in, and more sicknesses and doctors to be tormented with; ha, ha, ha! If this be all, much good may you do with it.

One of the most amusing scenes in the play is Julio's adventure with a generous bookseller, who begins by offering to let him have anything he likes. Books Julio declines on the ground he cannot understand 'em, whereupon the shopkeeper replies:[22]

> *Alphabet.* Understand 'em, ha, ha, ha! Lack-a-day, Sir, if no body bought any books but what they understood, what would become of us? Why, our best customers are those that never

---

[19] Act 1.
[20] Act 2.
[21] Act 2.
[22] Act 2.

look in a book; they buy 'em only to look at 'em; pray, observe how pretty a figure they make, all nicely rang'd, gilt and letter'd in so neat a manner.

Julio. Ay, Friend, but I'm afraid your books are like yourselves, fine outsides, and good for nothing within; so I'll have none of your glittering bawbles.

Books failing to please, the shopkeeper next tries to interest this visitor in pictures, with what success the following dialogue will disclose :[23]

Julio. Ay! I like this picture as you call it, I'll take this.

Alphabet. But what will your Honour give me for it?

Julio. My honour give ye! I have nothing to give ye, and indeed I am sorry for't.

Alphabet. I don't understand what you wou'd be at, Sir; I say I must have fifty shillings for it.

Julio. I have not one shilling, or so much as know what a shilling is.

Alphabet. Come, Sir, I'm not in jest, either pay me, or give me back my piece.

Julio. Why, you offer'd me your goods in a friendly manner here, and to oblige you, I have taken this, and now you talk of having it again; for shame, for shame, this is pitiful!

Alphabet. Come, come, Sir, no more words; either pay me or return the piece.

Julio. Hey-day! what's the matter now; begone this instant, or I'll drub you soundly, you rude unmannerly savage you.

Alphabet. How! Is it thus people are to be paid? Thieves, thieves; help, help, help.

Julio. I must scalp this rascal. (Laying hold of him, Alphabet runs off, leaving his wig in Julio's hand.)

Alphabet. Undone! ruin'd.

Julio. Ha! how? what's the meaning of this? the hair's not natural—by what I find, these people an't what they seem to be; and every thing they have is borrow'd; their very good-nature, their understanding, their wit, their very hair. O' my conscience, I begin to be afraid to live among'st 'em: the Captain said they were a good kind o' people, but I find 'em all as wicked as possible; or is it my ignorance makes me think so? Well, I'll go find out my master, that he may tell me the meaning of all these doings.

[23] Act 2.

Julio's attack upon civilization takes various forms: now it is against the distinction between rich and poor, now against the restraints of marriage, now against the lying and deceit he finds on all sides, in all of which, to be sure, the Indian seems himself more artificial than the vices he denounces. Possessing none of the characteristics of a genuine savage, he appears little more than an oratorical, verbose personification of naïveté, innocence, primitive simplicity, quite as meaningless as the oft-repeated abstractions, Reason and Nature. At the end of the play we find him in love with Violetta, whom he urges to go with him to America. When she replies, 'I think I do begin not to dislike thee much,' he exclaims:[24]

> Come along with me then, I'll take you to a country where we shall have no need of money to make us happy, nor laws to make us wise; our friendship shall be all our riches, and reason our only guide; we may not say a great many fine things but we'll take care to do 'em,—let us hear no more then of your laws, your arts, or your sciences, they are good for nothing, by what I have seen yet, but to give knaves an advantage over honest men, and fools authority over wise one's—no, no, let us go, and enjoy our selves, and be as happy as nature and common-sense can make us.

Although *Art and Nature* enjoyed no great success on the stage, the subject continued to interest dramatists. At least two other adaptations of *Arlequin Sauvage* appeared during the century, Cleland's *Tombo-Chiqui,*[25] 1758, and John Fenwick's farce, *The Indian,*[26] 1800. The former of these was never acted, and the latter met with little success. The representation of the Indian is in all these essentially the same, despite various minor differences of plot and situation.

History, rather than pure fancy, forms the basis of Colonel Robert Rogers's *Ponteach,*[27] a play never acted, but first pub-

---

[24] Act 5.
[25] Cf. *Monthly Rev.* 18 (1758). 648.
[26] Cf. Genest 7. 495.
[27] London, 1766. Cf. *Monthly Rev.* 34 (1766). 242.

lished in 1766. The action is supposed to take place about 1763-64, when Ponteach, the celebrated Indian chief, united a number of tribes, and led them against the English.[28] Realistic local color is most conspicuous in the first act, where an attempt is made to represent the different wrongs which have led the Indians to revolt. The first scene represents two unscrupulous traders who not only debauch the Indians by selling them rum, but cheat them as well in the purchase of their furs. One of them speaks thus of such dishonesty:[29]

> Our fundamental maxim then is this,
> That it's no crime to cheat and gull an Indian.

The next scene shows two hunters, who, having failed to find any game themselves, to make up for this ill fortune kill some of the Indian trappers, and seize their furs. One of them feels some misgiving for such a crime, but his companion makes light of killing an Indian:[30]

> *Osbourn.* But, Honnyman, d'ye think this is not murder?
> I vow I'm shock'd a little to see them scalp'd,
> And fear their ghosts will haunt us in the dark.
> *Honnyman.* It's no more murder than to crack a louse,
> That is, if you've wit to keep it private.
> And as to haunting, Indians have no ghosts,
> But as they live like beasts, like beasts they die.
> I've kill'd a dozen in this self-same way,
> And never yet was troubled with their spirits.

The third and fourth scenes show other examples of wrongs done the Indian. Of the thousand pounds which the king has sent to be given to the Indians, a token of his good will in return for their presents of furs and wampum, the greater part is kept by his agents, the dissatisfied savages being turned away with only a small portion. The unfairness of

[28] An entertaining account of the historical setting of the play is found in Parkman's *Conspiracy of Pontiac* (Boston, 1851).
[29] Act I, sc. I.
[30] Act I, sc. 2.

the English they view with the more resentment, because of the kind and friendly relations they had long maintained with the French.

The rest of the play, besides showing the course of Ponteach's conspiracy and final defeat, includes various fanciful and extravagant touches. One of his sons, Chekitan, is deeply in love with Monimia, daughter of Hendrick, chief of the Mohawks. Philip, the other son, jealous of his brother, murders Monimia, and is himself later killed by the despairing Chekitan. The introduction of a French priest becomes the means of exhibiting the hypocrisy of the Christians, in contrast with the credulity and simplicity of the savages. The wily Jesuit is here pictured, not at all as he was, but very much as he was viewed by the English of the eighteenth century. He enters the councils of the Indians in order to stir them up against the English, telling them that this is 'a course by Gods and saints espoused':

> *Priest.* You're going to fight the enemies of God;
> Rebels and traitors to the King of Kings;
> Nay those who once betray'd and kill'd his Son,
> Who came to save you Indians from damnation—
> He was an Indian, therefore they destroy'd him;
> He rose again and took his flight to Heaven;
> But when his foes are slain he'll quick return,
> And be your kind protector, friend, and King.
> Be therefore brave and fight his battles for him;
> Spare not his enemies, where 'e'r you find 'em;
> The more you murder them, the more you please him,
> Kill all you captivate, both old and young,
> Mothers and children, let them feel your tortures;
> He that shall kill a Briton, merits Heaven.
> And should you chance to fall, you'll be convey'd
> By flying angels to your King that's there
> Where these your hated foes can never come.

In support of these pretensions the priest produces a burning-glass, draws fire from Heaven, and thus secures a firmer hold on the loyalty of the superstitious savages:[31]

[31] Act 3, sc. 3.

> *Ponteach.* Who now can doubt the justice of our cause,
> Or this man's mission from the King above,
> And that we ought to follow his commands?
> *Astinaco.* 'T is wonderful indeed—it must be so—

Later this same priest tries to seduce Monimia, but the virtuous maiden is saved by the timely appearance of her lover, Chekitan, who expresses the greatest indignation at the priest's duplicity:[32]

> Oh vain pretence! Falsehood, and foul deception!
> None but a Christian could devise such lies!
> Did I not fear it might provoke your gods,
> Your tongue should never frame deceit again.
> If there are gods, and such as you have told us,
> They must abhor all baseness and deceit,
> And will not fail to punish crimes like yours.
> To them I leave you—but avoid my presence,
> Nor let me ever see your hated head.
> Or hear your lying tongue within this country.

The most realistic scene is probably that showing the torture of Honnyman (Act 4, sc. 4), whom the Indians thus justly punish for his having murdered one of their number. At first the savages plan to kill his wife and child also, but her tears and his entreaties finally procure her pardon. Although the Indian is pictured with much of his fierceness and cruelty, there is, in such scenes as this, a touch of sentimental idealization. There is also a certain amount of conventional praise for their primitive simplicity and hardihood, together with the usual idealization of their happy condition before the coming of the white men:[33]

> Our great forefathers, ere these strangers came,
> Liv'd by the chase, with nature's gifts content,
> The cooling fountain quench'd their raging thirst.
> Doctors, and drugs, and med'cines were unknown,
> Even age itself was free from pain and sickness.
> Swift as the wind, o'er rocks and hills they chas'd

---

[32] Act 4, sc. 2.   [33] Act 3, sc. 3.

The flying game, the bounding stag outwinded,
And tir'd the savage bear, and tam'd the tiger:
Nor then fatigu'd; the merry dance and song
Succeeded: still with every rising sun
The sport renew'd; or if some daring foe
Provok'd their wrath, they bent the hostile bow,
Nor waited his approach, but rush'd with speed,
Fearless of hunger, thirst, fatigue or death.
But we their soften'd sons, a puny race,
Are weak in youth, fear dangers where they're not;
Are weary'd with what was to them a sport.

During the last quarter of the century it becomes fairly common to introduce the Indians as a touch of picturesque local color for any play having its scene in America. Archibald Maclaren, who passed some time in America,[34] attempted this in two of his plays. In *The Coup de Main*,[35] a very light musical entertainment, one of the scenes shows some Indians dancing and singing, as they cook their supper around a fire in the woods. In *The Negro Slaves*,[36] the painted savage, with his war-whoop, his scalping-knife, his rude songs and dances, again appears, chiefly to add fanciful comic incident, and a slight touch of exotic realism.

The comic opera called *The Peruvian*[37] we may pass over briefly, inasmuch as the only Indian character, a Peruvian girl who has been brought over to England, is really Peruvian in name only. In Marmontel's tale, *L'Amitié à l'Épreuve*, on which the play is founded, the heroine is an Asiatic Indian, but her character in this drama is so vaguely indicated, and her part so much that of the conventional heroine, that the circumstances of her supposed origin, whether Peruvian or Asiatic, seem of slight importance.

[34] Cf. the preface to *The Coup de Main*.
[35] Perth, 1784. Cf. *Biog. Dram.* 2. 137.
[36] London, 1799.
[37] London, 1786. First performed March 18, 1786. Cf. Genest 6. 397; *Biog. Dram.* 3. 140.

In 1787 George Colman's opera, *Inkle and Yarico,* was produced at the Haymarket Theatre with great success. As the theme of this play, the love of a white man for a savage woman, was very popular all through the eighteenth century, it is necessary at this point to give some account of the different versions. The earliest mention of such an incident occurs in the *Voyages* of Jean Mocquet,[38] where the author relates how a shipwrecked sailor falls among the Indians, wins the love of a young savage, and later sails away in an English ship, unmindful of all the promises he has made her. His Indian bride, enraged at such ingratitude, tears in two the child she has borne him, hurling one-half into the sea as the boat sails away. Richard Ligon, in his *History of the Barbados,* 1657, tells how a white man who has been rescued by the Indian maid, Yarico, afterwards rewards his bene-factress by selling her into slavery.[39] This story of Ligon's is the basis of Steele's paper in the *Spectator,* No. 11, a good many details being added to increase the reader's sympathy

[38] Paris, 1616. For an account of this work, cf. Chinard's *L'Amér-ique et le Rêve Exotique,* pp. 24 ff.

[39] Ligon's narrative, found on p. 55, runs as follows: 'This Indian dwelling neer the sea-coast, upon the main, an English ship put into a bay, and sent some of her men ashoar, to try what victualls or water they could finde, for in some distresse they were: But the Indians perceiving them to go up so far into the country, as they were sure they could not make a safe retreat, intercepted them in their return, and fell upon them, chasing them into a wood, and being dispersed there, some were taken, and some kill'd: but a young man amongst them stragling from the rest, was met by this Indian maid who upon the first sight fell in love with him, and hid him close from her countrymen (the Indians) in a cave, and there fed him, till they could safely go down to the shoar, where the ship lay at anchor, expecting the return of their friends. But at last, seeing them upon the shoar, sent the long boat for them, took them abroad, and brought them away. But the youth, when he came ashoar in the Barbados, forgot the kindnesse of the poor maid, that had ven-tured her life for his safety, and sold her for a slave, who was as free born as he: And so poor Yarico for her love, lost her liberty.'

for the unhappy Yarico. A somewhat different love-affair between an Indian and a European is described in a long romance, called *Avantures du Sieur Le Beau,* first published at Amsterdam in 1738.[40] Of all such tales, however, that of Inkle and Yarico became the most popular, as well as the most varied in treatment. In the latter part of the century, Yarico is made the heroine of a large number of sentimental poems. To the dramatist, also, the subject made considerable appeal. An English version, not acted, appeared in 1742,[41] and in 1764 Chamfort treated the story in a play called *Jeune Indienne.*[42]

The exotic element in Colman's *Inkle and Yarico* is probably more closely connected with the negro than with the Indian. In the first act, located in America, the author introduces the natives, and at the same time speaks of them as blacks, thus creating a confusion which persists all through the play. Although Yarico is sometimes spoken of as an Indian, the main purpose of the play is to arouse our sympathy at her being sold into slavery,[43] which, with various other circumstances, seems to associate her pretty definitely with the sentimentalized negro, also a popular figure in the late eighteenth century.[44] There is not much attempt to

[40] Cf. Chinard, *op. cit.,* pp. 306 ff.

[41] Cf. *Biog. Dram.* 2. 325. The same work (3. 427) also lists *Yarico,* a pastoral drama, anonymous, and without date of publication.

[42] Presented at the *Théâtre Français,* April 30, 1764. For a discussion of its relation to the Inkle and Yarico theme, cf. Chinard, pp. 400 ff.

[43] Mrs. Inchbald, in her Introductory Remarks to the copy of this play included in the *British Theatre,* speaks of it as 'one of those plays which is independent of time, of place, or of circumstance, for its value. It was popular before the subject of the abolition of the slave trade was popular. It has the peculiar honour of preceding that great question. It was the bright forerunner of alleviation the hardships of slavery.'

[44] The magazines of this period contain a good many poems with a tone of sentimental appeal for the unfortunate negro. On the

secure atmosphere or local color, except in the broken negro dialect spoken by Yarico's companion, Wowski. Her love-affair with Trudge, Inkle's servant, together with various other comic elements, doubtless contributed to the popularity of the play,[45] as well as the more sentimental appeal of the wronged Yarico. One evidence of the continued interest in this subject is the fact that it was in 1792 made the basis of a play called *The American Heroine; or, Ingratitude Punished,*[46] much less successful on the stage than Colman's version.

In *New Spain; or, Love in Mexico,*[47] the Indians are introduced in a kind of sub-plot of love and adventure, in a comic opera dealing chiefly with the intrigues and disguises of a group of Spanish lovers. Iscagli, the Indian heroine, is loved by two warriors, Alkmonoak and Zempoalla, but before she can choose Alkmonoak, whom she prefers, she is carried off by the Spanish governor, who has also been charmed by her beauty. Alkmonoak, in trying to rescue her, falls into the hands of Zempoalla, and is threatened with torture. In the end, Iscagli escapes from her Spanish lover, and is happily united to the brave Ãlkmonoak.

In the picture of the Indian lovers, there is much of the conventional eighteenth-century hero and heroine, with here and there a touch of the exotic imagination.[48] Iscagli, when

stage, the negro first appeared in Southern's *Oronoko,* 1696, a tragedy founded on Mrs. Behn's novel of that name. The play was very popular, and produced various imitations and adaptations all through the eighteenth century. Montague Summers, in his edition of *The Works of Aphra Behn,* 5. 128, notes a number of later versions.

[45] Genest (6. 453) records twenty performances the first season and various other appearances down to 1825.

[46] Cf. *Biog. Dram.* 2. 24.

[47] This opera in three acts, attributed to John Scawen, was performed nine times, beginning July 16, 1790. It was also published at London in the same year. For an account of its success on the stage, cf. Genest 7. 3 and *Biog. Dram.* 3. 80.

[48] Act 2, sc. 1.

reminded how she must forego the comforts of polished society if she marries Alkmonoak, thus expresses her preference for idyllic simplicity :[49]

> No, ye powers bear me witness! how gladly would I forego the softness of the splendid couch for the fragrance of the rushy mat—the wretched imitating Theorbo for the sweet song of the nightingale. I would deck our humble wigwam for my love's approach with all the variegated plumage of our luxuriant Indian groves. It shou'd be my ozier cage, and my love, my Alkmonoak, my sweet bird—he should be my bird of paradise and convert my hut into a Heaven.

There are also passages referring more clearly to alleged Indian customs. The Spanish secretary mentions the speech of one of their chiefs, which, he says, was 'couch'd in the sublime expressions of these people.'[50] More realistic is the scene in which Alkmonoak sings his death-song,[51] and the other Indians joins in a war-dance. Besides Alkmonoak's song, there is a chorus of Indians, and another song which runs as follows :[52]

> In his ambush, wisely dark,
> Scarce distinguish'd from the bark,
> As he peeps behind a tree,
> Our ruddy painted foe we see,
> Hark, he took a deadly aim,
> My comrade falls, revenge is fame.
> Now the tomahawk I throw.
> In vain the Chieftain flies the blow,
> From him, panting as he lies,
> The scalp I bear, the victor's prize,
> This is war, advance, advance,
> Join the warrior's glorious dance.

[49] Act 2, sc. 3.
[50] Act 1, sc. 3.
[51] This is the well-known song beginning:
> The sun sets in night, and the stars shun the day.
> But glory remains when their lights fade away;
> Begin; ye tormentors, your threats are in vain
> For the son of Alkmonoak can never complain. Cf. chap. 6.

[52] Act 3. sc. 5.

The gentle Iscagli, however, like so many other Indian heroines, shows a refinement somewhat above the customs of her race, and when first invited to witness this scene of torture, exclaims :[53]

> Not for worlds! I know too well the savage manners of our people—their barbarous triumphs, even whilst I liv'd amongst them, often shook my frame with agony.

The contrast between the Indian and the European, though not very pronounced, is reflected in a few of the speeches. One of the Spaniards speaks of how nobly he was used when a prisoner among the Indians, how the hand of friendship was extended to him when he expected the grasp of torture; and Alkmonoak, hearing him, exclaims :[54]

> No more.—Torture, tho' often the test of fortitude, is the offspring of inhuman ferocity.—I was long a captive among Europeans—they taught me urbanity—but alas! their urbanity knew not integrity—they smiled on me while they robb'd my heart of its only treasure—my lov'd! my lost Iscagli.

Quite an ambitious attempt to dramatize the savages of North America was made in a play called *The Indians,*[55] attributed to Professor William Richardson of Glasgow. The scene is laid on the shore of Lake Huron, and the action begins about the time of the capture of Quebec by the English. Onaiyo, son of the aged Chief Onothio, has not returned with the other warriors, and the report of his death causes his wife Maraino great anxiety. Although deeply attached to her husband and the Indian way of life, Maraino is really a white woman, who had been captured by the savages when only a small child. A large part of the plot turns on the intrigues of Yerdal and Neidan—the

[53] Act 3. sc. 4.
[54] Act 1, sc. 2.
[55] London, 1790. According to the title-page, performed at the Theatre-Royal, Richmond. Genest (10.198) lists it among plays not acted.

former a warrior enamored of Maraino, and jealous of
Onaiyo, the latter a soothsayer who aims to overthrow
Onothio, and secure supreme power in the tribe. To accom-
plish these ends, they deceive Maraino into believing that her
husband is dead, and Onaiyo into thinking his wife has
deserted him for the English prisoner, Sidney. Everything,
however, is straightened out in the end. Sidney, rescued
from torture, proves to be the brother of Maraino, the
villains Yerdal and Neidan are exposed, Onaiyo and Maraino
are happily reunited.

The play is of importance for its many realistic details of
Indian life, combined with a sentimental idealization of the
characters, vaguely suggestive of certain passages in
Chateaubriand's *Natchez*. In Maraino's account of how her
parents were killed, and she herself carried off to captivity
among the savages, we see the cruel, bloody Indian painted
in bold colors:[56]

> O direful night! when at the dreary hour
> Of midnight, the tremendous yell arose:
> My father starting from sleep, beheld,
> By th' hideous light of his own roof in flames
> The scouling visages of savage fiends
> That yell'd with horrid howling. Dire event!
> The earliest image stamp'd on my remembrance
> Was that disastrous night!

Yet in the same scene she speaks of the 'increasing tenderness
and care' with which she had been reared, and the happiness
of her life with the venerable Onothio for father, and the
valiant Onaiyo for companion.

In the Indian's treatment of their prisoner, Sidney, another
vivid touch is added to the picture of the cruel savage.
Yerdal says they must kill him, in order to appease the
manes of their lost comrades:[57]

> To calm the fury of those angry powers.
> That have with dire calamity o'erwhelm'd us;

[56] Act 3.   [57] Act 1.

And soothe the melancholy ghosts, whose moan
Borne in the sighing breezes of the night,
Upbraids our tardy vengeance; while their limbs
Cold and unburied, and defil'd with gore,
Lie undeplor'd by Hoshelega's wave.

But such a course is opposed by the wise and aged Onothio, who argues against the spirits being pleased by any injustice:[58]

Those unseen spirits, as they are themselves
Pow'rful and happy, must approve the deeds
That flow from tender mercy; and must blame
Vindictive outrage. . . . Can I believe
That they are more inhuman than the most
Inhuman of mankind?

Onothio's persuasive reasoning is apparently not altogether without avail, for in the next act (Act 2, sc. 2) he reports that the elders, 'mov'd with becoming pity, have resolv'd to save our captive from inhuman outrage.' Neidan, however, continues revengeful, and tries to carry out the cruel custom. In the next scene[59] Sidney appears in fetters, the other Indians ranged about him singing the death-song:

1st Indian
Spirits of the dead, that fly!
All athwart the midnight sky,
When the sable-suited night
Bars the western gate of light
And with lamentable wail
Load the intermitting gale.

2d Indian
By your melancholy groans
Mangled carcases and bones,
That besmear'd with recent gore,
Lie on Hoshelga's shore,
Disembodied spirits come
And enjoy the victim's doom.

[58] Act 1.
[59] Act 3, sc. 1.

3d Indian
Come, my brethren, fierce and grim,
Fill the cauldron to the brim:
Fewel in the forest hue,
Cypress, pine and baleful yew,
Till the smoke and smould'ring fire
Round the sooty sides aspire.

4th Indian
With a thousand tortures slow
Vary his protracted woe:
Every nerve and every vein
Claims its destin'd dole of pain,
Till the wilds and rocky shore
Bellow with th' unpitied roar. . . .

In some ways the character of most interest is the aged Onothio, who, by his mild opposition to the excesses of his countrymen, reminds us of Chateaubriand's Chactas. His excuse for the violence of his people may perhaps reflect something of the writer's point of view toward the less ideal side of the Indian's character:[60]

They are indeed too vehement. They feel
Too ardently: too ardently resent
The suff'rings of their brethren. Yet their wrath
Is like the rushing of a mountain blast,
Sudden but soon appeas'd. I trust they know not
The hate that rankles in a vengeful breast.

At times, the dignified figure of Onothio is made very impressive, especially when he speaks of natural religion, the worship of the Great Spirit. His counsel to Maraino in the following passage reflects the pantheistic coloring of the romantic poets:[61]

Be assur'd
The mighty Spirit whose tremendous voice
Roars in the thunder, but whose bounty smiles
In the mild radiance of a vernal morn

[60] Act 3.
[61] Act 2.

All-powerful, all-discerning, unconfin'd,
Can see the meanest creature, and protect,
The lowliest reptile.

The poetic coloring which the play as a whole casts over
the life of the Indians, is not, however, to be taken as an
attack on the standards of civilization. This is brought out
in the way the play concludes. Maraino, who has become
acustomed to their primitive customs, has no desire to leave;
but Sidney, whom they think of adopting, prefers to return
to the kind of life he has always known. The contrasting
views of Sidney and Maraino are well brought out in the
following conversation, significant as expressing the rival
claims of civilization and the state of nature:[62]

Sidney.   He indeed deserves
        Every requital of unfeign'd affection.
        Yet pity it is such merit should be lost
        Amid this savage wild; nor have the aid
        Of European culture; those improvements
        That mend the heart, and dignify our nature.
Maraino. In truth my brother, I cannot but marvel
        At your regret. Think you that in the wild
        Amid the shades and silence of retirement
        Virtue may not be prov'd and have a field
        For exercise? I marvel much your schools
        Have not inform'd you, that true piety,
        From proud philosophy needs little aid,
        But may in ev'ry place be known and practis'd:
        And what should mend or dignify our nature
        But virtue and true piety, I know not.

John O'Keefe's opera, *The Basket Maker*,[63] is based upon
an earlier allegorical tale,[64] having its scene on a remote

[62] Act 5.
[63] Produced Sept. 4, 1790, and acted altogether five times. Cf.
Genest 8. 5; *Biog. Dram.* 2. 50. Not printed till 1798. Revived with
some alterations, Nov. 20, 1820, under the title, *Iroquois, or Canadian
Basket Maker* (Genest 9. 100).
[64] Published in the *Magazine of Magazines* 7 (1754). 270. Here is
no mention of the Indian, nor, in fact, local color of any kind. The
same tale may quite likely have appeared in other places.

island in the South Seas. Some of the original moral of the piece has been retained, but a good many new elements, comic and farcical, have also been introduced. William, the honest basket-maker, has a piece of land which the selfish Count Pepin covets. As William refuses to sell this, the Count takes revenge by setting fire to the willows from which he makes his baskets. Just at this point the Indians rush in, and carry them all off—William, the Count, Claudine his niece, and the Marquis de Champlain her suitor. The rest of the play is made up of a good many rather disconnected adventures. William wins the favor of the savages by weaving them basket-crowns, and the Count, having no skill in anything else, is compelled to gather reeds for William's use. Wattle, William's former assistant, steals the arrows of one of the Indians, and, as a punishment, is about to be burnt at the stake, when one of them decides to adopt him in place of his dead brother Kikapous. The other Indians then pay Wattle whatever they had owed Kikapous—a fowl, some fish, corn, and such things, whereupon Wattle demands more and more, until the Indians recall what Kikapous had owed them, and the fish, fowl, and corn are all taken away. This foolish sort of comedy is continued a while longer, as the following passage will illustrate:[65]

> *Wattle.* So then upon striking a balance, starvation is my sum total. These curs'd rascals. (aside) Pray my good people, didn't he owe you a few blows on the back?
> *Otchegros.* Dat put me in de mind, he did give me once a tump in cheek, I pay you. (strikes Wattle)
> *Sokoki.* He did vid Tamahawk once take my ear.
> *Wattle.* What! (puts his hand up to his ears—a large athletic Indian steps up to Wattle with two hatchets.)
> *Third Indian.* If Kikapous liv'd he was dis day to fight me vid hatchet—here. (offers hatchet).
> *Wattle.* Oh help! murder! (snatches a lighted brand, flourishes it, and runs into pavilion).

[65] Act 5, sc. 2.

The play concludes by having everybody restored to his proper possessions, Count Pepin much reformed by his life among the Indians. His friend, the Marquis de Champlain, advises him, when returned to the gay world, to tell the proud accomplished man of fashion that 'the best master of manners, is a wild savage,'—Rochefort, one of the other characters, adding, 'And the truest schools for civilization, are the forests of America.'

Despite various attempts to dramatize adventures among the North American Indians, the appeal of such plays was always more or less limited. It is the mild, semi-civilized natives of Peru, rather than the wilder savages of the northern continent, that aroused the greatest interest on the stage. The last years of the century are indeed marked by a considerable outburst of Peruvian drama, culminating in Sheridan's immensely popular play, *Pizarro*. The impulse to the whole movement may doubtless be traced, in part at least, to Marmontel's *Incas*, a long philosophical epic, first published at Paris in 1777, and translated into English the same year. The aim of the poem is to expose the Spaniards' greed and cruelty, attributed by the author to their religious fanaticism. He therefore tells at some length how Pizarro and his followers first entered and gained control of the country, and to these historic incidents he adds the pathetic love story of Alonzo and Cora, the Virgin of the Sun. In the realistic details concerning the customs of the Peruvians— their worship of the Sun, the authority of the Incas, the quarrel of the two brothers, Ataliba and Huascar—the influence of Garcilaso and other historians may be discerned; in the sympathetic picture of the Indian's sufferings, much has been taken from the narrative of Las Casas.

In the next play we are to consider, Thomas Morton's *Columbus; or, A World Discovered*,[66] the writer borrows

[66] London, 1792. First acted Dec. 1, 1792 (Genest 7. 99). Cf. also *Biog. Dram.* 2. 322.

from Marmontel the story of Cora and Alonzo, altering historical details to suit his taste. His chief source of confusion is in having Columbus land in Peru, a circumstance noted in his prefatory statement, though not very satisfactorily accounted for. Other incongruous elements are introduced, which lower the dignity and seriousness of the piece still more. A minor love-affair is carried on between Nelti, a Peruvian maiden, and Herbert, an Englishman, whose presence in Peru at that time might on strictly historical grounds be subject to question. Doctor Dolores and Bribon, a lawyer, two Spaniards who are supposed to have come there to get rich, add a good deal of light comic action, none of which is in good taste, or in keeping with the historical situation.

The reader's chief interest centres upon the love of Cora and Alonzo, where the writer, if untrue to history, is at least nearer to his source, Marmontel, and therefore more successful in his attempt to introduce exotic atmosphere. The opening scene shows us the temple of the Sun, the priests assembled in formal array, and the aged Solasco leading in his daughter, Cora, to take her vows as priestess. After Orozimbo, the Emperor, has addressed the assembly with due formality, Cora then becomes a Virgin of the Sun, but almost immediately afterwards meets and falls in love with Alonzo. Her vows prevent their seeing much of each other till some time later, when, a storm having wrecked a part of the temple, Alonzo rushes in, and leads Cora away with him. When he learns of the punishment which will befall her or her parents if this is found out, he takes her back to the temple, hoping her absence will not have been noticed. But Cora's flight has somehow been discovered, and her death is therefore ordered by the priests. Alonzo pleads with Orozimbo to secure her pardon, and finally convinces him that the punishment of Cora is contrary to the principles of justice, by which he aims to rule. The following passage reflects something of Marmontel's point of view in attacking superstition in the name of nature or reason.[67]

> *Alonzo.* (Points to the temple) Behold those walls! does thy exalted mind, which owns the noblest energies of reason, does it approve that structure, reared by mistaken zeal, to glorify the Deity, by the dire sacrifice of all his dearest blessings? . . .
>
> *Orozimbo.* I would aspire to reign beyond the limits of weak prejudice; but reflect, Alonzo, how sacred are a country's customs.
>
> *Alonzo.* There, there's the source of half the misery of human kind—custom is the vile confounder of virtue and of vice.—It checks the operation of our god-like reason, and makes the greatest glory of creation, a being void of will—Oh, Orozimbo, soar superior to the mists of error—when thy great soul displays unmanacled its glorious attributes—thou'lt cease to think that God delights in cruelty, whose blest intuition in the human heart breathes mercy and benevolence.

The conclusion of the play is quite different from that given by Marmontel. In *Les Incas* Alonzo is wounded, and dies in the course of the long struggle between the different factions of Indians and Spaniards, and Cora later dies at his tomb. In the play, Cora is about to be killed by the priests, contrary to Orozimbo's orders, when Alonzo rushes in and rescues her.

In his treatment of the Indians, Morton shows, without any particular originality, to be sure, a good deal of sympathy for the oppressions they are forced to undergo. Alonzo, the brave defender of their rights, thus reproaches Roldan, when he talks of attacking them:[68]

> Roldan, the conduct of these Indians obscures our European virtues, and we are come to be instructed not to teach . . . if yet thou needst a stimulus to virtue, look on that Indian, and in the name of heaven, do not stain thy honour and thy manhood with treachery and ingratitude.

[67] Act 5.
[68] Act 2, sc. I.

The Cherokee,[69] a light opera in three acts, has its scene in America, with the Indians introduced merely to add to the picturesque effect. There is a good deal of bustle and excitement from the various dangers and escapes, but very little genuine exotic atmosphere. The plot turns largely on the adventures of a certain mysterious lady called Zelipha, who finally proves to be the wife of Colonel Blandford, an English officer stationed in America. There is a good Indian, called Zamorin, and a bad Indian, called Malooko. Zamorin is friendly to the whites, and tries to have his tribe make peace with them. Malooko, who loves Zelipha, is angry when she refuses him, and tries to stir up all the mischief he can against the whites. The plot is made up of a good many adventures, strung together without much logical connection or probability. Zelipha's young son, Henry, is carried off by the hostile Indians of Malooko's band, but is later rescued by Zamorin, and brought back to his mother. In the latter part of the play, Colonel Blandford and Zelipha are both captured, and carried off to a hidden cave of Malooko's. The Indians are about to kill Blandford, when Henry, who has learned the secret path to the cave from an Indian boy, rushes in, just in time to rescue his father. Malooko, when he finds escape cut off, plans to blow them all up by firing the cave, which he had formerly stored with gunpowder. Just as his companion, Ontayo, is on the point of carrying this out, he is shot by Blandford. Malooko is then stabbed, and all ends happily. The whole thing is highly fantastic, and shows us the picturesque, rather than the real or the idealized Indian.

A serious attempt to show the superior morals of a people living in the state of nature is the aim of James Bacon's play, *The American Indians; or The Virtues of Nature,*

[69] First acted December 20, 1794, and published at London the following year. It is attributed to James Cobb. Cf. Genest 7. 186; *Biog. Dram.* 2. 94.

never acted, but published in 1795. As the plot and senti-ments of the piece are borrowed from Mrs. Morton's poem, *Onabi; or, The Virtues of Nature,* I postpone a discussion of the whole subject to a later chapter of this work.[70]

In *Harlequin and Quixotte; or The Magic Arm,*[71] a panto-mime produced at Covent Garden, December 26, 1797, the attempt is made to introduce some very highly fantastic Peruvian atmosphere. The following account of the action, published with the songs and choruses in 1797, will give some notion of the general character of the piece.

The pantomime commences with the representation of a Peruvian temple

> where an injured Inca and his son had taken refuge from the malice of their persecutors—the Inca in his retirement, mak-ing magic his study, persuades his son, by a happy presage, to attempt the re-obtainment of his right, by procuring the hand of his oppressor's daughter, who is a Spanish Grandee, and has betrothed her to the knight errant of La Mancha Don Quixotte: To prevent their union, he transforms his son to Harlequin, the *Magic Arm* appearing to guard him in the hour of peril—they take leave, and he commences his career of adventure, by darting through the ruined columns of the temple, and re-appears near the Grandee's house in Grenada.

After various adventures in Spain, the scene shifts to Eng-land, then to China, these changes being made, as the author expresses it, by a 'succession of whimsical transitions.'

Another strange, fanciful representation of the Indians is found in a musical entertainment, called *The Catawba Travellers: or, Kiew Neika's Return,* presented, according to the title-page, at Sadler's Wells in 1797, 'with Indian scenery, spectacle, etc.' Kiew Neika, the Catawba chief, is supposed

---

[70] Cf. Chap. 6. Bacon, in the *Preface*, says that his first knowl-edge of the story was derived from reading a criticism of Mrs. Morton's poem in the *Monthly Review* 19 (1793). 466.

[71] Attributed to J. C. Cross. Cf. *Biog. Dram.* 3. 281.

to visit England,[72] and his wife, Onora, during his absence sings the following song:

> One eve, near the lake as I stray'd,
> The winds blowing hollow and strong,
> I heard o'er the waves the wild maid
> That steals out the soul with her song.
>
> Grieve no more for your husband, she cried,
> His bed now of coral is made;
> With me he at midnight doth glide,
> And sits on the rock a wan shade.
>
> The sea bird then scream'd o'er the deep,
> The fire came in sheets from the sky,
> My blood with cold horror did creep,
> And methought in a cloud he pass'd by.

The rest of the piece is made up of a very trifling sort of comedy, still less suggestive of anything that pertains to the Indians. Tom Bowling, an English sailor, has run away from his wife, Doll, and settled among the Catawbas, with the savage maid, Chicka, as his temporary partner. When Kiew Neika returns to America, Doll Bowling comes with him, in pursuit of her lost husband. Chicka then falls in love with a Jew peddler, who for some mysterious reason is traveling among the Catawba Indians. The following song of Chicka's illustrates the writer's attempt to introduce Indian dialect:

> Chicka lika sailor man,
> Tom lik'a Chicka too;
> He come home, he shakee hand,
> And me say how dye do?

[72] The following introductory note indicates a connection with some Indians who visited England: 'The piece, written and arranged by Mr. Lonsdale after the manners and customs of the American Indians, as correctly obtained from two Catawba chiefs who first performed at Sadler's Wells in 1795.—The occasional barbarisms interspersed among the songs and recitatives, are genuine words and expressions of the Catawba language.'

Tom no to Ningland go,
  Doll nibber come so far—den—
Ickle Chicka happy squaw,
  With a jolly tar!—

Tom shoot a cockatoo,
  Chicka put him in a pot,—
Tom fill a wamessou,
  And puxa till he hot;
Him call for grog, a ho!
  Me drinka swipe galore;—hee—ee!
Ickle Chicka happy squaw,
  Wid a jolly tar.

But, Doll 'o Wapping is she dead,
  Chicka, den a Ningland goes,—
Yellow fedder on a head,
  And silber at ee nose;
Gold ring on ebery toe,
  Blue cheek and shinee hair;—Oh la!
Ickle Chicka pretty squaw,
  For a jolly tar!

Of all the Peruvian dramas, by far the most popular was Sheridan's *Pizarro,* one of the many adaptations from Kotzebue's play on the same subject.[73] The German dramatist,

---

[73] *Die Spanier in Peru, oder Rolla's Tod* (Leipzig, 1795). The large number of translations appearing in the same year is an indication of Kotzebue's popularity, and of the widespread interest in the whole subject. Besides Sheridan's version, first published in 1799, the following translations or adaptations also appeared:

Pizarro in Peru; or, The Death of Rolla, tr. Thomas Dutton (London, 1799).

The Spaniards in Peru; or, The Death of Rolla, tr. Anne Plumptre (London, 1799).

Rolla; or, The Peruvian Hero, tr. M. G. Lewis (London, 1799).

Pizarro, tr. M. West (Dublin, 1799).

Pizarro; or, The Death of Rolla, tr. Richard Heron, 1799.

Pizarro. Tragedy in five acts; differing widely from all other *Pizarro's* in respect of characters, sentiments, language, incidents, and catastrophe, by a North Briton (London, 1799).

it is said, planned a trilogy of Peruvian plays,[74] of which only the first two parts were ever written. *The Virgin of the Sun,*[75] the first of these, deals with the story of Cora and Alonzo, also the subject of Marmontel's *Incas* and Morton's *Columbus,* already discussed.[76] Much of the interest in this piece centres in the figure of Rolla, the brave Peruvian hero, Cora's lover, rejected, but still faithful. In the character of Rolla, who has been compared to Rene and Werther,[77] there is a suggestion of Rousseauism, a point of view more fully expressed in the arguments by which the conduct of Cora and Alonzo is justified. A Virgin of the Sun, by the nature of her office devoted to perpetual chastity, breaks her vows, and runs away with her Spanish lover. When she is condemned to death, according to the laws of her country, the high priest himself urges her acquittal on the ground of reason and mercy. Pleading with Ataliba, the king, he exclaims, 'Mercy is the will of Heaven,' and goes on to relate how Manco Capac, the founder of their race, had established

Pizarro; or, The Death of Rolla, tr. Benjamin Thompson (London, 1800).

The *Biog. Dram.* 3. 158-9, gives some information regarding these different versions. None of them, so far as I can learn, was ever performed.

[74] This statement is made in Ch. Rabany's *Kotzebue, sa Vie et son Temps, ses Oeuvres Dramatiques* (Paris, 1893), p. 155. This work contains a good account of both the Peruvian dramas.

[75] *Die Sonnenjungfrau* (Leipzig, 1791). This play, though never very popular in England, appeared in the following translations:
The Virgin of the Sun, tr. James Lawrence (London, 1799).
The Virgin of the Sun. tr. Anne Plumptre (London, 1799).
Rolla; or, The Virgin of the Sun, tr. Benjamin Thompson (London, 1800). Cf. *Biog. Dram.* 3. 216. This play was not acted at London till 1812, and then in a version by Reynolds, considerably altered from the original. Cf. Genest 8. 288-290. An alteration of the German drama was acted at New York in 1800 (Genest 8. 290).

[76] For Kotzebue's relation to Marmontel, Voltaire, and others in these plays, cf. Rabany, p. 156.

[77] Cf. Rabany, pp. 156-7.

the law of chastity to protect the virgins of the temple, because at that time 'sensuality prevailed, and Reason was a child.' By now a long train of years has so changed their dispositions that the stricter rule is no longer needed. 'Therefore, Ynca,' he concludes, 'I stand here in the name of all the Gods, and call upon thee, the benefactor of thy people, to crown thy noble deeds by offering a sacrifice to Reason, and thereby to Heaven.' In such passages as this, it is clear that remoteness of the scene in time and place was not intended to prevent the reader from relating it to matters nearer home,[78] the implied moral being the overthrow of the customs of the country in favor of Rousseauistic, or strictly *natural*, principles of action.

In the sequel, *The Spaniards in Peru, or, The Death of Rolla,* the sources of interest are various—the war between the Spaniards and Peruvians, the bravery of Alonzo, and the unselfishness of Las Casas, in opposing Pizarro's cruelty, the heroic self-sacrifice of Rolla in rescuing the child of Cora, the relations of Pizarro with his dissatisfied mistress, Elvira. The plot is briefly as follows: A battle is impending between the Peruvian and the Spanish forces, and Alonzo, fearing he may be killed, sends a parting message to Cora, urging her to marry Rolla in case he does not return. In the struggle which follows the Peruvians are victorious, but

---

[78] Rabany (p. 159) speaks thus of the king's attitude: 'Alors Ataliba, qui ne craint plus de paraître céder à la violence, proclame l'abolition de la loi qui punissait de mort les prêtresses compables. Son discours est une sorte d' "exposé des motifs," comme nous dirions anjourd'hui, ou plutôt un préamble d'édit, dans le genre de ceux où Turgot faisait parler Louis XVI avec tant d'amour pour le peuple.

'L' occasion était belle pour déclamer en faveur des lois de la nature. Sous le voile transparent des mœurs américaines au temps de la conquête, le spectateur voyait avec plaisir célébrer l'affranchissement de ces jeunes novices, à qui la Révolution, en France, et Joseph II, en Autriche, venaient d'ouvrir les portes de leurs couvents. Il s'unissait de cœur aux tirades qui flétrissaient les abus alors commis au nom de la religion.'

Alonzo is among the missing, by some reported dead. Rolla, innocently crediting the latter story, delivers his request to Cora, who becomes wild and distracted in her grief, even blaming him for Alonzo's death. Resolved to convince Cora of his devotion, he goes to the Spanish camp dressed as a monk, makes his way to the cell of Alonzo, and forces him to escape in the disguise, while he takes his place as Pizarro's prisoner. Just as Alonzo seems to be happily reunited to Cora, another accident happens. In rushing through the woods to meet her husband, she leaves her baby under a tree. While she is gone, two Spanish soldiers find the child, and carry it to the camp of Pizarro. Rolla, who has been pardoned by Pizarro, finding that the child is Cora's, seizes it in his arms, and rushes off fighting for his life. He escapes, but so severely wounded that his strength is barely sufficient for him to reach the Peruvian stronghold, lay the child in Cora's arms, and expire at her feet. Besides the principal action of the play, as here stated, various subordinate episodes are introduced. A good deal is made of the part of Pizarro's mistress, Elvira, a runaway nun, now disgusted with her lover, and bent on his death. Her final repentance, if such it may be called, is due largely to the influence of Las Casas, with whom she joins in denouncing Pizarro's cruelty and oppression.

Sheridan's *Pizarro,* based on the second of these two plays, follows the broad outlines of the original story, at the same time changing the language and the incidents in a rather free way, not always for the better. One of the most striking and perhaps least happy of these changes is in the matter of ending. Instead of stopping with the death of Rolla, as did Kotzebue, Sheridan has more fighting between the Peruvians and Spaniards, and a duel between Alonzo and Pizarro, in which the latter is killed.

The prominence thus given to the Pizarro-Alonzo quarrel tends more or less to obscure the pathetic situation of the Indians. As regards Sheridan's treatment of the unfortunate Peruvians, one can only say that they seem a simple, harmless, innocent people, whom the rapacious invaders have greatly wronged. This familiar point of view is reflected in the following speech of Las Casas :[79]

> Is then the dreadful measure of your cruelty not yet complete?—Battle!—gracious Heaven! Against whom?—Against a king, in whose mild bosom your atrocious injuries even yet have not excited hate! but who, insulted or victorious, still sues for peace. Against a people who never wronged the living being their Creator formed: a people, who, children of innocence! received you as cherished guests with eager hospitality and confiding kindness. Generously and freely did they share with you their comforts, their treasures, and their homes: you repaid them by fraud, oppression, and dishonour. These eyes have witnessed all I speak—as gods you were received; as fiends have you acted.

Sympathy for the unhappy natives is also shown when, a little later in the same scene, an old cacique is dragged in, and unjustly put to death. First the Spaniards try threats, in order to extort from the old man information concerning the strength of his countrymen. Then they offer him wealth if he will show them a secret path to the Peruvian stronghold, and this the cacique also rejects with scorn:

> *Pizarro.* Dost thou despise my offer?
> *Orozembo.* Thee and thy offer!—Wealth! I have the wealth of two dear gallant sons.—I have stored in heaven the riches which repay good actions here—and still my chiefest treasure do I bear about me.
> *Pizarro.* What is that? Inform me.
> *Orozembo.* I will; for it never can be thine—the treasure of a pure unsullied conscience.
> *Pizarro.* I believe there is no other Peruvian who dares speak as thou dost.
> *Orozembo.* Would I could believe there is no other Spaniard who dares act as thou dost!
> *Gonzalo.* Obdurate pagan!—How numerous is your army?
> *Orozembo.* Count the leaves of yonder forest.

[79] Act I, sc. I.

Almagro. Which is the weakest part of your camp?

Orozembo. It has no weak part—on every side 't is fortified by justice.

Pizarro. Where have you concealed your wives and your children?

Orozembo. In the hearts of their husbands and their fathers. . . .

Pizarro. Romantic savage!—I shall meet this Rolla soon.

Orozembo. Thou hadst better not! The terrors of his noble eye would strike thee dead.

Davilla. Silence, or tremble!

Orozembo. Beardless robber! I never yet have trembled before God—why should I tremble before Man?—Why before thee, thou less than Man!

Davilla. Another word, audacious heathen, and I strike!

Orozembo. Strike, Christian! Then boast among thy fellows—I too have murdered a Peruvian!

Davilla. Hell and vengeance seize thee! (Stabs him)

Pizarro. Hold!

Davilla. Couldst thou longer have endured his insults?

Pizarro. And therefore should he die untortured?

Orozembo. True! Observe, young man—your unthinking rashness has saved me from the rack; and you yourself have lost the opportunity of a useful lesson; you might have seen with what cruelty vengeance would have inflicted torments—and with what patience virtue would have borne them.[80]

The attempt to make a striking impression by the introduction of Peruvian customs is nowhere better illustrated than in the second scene of Act 2. The setting discloses the temple of the Sun, with its altar in the centre, and a solemn march of king and warriors entering from one side, all supposed to represent 'the magnificence of Peruvian idolatry.' After a very bombastic speech by Rolla, in which the Spaniards are denounced, and the Peruvians urged to resistance, Ataliba, king and priest, offers the solemn sacrifice to their ancient deity, the Sun. The following stage-directions show that the dramatist had not overlooked this opportunity of securing spectacular effect:

[80] Act 1.

A solemn procession commences from the recess of the temple above the altar. The Priests and Virgins of the Sun arrange themselves on either side. The High-priest is followed by the choruses of the Priests and Virgins. Fire from above lights upon the altar. The whole assembly rise, and join in the thanksgiving.

Such an attempt to exploit upon the stage the picturesque religious rites of the Incas, though highly significant and interesting as a manifestation of Peruvian exoticism, has always its ridiculous aspects, very well brought out in the following contemporary criticism:[81]

> The High-priest begins an invocation, which is followed by choruses of Priests and Virgins. A ball of fire lights upon the altar, and the whole assembly then join in a prayer and thanksgiving. Observe the succession of incidents—A solemn march! a speech! a procession! an invocation! a chorus of priests and virgins! a ball of fire! and a thanksgiving!!! following one another with the *rapid variety* of a magic lantern. This is tragedy!!! To introduce fire falling from *heaven* at the invocation of *mankind,* is a stride of fancy that gives us room to hope that in the course of the next season we shall be presented with the *Deity in propria persona.* And instead of *playing off* a single insignificant *feu de joye,* he will, to the great edification and *delight* of a *gaping audience,* introduce the planets in a *country dance,* or the sun and moon in a *pas de deux,* to the tune of
>
> High diddle diddle,
> The cat's in the fiddle:
> The cow's *jump'd* over the moon, etc.
>
> Should this piece ever be cut down to *pantomime* (an event by no means improbable), we may then *fairly* criticize this wonderful

[81] From an anonymous pamphlet called *A Critique of the Tragedy of Pizarro* (London, 1799). The writer also makes a good many other unfavorable comments. Speaking of the choice of subject, he says that the 'policy of an author who dramatizes a nation of men of whom he knows little, merely because his readers know less, and his audience nothing, resembles the humble art of a juggler, whose success depends not upon his being a *great conjuror himself,* but upon his spectators being *no conjurors at all. . . .* There therefore appears to me a fundamental error in the choice of the subject of this drama, which, I think, is not made amends for by the execution of it.'

incident, unless it should be *wisely omitted,* as being too *outré*
for that species of composition, in which I recollect to have once
seen represented the vulture feeding on the bowels of Promethus;
but the author, having no *precedent,* did not venture to introduce
him stealing *fire* from *heaven.* Shall we say of this whole scene,
that it 'goes entirely for what we call *situation* and *stage effect,*'
by which the *greatest applause* may be obtained without the
assistance of *language, sentiment* or *character?*

Yet, despite this, and other adverse criticisms,[82] *Pizarro*
continued to hold the stage all through the early part of the
following century.[83] This circumstance, together with the
extraordinary pecuniary success of the piece,[84] make *Pizarro*
the most significant of the Peruvian dramas, whatever may
be said concerning its artistic defects.

And so the Indian has at last, it would appear, attained
a position of prominence on the English stage; but at the
same time has also, as it were, lost much of his identity. He
is, for the most part, Indian or Peruvian in name only. His
customs, his beliefs, his character, are not of much interest
in themselves; and his appearance on the stage, never taken
very seriously, is in the end almost wholly separated from
reality. His picturesqueness is, in brief, the quality which
makes the greatest appeal. To be sure, as we look back

[82] Besides several critical pamphlets, contemporary estimates may
also be found in *Crit. Rev.* 26 (1799). 308 ff.; *Monthly Rev.* 29
(1799). 341 ff.; *Brit. Crit.* 14 (1799). 69.

[83] I have obtained a fairly complete list of the number of times the
play was acted, by examining Genest year by year. After its first
performance, May 24, 1799, it was acted thirty-one times that season.
During the season 1799-1800 it appeared seventy-three times, during
the following season twenty-four, and after this an average of two
or three performances a year. The last of which I have found any
record was in 1834, and the total number of appearances reaches two
hundred. The part of Elvira was a favorite rôle for Mrs. Siddons,
and other popular actresses.

[84] W. Fraser Rae, in his *Sheridan, a Biography* (London, 1896) 2.
177, states that the performance of *Pizarro* caused fifteen thousand
pounds to flow into the treasury.

over the century, we see him represented now in a sentimental, now in a picturesque posture, now as the embodiment of primitive simplicity; but, judging from the success of all these different plays on the stage, it is clear that philosophic or even sentimental exoticism is ever subordinate to the fanciful and the bizarre. The practical dramatist found that he could put to most effective use the North American Indian with his feathers, war-paint, and tomahawk, or the more refined Peruvian with his gorgeous spectacle of pagan idolatry, both exploited in opera, comedy, farce, pantomime, the latter brought to the height of scenic picturesqueness in Sheridan's *Pizarro*.

CHAPTER VI.

The confusion of America with the Orient, a circumstance of such immense importance in determining the course of early exploration and discovery, is also reflected in the first poetical references to the newly discovered land. When an Elizabethan poet speaks of the Indies, one is seldom sure whether he means the East or the West, or the two viewed as one and the same; nor is the reader's uncertainty removed by the mention of such details as pearls, flowers, spices, or other indications of exotic coloring. As to the people whom Columbus and his followers found here, the poet is not much concerned with them except to wonder at their strange appearance, the pleasing novelty of bow, arrows, and feathery adornments, which he had no doubt seen pictured in some quaint old print. Even as early as Spenser we find no little interest in the picturesque Indian, as the following passages may serve to illustrate:[1]

> And in his hand a bended bow was seene,
> And many arrowes under his right side,
> All deadly daungerous, all cruel keene,
> Headed with flint, and feathers bloody dide,
> Such as the Indians in their quivers hide. . . .

> His garment nether was of silke nor say,
> But paynted plumes, in goodly order dight,
> Like as the sunburnt Indians do aray
> Their tawny bodies, in their proudest plight.

Milton also, as regards the natives of the new world, continues the tradition of Spenser. Besides a good many vague allusions to India and Ind, we find at least one clear refer-

[1] *Faerie Queene* 2. 11. 21; 3. 12. 8.

ence to the American Indian. Their feathery covering is compared to the leafy dress adopted by our first parents after the fall:[2]

> Those leaves
> They gathered, broad as Amazonian targe,
> And with what skill they had, together sowd,
> To gird their waste, vain covering if to hide
> Their guilt and shame; O how unlike
> To that first naked glorie. Such of late
> Columbus found th' American so girt
> With feathered cincture, naked else and wilde
> Among the trees on iles and woodie shores.

This early view of the Peruvians and Mexicans continued, with various modifications, through the next two centuries. Oftentimes it is revealed quite casually, as in Thomson's reference to birds as the 'plumy nations' and the 'gaudy robes they lent proud Montezuma's realm.'[3] Our study of the drama has already shown us something of the Spanish conquest, and its effect upon the Indians. This also appears in various poems during the latter part of the century, where the writer often shows less appreciation of the Indian's picturesqueness than sympathy with the wrongs he had received at the hands of the Spaniards. Much of this interest may be due to the writings of the historian Robertson, or the earlier Spanish writers from whom he drew most of his material. Or perhaps the dawning humanitarian tendencies of the time[4] found in these far-off times and

---

[2] *Paradise Lost* 9. 1110 ff.

[3] *Summer*, 741-2.

[4] An example of this kind of interest in the oppressed Indian is supplied by one of the letters of James Boswell. On September 6, 1770, he wrote to Temple: 'There is a history of the barbarous conquest of Mexico, written by one of the princes of India who lived at the time. It is an authentic book, and is translated into French. . . . I have undertaken to read it, and I shall do it with great pleasure. If the Indian prince writes of the horrible transactions of the Spaniards in his country, as I imagine he must do, his history will be

places a fitting object for sentimental effusions. Besides the expression of this point of view in several long epics, we may also see it reflected in various shorter poems. John Farrer's *America*,[5] though devoted largely to a long and tiresome account of how Britannia chides her disobedient daughter, does not fail to give some account of the early wrongs done the Indians:[6]

> Hesperian Indian sighs
> And tears of blood her swarthy cheeks bedew,
> While through her soul relentless Memory flies,
> And still recalls the horrid scene to view,
> When chased by dogs and human fiends more dread,
> Wild in their fear her naked millions fled,
> In vain they 'scaped the glutton eagle's ire,
> Deep in their breasts they felt the lightning's fire;
> Surpris'd by flames the peaceful hamlet fell.

William Richardson also has an ode called *The Indians*,[7] which he says was 'occasioned by reading an account of the barbarities perpetrated by the Spaniards in America.' He brings out the peace this simple people had enjoyed before the coming of the invader, and the afflictions they were later obliged to undergo:

> Blameless, beneath Elysian climes,
> Remote from Europe, and her crimes,
> Peaceful ye liv'd till from afar,
> The minister of impious war,
> By avarice prompted, swoln with pride,
> Th' Iberian plough'd the western tide. . . .

very striking.' Boswell probably refers to Garcilaso de la Vega's *Royal Commentaries of the Incas,* a French translation of which had appeared in 1737.

[5] A poem of twenty-four pages published at London, 1780. The John Carter Brown Library, Providence, contains a copy of this rare work. For a contemporary estimate cf. *Monthly Rev.* 64. 152.

[6] P. 2.

[7] This may be found in vol. 1, pp. 106-9, of the edition of his poems published at London, 1805. I have not had opportunity to consult the earlier editions to determine when this poem was first published.

No more, beneath the citron grove,
Warbling the liquid notes of love,
Will ye in harmless pastime gay,
Enjoy your inoffensive day.
The sable hours are on the wing;
Soon will your valleys cease to sing;
Soon will the voice of weeping rise,
And lamentation rend the skies.

Another short poem touching upon the enmity between Spaniards and Peruvians is Joseph Warton's *Dying Indian*.[8] Here a Peruvian, who appears to be of royal rank, has been slain by a poisoned arrow of the Spaniards, and, as he feels the approach of death, he calls his son to him to receive the crown. After relating how he dealt with one of the Spaniards who first dared deflower a virgin of the Sun, he pictures the future life awaiting him, and the possibilities for further vengeance upon the invaders:

                              I shall soon arrive
At the blest island, where no tigers spring
On heedless hunters; where ananas bloom
Thrice in each moon; where rivers smoothly glide,
Nor thund'ring torrents whirl the light canoe
Down to the sea; where my forefathers feast
Daily on hearts of Spaniards!

Two short poems of Southey's also reflect the Peruvian's hostility toward his conqueror. *The Song of the Araucans* (1799) is a vague and highly fanciful account of how the Indians, during a thunderstorm, imagine that their forefathers are coming from the Islands of Bliss to join the

---

[8] Included in Dodsley's *Collection of Poems* (London, 1758, 2d ed.) 4. 205. Published anonymously in the *American Museum* 2 (1787). 414. Anna Seward, writing to Henry Cary, March 16, 1790, comments as follows on this poem: 'But Joseph Warton has written very fine poetry. His dying Indian is sublime. The shortest work, if it is executed finely, almost equally with the longest, ascertains the possession of genius.'—*Letters of Anna Seward* (Edinburgh and London, 1811) 2. 394.

Strangers in the 'war of the winds.' In *The Peruvian's Dirge over the Body of his Father* (1799), he pictures a faithful son stealing the body of his father from the Spaniards' burying-place, and piously bearing it to where the departed spirit may rest in peace. The 'bloody and merciless priest,' he says, 'mumbled his magic hastily,' placed the cross in the hands of the dying man, and then buried him in the 'Stranger's field of death.' The son, in the following lines, laments the misfortunes of his country and calls upon the god of his fathers:

> Visible God of the Earth,
> The Strangers mock at thy might!
> To idols and beams of wood
> They force us to bow the knee;
> They plunge us in caverns and dens,
> Where never thy blessed light
> Shines on our poisonous toil!
> But not in the caverns and dens,
> O Sun, are we mindless of thee!
> We pine for the want of thy beams,
> We adore thee with anguish and groans.

Of the longer poems dealing with the Spanish conquest, the earliest to appear was Edward Jerningham's *Fall of Mexico*,[9] a composition of between eight and nine hundred lines. Though hopelessly dull, the work is yet of some significance, as reflecting the interest in the early relations between the Spaniards and the Indians. Of the various events the poet attempts to describe, we may pass over his account of the marriage of Guatamozin and Andalusia, as well as the different battles fought between the Mexicans and the followers of Cortez, and focus our attention upon one or two of the more dramatic episodes of the conflict. One of the most impressive scenes in the whole poem is that showing the death of the two friends, Janellan and Venzula.

[9] London, 1775. Cf. *Monthly Rev.* 54. 165.

Borrowing the details of this story from the history of Antonio de Solis,[10] Jerningham tells of their plan to seize Cortez, and drag him from the lofty height of the temple. Failing to secure their victim, Janellan and Venzula meet an untimely end, friendship, however, uniting them to the last :[11]

> Then, in each other's circling arms compress'd,
> The last and dear farewell in sighs express'd :
> 'Twas Friendship burning with meridian flame,
> One cause—one thought—one ruin—and one fame—
> Tremendous moment! See, they fall from light,
> And dauntless rush to never ending night!

The poem throughout reflects the writer's sympathy with the oppressed Mexicans. This appears in the introduction of the virtuous Las Casas, friend and protector of the Indians, as well as the instructor of their priest, Talepo, in the mysteries of the Christian religion. In the scene showing the torture of Guatamozin, the cruelty and greed of the Spaniard are contrasted with the lofty heroism of the Indians; Guatamozin, after an eloquent exhortation to his companion, gives himself up to his torture :[12]

> He said—and to his rigid doom resign'd
> Along the flaming couch his form reclin'd :
> The partner of his fate submissive bends,
> And o'er the tort'-ring bed his frame extends;
> Yet then unequal to the conq'ring pain,
> He spoke his suff'ring in lamenting strain:
> 'O, royal master, give me to disclose
> Where in the mine the golden treasure glows—
> I shrink, I faint, inferior to my part,
> And this frail frame betrays my daring heart.'

---

[10] Cf. *Historia de la Conquista de Mejico* (Madrid, 1684), Bk. 4, chap. 16.
[11] ll. 302-315.
[12] 775-792. For Dryden's account of this famous scene, cf. chap. 5.

> Amidst the raging flames that round him blaz'd,
> The royal chief his martyr'd figure rais'd,
> Cast on the youth a calm-reproaching eye,
> And spoke—oh eloquent, sublime reply!
>> Oh heav'n! oh earth! attend 'Do I repose
>> All on the silken foliage of the rose?'
>> He ceas'd—and deep within his soul retir'd,
>> To honour firm, triumphant he expir'd.

In 1784 Helen Maria Williams published an epic in six cantos, called *Peru*,[13] a work of some popularity in its day, but now neglected by all but the most curious investigators. With more sentiment than imagination, she attempts, somewhat after the manner of Marmontel, to relate in verse various incidents attending the Spanish conquest of Peru. The chief fault of the piece is its lack of unity: a good many striking situations are sketched, but the thread of narrative connecting the different cantos is sometimes very slight.

The opening of the poem shows the happiness the Peruvians enjoyed under the mild reign of Ataliba. Nature is pictured as calm and serene, the luxuriant tropical atmosphere supplying a suitable background for the Peruvians' gentleness and docility :[14]

> Where the pacific deep in silence laves
> The western shore, with slow and languid waves,
> There, lost Peruvia, rose thy cultur'd scene,
> The wave an emblem of thy joy serene :
> There nature ever in luxuriant showers
> Pours from her treasures, the perennial showers;
> In its dark foliage plum'd, the towr'ing pine
> Ascends the mountain, at her call divine;
> The palm's wide leaf its brighter verdure spreads,
> And the proud cedars bow their lofty heads;
> The citron, and the glowing orange spring,

---

[13] For contemporary criticism cf. *Crit. Rev.* 52 (1784). 376-380. A highly laudatory sonnet to Miss Williams on her achievement appeared in the *Gentleman's Magazine* for June, 1786, p. 513.

[14] I. 1-14; 41-54.

And on the gale a thousand odours fling;
The guava, and the soft ananas bloom.
The balsam ever drops a rich perfume. . . .

Nor less, Peruvia, for thy favour'd clime
The virtues rose, unsullied, and sublime:
There melting charity, with ardor warm,
Spread her warm mantle o'er th' unshelter'd form;
Cheer'd with the festal song, her lib'ral toils
While in the lap of age she pour'd the spoils.
Simplicity in every vale was found,
The meek nymph smil'd, with reeds, and rushes crown'd;
And innocence in light, transparent vest,
Mild visitant! the gentle region blest:
As from her lip enchanting accents part,
They thrill with pleasure the responsive heart;
And o'er the ever-blooming vales around,
Soft echoes waft each undulating sound.

The first canto then describes the nuptials of Ataliba and Alzira, daughter of Zorai, and closes with a dire prophecy by the genius of Peru, in which the coming of the foreigners and the unhappy fate of the empire is foretold. In the second canto, Pizarro lands with his ̄forces, and the misfortunes of the natives begin. Zorai dies, Ataliba is imprisoned and strangled, Alzira's despair drives her to madness. The canto closes with an account of how she seeks her lover in death.

In the third canto, the effects of Spanish fanaticism are vividly depicted. Valverda, a bigoted ecclesiastic, tortures an aged priest, the father of Zilia. Her lover generously rushes to the rescue, but is immediately 'pierc'd by a thousand wounds.' The courage of the Peruvian and the inhumanity of the Spaniard are revealed in the following passage:[15]

'Vain man,' the victim cried, 'to hoary years
Know death is mild, and virtue feels no fears:
Cruel of spirit, come! let tortures prove

[15] 3. 77-86.

The Power I serv'd in life, in death I love.'—
He ceas'd—with rugged cords his limbs they bound,
And drag the aged suff'rer on the ground;
They grasp his feeble form, his tresses tear,
His robe they rend, his shrivell'd bosom bare.
Ah, see his uncomplaining soul sustain
The sting of insult and the dart of pain.

Shortly after Las Casas rushes to the rescue, but his aid comes too late. The aged priest dies from the effects of what he has undergone, and his daughter Zilia soon expires of grief.

The following canto deals with a variety of events, historical and semi-historical.[16] Almagro, a companion of Pizarro, invades Chile, and encounters many difficulties in his attempt to subdue the wild, freedom-loving natives. In the meantime the Peruvians, under Ataliba's successor, Manco Capac, revolt, and regain a large part of the city. The pathetic love-story of Manco Copac and his faithful wife, Cora, is here introduced, and again resumed in a later canto.

Canto five is largely taken up with the romantic episode of Zamor and Aciloe. A battle takes place between Spaniards and Peruvians, in which Aciloe's father is taken prisoner, and her lover is supposedly killed. The victorious Alphonso then demands the hand of Aciloe, who resists his entreaties for some time. When, however, her aged father is bound on the rack and tortured, she yields to Alphonso's demands, in order to save her parent's life. Soon after Zamor appears, and the two lovers are lamenting the obstacles which separate them, when suddenly Las Casas appears at the scene, and offers to plead her cause with Alphonso. The united entreaties of the priest and the lovers finally move his heart: Aciloe is freed from her unwelcome bond, and with Zamor plans to seek safety in Chile.

[16] Many of these events are described by Robertson in the sixth book of his *History of America*.

The last canto traces the course of various quarrels between the Spaniards and Peruvians, as well as between the Spaniards themselves. Manco Capac attacks Almagro and Alphonso, is defeated, and forced to fly with the rest of his forces. Cora undergoes various dangers and hardships, and finally dies just after she has become reunited to her husband. The deaths of Almagro, Pizarro, and Las Casas soon follow one another, and the poem closes with a prophecy of the future freedom and greatness of Peru.

A different aspect of Peruvian history is brought out in Joel Barlow's *Vision of Columbus*. He begins his account of that people with the story of Capac and Oella, legendary founders of the Peruvian empire. Before their time, the people were in a state of barbarism. Capac conceives the idea of reforming their customs—doing away with human sacrifice, making the sun the supreme object of worship, establishing a rational system of religion and government. He thus describes his plan to Oella :[17]

> My anxious thoughts indulge the great design,
> To form those nations to a sway divine ;
> Destroy the rights of every dreadful Power,
> Whose crimson altars glow with human gore ;
> To laws and mildness teach the realms to yield,
> And nobler fruits to grace the cultured field.

Aiming, therefore, to reform his country, and 'build his greatness on the bliss of man,' Capac has Oella weave them robes of white, that they may by their appearance deceive the people into thinking them children of the Sun.

After they have established laws and the mild and rational worship of the sun in Peru, Capac and his descendants try to extend their beneficent rule over other parts of South America. Barlow gives a long account of how Capac sent his son, Rocha, to win the allegiance of various savage tribes. The capture of Rocha by Zamor and his followers,

[17] Bk. 2, p. 71.

a wild mountainous people, leads to a war between them and the Peruvians. At first, victory inclines to the side of Zamor; for the Incan army, terrified by an eclipse of the sun, had fled behind the walls of Cuzco. Later, however, when the sun again breaks forth, they recover their spirits at this renewed proof of their great parent's favor, and rush forth upon the enemy. Rocha, who was just about to be sacrificed, is happily rescued by his countrymen, and the invading savages are soon put to flight. Zamor, when offered his life, scornfully rejects all offers of clemency.

The future course of the Incas' sway over Peru, Barlow does not attempt to relate in any detail; its general course is, however, sketched in the following lines :[18]

> In one dark age, beneath a single hand,
> Thus rose an empire in the savage land,
> Her golden seats, with following years, increase,
> Her growing nations spread the walks of peace,
> Her sacred rites display the purest plan,
> That e'er adorn'd the unguided mind of man.

Here Barlow's idealization of Peruvian government and society, like his description of the founding of the empire, bears a strong resemblance to the account of these circumstances by Garcilaso de la Vega. Directly or indirectly, Barlow drew from the early Spanish historians, and possibly from Spanish or Portuguese poems on America.[19]

The North American Indian, as he is represented in English poetry, has frequently very little in common with the idealized Peruvian or Mexican whom we have thus far been considering. These far-off, tropical lands, it should be recalled, were viewed largely through the medium of literary accounts, usually second or third hand, and always more or

---

[18] Bk. 4, p. 129.
[19] In a note, he gives a long account of the tradition of Capac and Oella, and speaks of his interest in the *Araucana* of don Alonso de Ercilla, and the *Lusiad* of Camoens (cf. Bk. 2. 66-68).

less colored by the writer's imagination. North America, on the contrary, was more of a reality. The English settlers, in a long series of wars, had gained no little experience of the savages' fierceness, cruelty, and revenge; hence we are not surprised to find some reflection of this in poetry, as well as in histories and narratives of Indian captivity. In one of the earliest poems dealing with America, we find that the writer, though in general favorable to the Indian,[20] gives us a good deal of realistic description of his customs and ways, and at the same time brings out his fondness for revenge. In so far as less pleasing traits are omitted from this picture of the savage, we may conclude that it is due to the author's desire to interest colonists in America, the primary object of his poem.

In a number of eighteenth-century poems, we find the Indian represented as living in a condition of ignorance, superstition, and continual warfare. Timothy Dwight, in his poem entitled *America*,[21] speaks thus of the universal state of savagery existing before the arrival of Columbus:

> Sunk in barbarity these realms were found,
> And superstition hung her clouds around.
> O'er all, the impenetrable darkness spread
> Her dusky wings, and cast a dreadful shade;
> No glimpse of science through the gloom appeared;
> No trace of civil life the desert chear'd;
> No soft endearments, no fond social ties,
> Nor faith, nor justice calm'd their horrid joys:
> But furious vengeance swell'd the hellish mind,
> And dark ey'd malice all her influence join'd,
> Here spread broad plains, in blood and slaughter drown'd;
> There boundless forests nodded o'er the ground;

[20] William Morrell, *New England, or a Briefe Ennaration of the Ayre, Earth, Water, Fish, and Fowles of that Country, with a Description of the Natures, Orders, Habits, and Religion of the Natives, in Latine and English Verse* (London, 1625). A reprint of this may be found in the *Mass. Hist. Soc. Coll.* (Boston, 1792) I. 125-139.

[21] New Haven, 1780.

Here ceaseless riot and confusion rove;
There savage roarings shake the echoing grove.
Age after age rolls on in deepening gloom,
Dark as the mansions of the silent tomb.

The same poem also contains a lurid picture of the Indians'
attacks on the colonists: the burning of the houses, the yells
of the savages, the scalping of the victims—all familiar
scenes in the early history of New England. The following
lines bring out the horror and confusion attending an Indian
raid:

Oft when deep silent night her wings had spread,
And the vast world lay hid in peaceful shade,
In some lone village mirth led on the hours,
And swains secure to sleep resign'd their powers;
Sudden the fields resound with wars alarms,
And earth re-echoes,—arms, to arms, to arms;
Faint through the gloom the murd'ring bands are seen;
Disploded thunder shakes the darksome green
Broad streams of fire from falling structures rise,
And shrieks and groans and shouts invade the skies:
Here weeping mothers piercing anguish feel;
There smiles the babe beneath the lifted steel;
Here vig'rous youth from bloody vengeance flies;
There white-hair'd age just looks to heaven and dies.

In a poem of Francis Hopkinson's, called *The Treaty*,[22]
we find the Indian captivity-motive treated with a good deal
of vividness, as well as sentiment. After picturing, in
the manner of Dwight, the peaceful village attacked by the
murderous savages, the slaughter of the settlers, the hard
fate of the children carried off to captivity, the poet introduces an idyllic theme, the love of Doris, the gentle shepherd,
and Rosetta, 'fairest maid that grac'd the plains.' One evening, as she strays from the cottage 'to seek a wand'ring lamb-
kin of her fold,' she is seized and carried off by the savages.

[22] Included in *Miscellaneous Essays and Occasional Writings*
(Philadelphia, 1792), pp. 120-128. The episode of Doris and Rosetta
was published in the *Massachusetts Magazine*, I (1789). 521.

Her lover, hearing her cries, rushes fearless upon her captors, but is soon forced to yield to the power of numbers:

> Long did the youth th' unequal fight maintain;
> But what, alas! could valour then avail?
> An Alexander must have strove in vain,
> Superior force and numbers will prevail.

Rosetta and Doris are then carried off by different bands, and do not see each other till the torture of the prisoners is prepared. Then one day Rosetta, hearing a familiar voice, rushes forth only to find her lover bound to the stake:

> Oh! mournful object for a soul distrest!
> Fast to a tree she sees her shepherd bound:
> A mortal arrow planted at his breast,
> And his life bubbling from the recent wound!
> Struck with an instant frenzy of despair,
> Thro' all her frame she feels the chill of death;
> Flies to her just expiring love, and there
> Sinks at his feet with closing eyes, and sighs her latest breath.

The Treaty is also of interest for the description it gives of the mysterious war-dance. The wild frenzy which seizes upon the actors in this barbarous spectacle is well brought out in the following lines:

> And now the chiefs for awful rites prepare,
> And hand in hand in horrid rounds unite,
> Where curling blazes lash the misty air,
> And pierce their radiance thro' the gloom of night.
> —The dance of war begins, their eye-balls roll,
> And dart their fierce enraged glances round;
> More than internal madness fills the soul,
> And distant rocks their fearful yells resound.
>
> No greater frenzy e'er the priestess shook,
> When on the sacred tripod mounted high,
> Her tender, shiv'ring, panting frame was struck
> With the rough presence of the deity.
> Each village now convulsed looks aghast,
> Their limbs are all in rude contortions thrown,

Their wild enthusiasm heightens fast,
And they for devils, not for men are known:
Till wasted nature can no more sustain,
And down in sleep their wearied bodies fall;
Silence profound resumes her awful reign,
And midnight's thickest mantle covers all.

Many of the historic poems on America portray the activities of the Indians, not only in their perpetual wars among themselves, or in their attacks upon the settlers, but also in the longer struggles between the English and the French, or the Americans and the British.[23] Barlow, in the fifth book of *The Vision of Columbus,* describes the part they played in the French and Indian War. A short poem on the same subject appeared in the *London Magazine* for 1756 (25, 189). As the poem was apparently occasioned by General Braddock's defeat, it may doubtless be taken to reflect contemporary sentiment over the British losses. The writer speaks with considerable feeling of the fate of those who have fallen victims to the Indians' barbarity:

Unhappy youths, far from their native sky,
In India's darksome woods untomb'd they lie,
While ghastly wounds deface their mangled clay
Of ruthless savages, the destin'd prey;
Who wildly fierce each prostrate coarse deride.
And with fell shouts the reeking scalps divide.

[23] The cruel, warlike Indian receives passing notice in a number of poems, which need not be discussed here. The *Gentleman's Magazine*, 65 (1795). 742, contains a sonnet by Mrs. Charlotte Smith, describing an Indian's attempt to escape from his captors. In *Columbia and Ivor*, a short poem published in the *Town and Country Magazine* for 1778, pp. 45-6, the savage, warring Indian furnishes an element of picturesqueness and adventure. In this connection we should also mention *The Indian Scalp, or, Canadian Tale* (London, 1778), a rare poem, which the writer has not had opportunity to consult. Cf. *Monthly Rev.* 58. 308, and *Crit. Rev.* 45. 227.

A poem called *The Desolation of America,* London, 1777, relates, with a good deal of bitterness against British as well as Indians, how the savages were incited to commit atrocities against the Americans. Not all of these works, however, show such an entire lack of sympathy with the Indians. A poem called *Defeat of Stuart's Indians in the South*[24] shows something of the unfortunate state of the savages, defeated and driven back into the wilds, yet still angry and revengeful against the whites. In Timothy Dwight's long poem, *Greenfield Hill,* the series of events which resulted in the destruction of the Pequots are related with some fulness of detail. The most pathetic part is that which describes the cruel, yet necessary, extermination meted out to those last survivors who in a remote swamp had sought refuge from impending death. One of their number, unluckily taken captive by the English commander, Stoughton, is compelled to reveal the hiding-place of his companions, who, with the exception of the hundred who surrendered, were all put to death. The terror of this wild scene, and the writer's sympathy for the unhappy victims, are well brought out in the closing stanzas of Part Four:

> Through the sole, narrow way, to vengeance led,
> To final fight our generous heroes drew;
> And Stoughton now had pass'd the moors black shade,
> When hell's terrific region scream'd anew,
> Undaunted, on their foes they fiercely flew;
> As fierce, the dusky warriors crowd the fight;
> Despair inspires; to combat's face they glue;
> With groans, and shouts, they rage, unknowing flight,
> And close their sullen eyes, in shades of endless night.

> Indulge, my native land! indulge the tear,
> That steals, impassion'd o'er a nation's doom:
> To me each twig, from Adam's stock, is dear,
> And sorrows fall upon an Indian's tomb.

[24] Published in the *Massachusetts Magazine* 4 (1792). 51.

And, O ye Chiefs! in yonder starry home,
Accept the humble tribute of this rhyme,
Your gallant deeds, in Greece, or haughty Rome,
By Maro sung, or Homer's harp sublime,
Had charm'd the world's wide round, and triumph'd over time.

The unhappy fate of the dispossessed Indian, here the
subject of little more than a passing regret, received in
several other poems much more extended comment. The
Gentleman's Magazine for 1785[25] includes a short piece
called *An Indian's Speech to His Countrymen,* in which an
aged chief addresses his followers on the injuries they have
received from the white man. First we see pictured the
English army spread out to besiege Quebec, and the savage
warrior standing upon a distant rock, silently contemplating
the art of European war. Then he turns to his followers and
tells them of the happy time when their bold ancestors 'had
sole dominion o'er these boundless woods.' After numberless
ages had passed in plenty and security, the unknown race of
men came from across the ocean. Having seized the Indian's
land, they sought protection in 'fastnesses of stone' or issued
forth,

and over all our realms
Rang'd uncontroul'd, and slaughter'd in their rage
Th' opposers, the submissive, in their mirth;
Some of the poor remains of our lost country,
Buried in caverns, were compell'd to dig
Metals for their insulting lords; and some
Employ'd to till the ground, whose large increase
Supply'd the idleness of foreign tyrants.

Yet the Indian now hopes that this period of injustice is
nearing an end. He has been deprived of his right to hunt
and fish, openly driven from the lands of his fathers, or
more basely defrauded by those who pretend to have bought

[25] 35. 526. The writer admits that his poem is an imitation of a
paper in Johnson's *Idler,* No. 81.

them; but he sees that the whites are at war with one another,
and he rejoices in the anticipation of their mutual destruction:

> Let us
> Look on with pleasure, still remembering
> That when an European falls, there falls
> A tyrant and a robber; for what claim
> Has either hostile nation, but the claim
> Of the rapacious vulture to the hare,
> Or of the tiger to the helpless fawn?
> Let them continue to dispute their title
> To realms they cannot people, and by blood
> And danger purchase a dominion
> O'er airy mountains which they will not climb.
> O'er rapid rivers which they will not pass.
> Let us, mean time, observe their discipline,
> And learn to forge their weapons, that, at last
> When they are weaken'd with a mutual slaughter,
> Unable to resist, we may rush down
> Impetuous on them, from our mountains heights,
> Force them to seek for shelter in their ships,
> And once more govern in our native realms.

Another *Speech of an Indian Chief* appeared in the
American Museum for 1788 (4. 481). Here, also a despairing warrior is represented as lamenting the departed glories
of his race, eloquently recalling to his countrymen the ills
which have followed in the train of the invader. Perhaps,
however, the best example of this feeling for the wrongs of
the Indian is contained in a poem by Josias Arnold, called
Translation of an Indian Prophecy.[26] Similar to the works
just discussed in point of style and subject-matter, the dire
prophecies of this 'Indian Sage' are made the more impressive by the writer's choice of a suitable natural background,
the majestic falls of Niagara:

> Where the rough cataract of Erie pours
> Down headlong bellowing through Ontario's shores,

[26] Contained in a volume of his *Poems,* published at Providence,
1797.

Where vapouring clouds in pomp sublime arise,
And shew a thousand rainbows in the skies;
Seated beneath a heaven-pervading oak,
An Indian Sage prophetically spoke.

Most of his speech is upon the old themes—the European's craving for gold, the war and bloodshed he has brought among the happy children of nature. The prophet thus mournfully laments the passing of the Indian's peace and contentment:

No more within these venerable groves
Shall the young suitors breathe their ardent loves;
No more we chase the wild deer o'er the hills,
For moose nor ambush by the shady rills;
No more the wily beaver we ensnare,
But hasten, headlong hasten, to the war.
A long, a long adieu, shall sigh fair peace,
And halcyon days and blissful quiet cease.

A variation of the prophetic Indian motive may be found in Freneau's *Prophecy of King Tammany*,[27] where the dispossessed savage is viewed in a heroic, as well as in a pathetic light. Tammany, according to tradition the first Indian to welcome William Penn to America,[28] is here pictured in despair over his country's fallen pride. Realizing the futility of the Indian's attempt at resistance, he prepares his funeral pyre, and resolves to find an escape in death:

Yes, yes,—I see our nation bends;
The Gods no longer are our friends;—
    But why these weak complaints and sighs?
Are there not gardens in the west,

[27] Published in the *Freeman's Journal*, Dec. 11, 1782. Also in Freneau's poems, ed. Pattee, 2. 187.

[28] Drake, in his *Book of the Indians* 5. 6-17, gives some information on the life of this famous Delaware chief. John Heckewelder, in his *Account of the History, Manners, and Customs of the Indian Nations* (Philadelphia, 1819), pp. 299-300, writes at length concerning the legend which attaches to King Tammany.

Where all our far-famed sachems rest?—
I'll go, an unexpected guest,
   And the dark horrors of the way despise. . . .

      Around him soon the crackling flames ascend;
He smiled amid the fervours of the fire
   To think his troubles were so near their end,
'Till the free soul, her debt to nature paid,
Rose from the ashes that her prison made,
And sought the world unknown, and dark oblivion's shade.

The virtue and bravery of King Tammany, or Saint Tammany, as he was afterward called, were also celebrated in a poem published in the *American Museum* for 1789.[29]   Here the writer, one William Prichard, recalls not only the chief's heroic death, but his love of country, his courage in war, his swiftness in the chase:

Immortal Tamany, of Indian race,
Great in the field and foremost in the chase!
No puny saint was he, with fasting pale,
He climb'd the mountain and he swept the vale,
Rush'd thro' the torrent with unequall'd might;
Your ancient saints would tremble at the sight,
Caught the swift boar, and swifter deer with ease,
And work'd a thousand miracles like these.
To public views he added private ends,
And lov'd his country most, and next his friends;
With courage long he strove to ward the blow,
(Courage we all respect ev'n in a foe,)
And when each effort he in vain had tried,
Kindled the flame in which he bravely died!
To Tamany let the full horn go round,

---

[29] 5. 104.   The same poem also appeared in the *Columbian Muse* (New York, 1794), pp. 223-4.   Richard B. Davis, in his *Poems* (New York, 1807), pp. 120-2, has a *Prologue to Mrs. Hatten's Opera of Tammany,* most of which had already appeared in the *New York Magazine* 5 (1794). 187.   Wegelin, in his *Early American Plays* (New York, 1905), p. 43, mentions an opera, *Tammany, or The Indian Chief,* performed in 1794.

His fame let every honest tongue resound!
With him let ev'ry gen'rous patriot vie,
To live in freedom or with honour die.

The Indian as a heroic figure is nowhere seen to better
advantage than in some of the poems picturing his stoical
endurance under torture. A good deal of realism colors
these accounts of savage cruelty and revenge, in which the
sufferer's fortitude can hardly fail to arouse the reader's
wonder and admiration. The circumstance of most striking
appeal in these situations is, of course, the victim's composure
under the utmost extremity of pain. As his torturers strive
to outdo one another in ferocity, he calmly chants his death-
song—taunts them with a recital of the number he has killed,
threatens them with the revenge his countrymen will take for
his death, and defies their utmost ingenuity to extort a groan
or a sigh. This type of Indian is best portrayed in a poem
of disputed authorship,[30] immensely popular in its day, generally known under the title, *The Death Song of a Cherokee
Indian:*[31]

The sun sets in night, and the stars shun the day,
But glory remains, when their lights fade away.
Begin, ye tormentors: your threats are in vain;
For the son of Alknomock can never complain.

Remember the woods, where in ambush he lay,
And the scalps which he bore from your nation away.
Why do ye delay? . . . 'till I shrink from my pain?
Know, the son of Alknomock can never complain.

[30] Farley, in his paper, *The Dying Indian* (*Kittredge Anniversary Papers*, Boston, 1913, pp. 251-260), gives an extended discussion of the three claimants to this piece, Philip Freneau, Thomas J. McKee, and Mrs. Anne Hunter, but in the end decides that 'the evidence does not seem conclusive in the case of any one of the three candidates.' Farley also comments on many other points of interest relative to *The Dying Indian.*
[31] First published in the *American Museum* I (1787). 77.

Remember the arrows he shot from his bow:
Remember your chiefs by his hatchet laid low.
The flame rises high. You exult in my pain:
But the son of Alknomock will never complain.

I go to the land, where my father is gone:
His ghost shall exult in the fame of his son.
Death comes like a friend. He relieves me from pain:
And thy son, O Alknomock, has scorn'd to complain.

An interesting parallel to the son of Alknomock is found in the hero of Josias Arnold's poem, *The Warrior's Death Song*.[32] His fortitude is displayed when he bids his enemies try his endurance with fiercer flames, but his defiance is also colored with a tinge of poetic fancy when he tells how death

the sooner shall disclose
The land where every torment flies,
Where endless joys and pleasures rise.

This notion of a future state, quite un-Indian in its lack of tomahawks, arrows, and war-songs, is expressed with some picturesqueness in the following lines:

Thus, tho' the raging flame destroy
This mortal frame, to scenes of joy
The soul shall fly, where Podar reigns
O'er pleasant woods and fertile plains.

There nations shall no more be foes,
Nor warriors tribe to tribe oppose;
No hideous war-song shall be heard,
But peace inspire the ravish'd bard.

No arrows tipt with polish'd bone,
Nor tomahawk shall there be known;
But all, till time itself shall cease,
Shall live in harmony and peace.

[32] Included in his *Poems* (London, 1797), pp. 50-2.

In Thomas Gisborne's *Dying Indian*,[33] we have an unusually lurid account of how a Mohawk brave, who had fallen into the hands of the enemy, derides the feeble powers of his tormentors, at the same time reminding them of the fierce atrocities he has himself committed:

> Is this your vaunted art?
> Is this to act the torturer's part?
> Go, rival a mosquito's smart!
> Your bravest chiefs of yore
> I seized: their flesh my burning pincers tore:
> Round them I wove the glowing cane:
> Red splinters pierced each hissing vein:
> While from my back, in bloody triumph hung,
> Scalps of their slaughter'd brethren swung.
>   The woods return'd their moan.
> I watch'd the writhing limb,
> Saw the rack'd eyeball swim,
>   And laugh'd at every groan!

Despite any seeming incongruity, the writer detects a parallel between his Indian hero's death and that of the martyr Stephen, which he brings out in the following lines:

> He spoke, he laugh'd, he died,
> 'Hail, my unequall'd Son,' said Pride.
> 'Not so;' a voice from Heaven replied.
> 'Is he the truly brave,
> Victor of pain, but thine and Passion's slave?
> His holy head see Stephen bow:
> See meekness calm his angel brow.
> Around see Malice scowl, see Vengeance glare;
> See Rage the murderous stones prepare;
> And Saul the garments keep.
>   Hark!—"Lord, their sin forgive!
>   My spirit, Lord, receive!—"
> He spake, and fell asleep.'

---

[33] Included in his *Poems, Sacred and Moral* (London, 1799), pp. 29-33. In his preface he cites a lurid account of Indian torture from Carver's *Travels into the Interior Parts of North America*.

One of the most dramatic of these poems of captivity and
torture is William Dunlap's *Cololoo, an Indian Tale*.[34]   As
this Cayugan brave is being tortured by his enemies, he sings
a death-song recounting the famous exploits of Logan, a
famous chieftain of his tribe.   His account of how Logan
once spared a white warrior who was in his power so moves
his hearers that they are induced to adopt a similar forbear-
ance toward Cololoo himself.   The poem closes by showing
his enemies so changed that they now wish to adopt him:

> Reldor then with sullen stride,
>   His knife was in his hand,
> Advanc'd, and thus aloud he cried,
>   And cut the twisted band.
>
> Reldor takes thee for his son,
>   Colwall in battle slain;
> In many a fight his fame he won,
>   Nor shrunk from death or pain.
>
> Silent now the warrior train
>   Bear the blood-stain'd chief,
> No more they weep for Colwall slain,
>   No more is known of grief.

Although the heroic sentiments ascribed to the Indian are
most conspicuous in these scenes of torture at the stake, his
death under altogether different circumstances is also the
occasion for considerable fanciful elaboration and picturesque description, frequently without basis in any of his
known customs or beliefs.   His conception of the future life,
which has already been touched upon in the discussion of
Warton's *Dying Indian* and Arnold's *The Warrior's Death*

---

[34] The first appearance of this poem, according to Professor Farley,
was in a collection of *American Poems*, published by Collier and
Buel at Litchfield, Connecticut, in 1793. I have used the version
printed in The *Columbian Muse* (New York, 1794), pp. 187-190.
For the historic character, Logan, cf. Farley's *Dying Indian*, or
Drake's *Book of the Indians*, Bk. 5, pp. 41 ff.

Song, is also the subject of several other poems, of some interest for their difference in point of view and treatment. The *Dying Indian, or the Last Words of Shalum,*[35] differs from most poems of its kind in attributing to the aged warrior a sombre view of his condition in the world of shades. He meditates regretfully on the bright world he is to leave, and asks,

> What solitary streams,
> In dull and dreary dreams,
> All melancholy, must I rove along?

> To what strange lands must Shalum take his way!
> Groves of the dead, departed mortals trace;
> No deer along these gloomy forests stray,
> No huntsmen there take pleasure in the chase:
> But all are empty, unsubstantial shades.

In *The American Warrior,* an anonymous piece published in *The Columbian Muse,*[36] the hero, Carandoc, after describing how he has been driven from his home by the enemy, the village burned, his companions killed, decides that honor and glory now bid him cease to live. In the following speech of farewell he expresses the hope of being united with his sweetheart, Lamuna:

> 'Farewel, ye dreary wilds! for now I go
> To visit peaceful realms unknown to woe;
> Whose vales are blooming with perennial flowers,
> And meadows water'd by refreshing showers,
> There shall I see my lov'd Lumuna's shade,
> Stray o'er the fields, and haunt the blossom'd glade;
> Clasp to my breast the idol of my heart,
> And (oh! the pleasing thought) no more to part:

[35] This piece is also of disputed authorship. It was published in the *American Museum* 3 (1788). 190, under the name of Freneau, and in the *Freeman's Journal* of March 17, 1784. Cf. note in Pattee's edition of Freneau 2. 243. It is also included among the poems of Josias Lyndon Arnold (Providence, 1797).

[36] Pp. 126-8. Said to be by a South Carolinian, aged 17, reprinted from *The (Charleston) Star.*

But, while she wanders spicy vallies o'er,
I'll hunt the stag or rouse the mountain bear.
—She glides before me on the gentle wind!—
And bids me cease to tarry long behind!—
I come.—I come,—Lumuna dear—I come!
And joyful seek th' embraces of the tomb!'
Carandoc plung'd a weapon in his breast,
Clos'd his dim eyes, and sunk to endless rest.

More picturesque is the manner of meeting death adopted
by the aged Weimar, hero of a piece called *The Indian Warrior's Lamentation,* published in the *Massachusetts Magazine*
for 1792 (4. 120). The first part of the poem is taken up
with Weimar's account of the wrongs done by the whites,
the fading fame of his nation, and the deeds of valor he
has himself performed.   Then, after lamenting the death
of his son Lorad, and bidding his native woods farewell, he
leaps from the heights of Niagara, and is supposedly
reunited with the spirits of his departed friends:

'I see the blooming regions rise;
My father's spirits hail my eyes,
    Among the happy bowers.
I come, I come, ye sons of light,
No more I fear the storms of night
    Whom feeble man adores.'

He said and shook his hoary locks.
As down he plung'd the craggy rocks,
    A kindred spirit came:
Rob'd in the cloudy vests of morn;
On flaming plumes triumphant borne
    They hail the realms of fame.

Another and more pathetic view of the dying Indian
appears in one or two poems on the treatment of the aged
or infirm by the more active members of the tribe.[37]   In

_____

[37] Various writers on the Indian and his customs discuss the treatment accorded the old and helpless. Long in his *Voyages and
Travels,* pp. 73-75, gives a graphic account of their manner of dis-
posing of those who have become burdensome.

William Preston's *Speech of an Old Savage to his Son, Who, in a War with a Neighboring Tribe, Was Preparing to Bear his Feeble Father on his Back,*[38] the aged warrior generously refuses to continue a burden to his affectionate son:

> No more, my son; thy pious care is vain.
> Bow not thy back, with age's useless weight.
> I am not worth preserving: would'st thou wish me
> To drag about a loathed crazy mass,
> A vile memento of strength's frailty,
> Cumb'rous to others, grievous to myself,
> And die of old age, like a dog or Christian?—
> Thou wert not form'd to bear a weak old man.

After urging his son to fight valiantly against the enemy, the old man requests that he may be killed, rather than left to the chance of capture and disgrace:

> But first strike here; leave not thine aged father,
> To feel their rage, whose kindred he has mangled;
> Nor let his tortur'd members feast the sight
> Of those that hate him and his tribe!—Farewell,
> Be kind and quick.—Thy lance be sharp as now,
> Thine arm as strong, my son, in all thy warfare!

In Wordsworth's *Complaint of a Forsaken Indian Woman,*[39] there is a picture of the involuntary suffering doubtless more generally accorded the unfortunate victim of disease or old age.[40] Here much of the pathos lies in the

[38] Professor Farley states that this was published in Preston's *Poetical Works* (London, 1795), which I have not had an opportunity to consult. It was also included in the *Monthly Review* 16 (1795). 168, and in the *Scots Magazine* for the same year (57. 173).

[39] Composed in 1798, and published in the *Lyrical Ballads,* the same year.

[40] Wordsworth acknowledges his indebtedness to Samuel Hearne's *Journey from Prince of Wales's Fort in Hudson's Bay to the Northern Ocean* (London, 1795). The source of Wordsworth's realistic details may be found in the passage from chap. 7, pp. 218-9, ed. Tyrrell (Toronto, 1911).

mother's grief over the loss of her child, whom her companions took from her when they left her to perish:

> My Child! they gave thee to another,
> A woman who was not thy mother.
> When from my arms my Babe they took,
> On me how strangely did he look!
> A most strange working did I see;
> —As if he strove to be a man,
> That he might pull the sled for me:
> And then he stretched his arms, how wild!
> Oh mercy! like a helpless child. . . .
>
> Young as I am, my course is run,
> I shall not see another sun;
> I cannot lift my limbs to know
> If they have any life or no.
> My poor forsaken Child, if I
> For once could have thee close to me,
> With happy heart I then would die,
> And my last thoughts would happy be;
> But thou, dear Babe, art far away,
> Nor shall I see another day.

The Indians' affection for their dead, and some of the picturesque customs in their mode of burial, are also noted in various poems. Farrer, in *America*, pictures their grief for their lost companions, whose bones they carry about with them, and finally bury or deposit together in a selected spot, with a ceremony called 'The Feast of Souls.' Dwight's *Greenfield Hill* represents a widow lamenting over the tomb of her buried lover, whose shade comes to visit her in her sleep:[41]

> There, on her lover's tomb, in silence laid,
> While still, and sorrowing, shower'd the moon's pale beam,
> At times, expectant, slept the widow'd maid,
> Her soul far-wandering on the sylph-wing'd dream.
> Wafted from evening skies, on sunny stream,
> Her darling youth with silver pinions shone;

[41] 217-225.

With voice of music, tun'd to sweetest theme,
He told of shell-bright bowers, beyond the sun,
Where years of endless joy o'er Indian lovers run.

Southey treats a similar theme in his *Song of the Chik-kasah Widow* (1799), in which an Indian woman imagines she hears the voice of her dead husband borne to her on the gale, crying for revenge on his enemies. She sees his hatchet idly hanging on the war-pole, his bow waving in the wind, and the still greater evidence of his bravery, the many scalps taken in war. Then she speaks of her grief when her companions returned without him, and the joy she will take in the revenge to be inflicted on the prisoners.

Southey also has a poem, called *The Huron's Address to the Dead* (1799), in which a warrior indulges in a lament over his lost companion, and records his many feats of valor. The most interesting, however, of these poems touching the Indian's attitude toward the dead is Freneau's *Indian Burying Ground*. The white man's custom of laying the dead in a position suggestive of their eternal sleep is contrasted with the Indian's custom of placing them in a sitting posture, surrounded by bow, arrows, and other belongings—symbolical, he thinks, of the continued life the Indian imagines for his friends, the 'activity that knows no rest.' The latter part of the poem pictures the shades of the departed redskins haunting the scenes they had known during life:

Here still an aged elm aspires,
  Beneath whose far-projecting shade
(And which the shepherd still admires)
  The children of the forest played!

There oft a restless Indian queen
  (Pale Shebah, with her braided hair)
And many a barbarous form is seen
  To chide the man that lingers there.

By midnight moons, o'er moistening dews;
  In habit for the chase arrayed,
The hunter still the deer pursues,
  The hunter and the deer, a shade!

> And long shall timorous fancy see
> The painted chief, and pointed spear,
> And Reason's self shall bow the knee
> To shadows and delusions here.

Passing over several pieces in which other picturesque Indian customs are noticed,[42] we shall next consider a few poems which treat of his religion, his conversion, or his attitude toward Christianity. The heathen worship of the Indian, and his need of Christian faith, is mentioned in Morrell's early poem on New England. Although they have traditions of a supreme being who created all things, most of them worship two Gods,

> One good, which gives all good, and doth preserve;
> This they for love adore; the other bad,
> Which hurts and wounds, yet they for fears are glad
> To worship him.

Yet, though without a true knowledge of God, they own his laws are good, all except one, 'whereby their will's withstood in having many wives.' The notion of a superstitious, uninstructed savage, awed by the wonders of nature, which he colors with his own poetic fancy, is probably best expressed in Pope's well known lines:

> Lo, the poor Indian! whose untutor'd mind
> Sees God in clouds, or hears him in the wind;
> His soul proud Science never taught to stray
> Far as the solar walk or milky way;
> Yet simple nature to his hope has given,

---

[42] I refer to such poems as the following:

Description of a Mohawk Chief, Massachusetts Magazine 4 (1792). 329.

Fragment of an Indian Sonnet, by Josias L. Arnold, p. 53 of his *Poems* (London, 1797).

The Indian Chief, by Edward Jerningham, pp. 133-5 of Vol. 1 of his *Poems* (London, 1786).

Old Chikkasah to his Grandson, by William Southey, in a group of Indian poems dated 1799.

> Behind the cloud-topp'd hill, an humbler heaven;
> Some safer world in depth of woods embraced,
> Some happier island in the watery waste,
> Where slaves once more their native land behold,
> No friends torment, no Christians thirst for gold.
> To be, contents his natural desire,
> He asks no angel's wings, no seraph's fire;
> But thinks, admitted to that equal sky,
> His faithful dog shall bear him company.[43]

The picturesque side of the Indian's belief and worship receives casual mention in various poems toward the close of the eighteenth century. Dwight paints with a good deal of imagination the dark mysterious rites of the savage priest.— The hoary priest, dressed in a magic cincture, strews the altar with mystic dust and spicy herbs, while rich perfume rises from the curling flame. No less impressive is his account of the part played by the Great Spirit, the vague pantheistic deity disclosed in the phenomena of nature— cloud, rainbow, and sunset:[44]

> Then (so tradition sings), the train behind,
> In plumy zones of rainbow'd beauty dress'd,
> Rode the Great Spirit, in th' obedient wind,
> In yellow clouds slow-sailing from the west.
> With dawning smiles, the God his votaries bless'd,
> And taught where deer retir'd to ivy dell;
> What chosen chief with proud command to invest;
> Where crept th' approaching foe, with purpose fell,
> And where to wind the scout, and war's dark storm dispel.

English accounts of the Indian's relations with the missionary have little to compare with the marvels and wonders that abound in such narratives as those composing the French *Jesuit Relations.* As the introduction of Christianity among the savage people was perhaps on the whole taken less seriously by the English missionaries, the occasional references to their labors which we find in poetry sometimes show

[43] *Essay on Man,* Epistle I, 99-112.
[44] *Greenfield Hill,* p. 99.

sympathy and appreciation, more often amusement and mild satire. One of the most celebrated of these missionaries, George Whitefield,[45] is referred to in a poem by Joseph Williams, called *The Indian Convert*.[46] Here an Indian is represented as describing his experiences when converted by Whitefield's powerful preaching. First he pictures his condition before he learned of the Christian religion:

> Wild as the wilderness in which I trod,
> By nature stupid as the bestial train:
> Lost to myself—a stranger to my God,
> Thoughtless I wander'd o'er my native plain.

Then came the missionary, at whose accounts of the sorrows of Jesus even the savage Indians, assembled from far and near, are moved to repentance and submission:

> How did our sable sons from afar and near
> By night, by day, their eager steps pursue?
> No threats nor dangers! stop'd their glad career,
> 'T was Jesus call'd, and Jesus led them thro'.

> Sweet was the scene! Delightful was the hour!
> When round the prophet of the Lord we stood,
> Heard him declare his Savior's mighty power,
> And tell the virtues of His precious blood.

It is said that Whitefield frequently addressed his savage audience under a large tree, on the bank of a stream near Savannah. To this place, therefore, the scene of his first conversion, the Indian comes for meditation, and at the end of the poem expresses the hope that he may at last be buried in this hallowed spot:

---

[45] Whitefield first visited Georgia in 1737. For an account of his preaching here, and his other trips to America, cf. Joseph Belcher's *George Whitefield, a Biography, with Special Reference to his Labors in America* (New York, 1757).

[46] Included in his *Poetical Works* (*Shrewsbury*, 1786), p. 39.

And (if 't were blameless to indulge the claim)
  When death propitious hath discharg'd his trust,
Fain would I sleep near this thrice hallow'd stream,
  'Till the last trumpet animates my dust.

Then! Christian, then! the sacred morn shall rise,
  Then, all the kingdoms of the ransom'd come,
Mount up in triumph! through dissolving skies,
  And take possession of their promis'd home.

Here cease my song—for who hath rent the vail?
  Or dar'd to look within the Holy Place?
Enough for us, that Christ will there reveal
  Th' unclouded visions of His lovely face.

A poem by Hildebrand Jacob, called *The Indian,*[47] brings
out, like several others of the same kind, certain more humorous aspects of the missionary's labors, the Indian's naïve
misunderstanding or affected stupidity. A Spanish priest
goes to convert the savage Americans, and is succeeding in
winning a good many to the faith, till one day a 'sly, bold
savage, hard of heart,' questions the rule which requires him
to have only one wife:

    Hold, Father, first I fain, wou'd see,
    Why I, who ever have been free.
    And whom you lord of all declare
    On earth, in water, and in air,
    Shou'd yet be forc'd, to take a wife
    For better, and for worse; for life;
    Keep all the children, she provides;
    Renouncing all the sex besides?
    The Father, staring in his face,
    My son, you yet are void of grace:
    The devil baffles all I say!
    The savage sneer'd, and ran away.

The failure of another missionary to impress his Indian
disciple with the value of the unsubstantial rewards of

[47] Pp. 91-3 in his *Works* (London, 1785).

religion is recorded in a poem of Freneau's, called *The Indian Convert*.[48]   This Indian, who had only been won by a great deal of coaxing and urging, one day asks the minister if the heaven he talks of has liquors in plenty; if so, he decides he will soon put himself down in the heavenly spot:

> You fool (said the preacher) no liquors are there!
> The place I'm describing is most like our meeting,
> Good people, all singing, with preaching and prayer;
> They live upon these without eating or drinking.
>
> But the doors are all locked against folks that are wicked;
> And you, I am fearful, will never get there:—
> A life of repentance must purchase the ticket,
> And few of you, Indians, can buy it, I fear.
>
> Farewell (said the Indian) I'm none of your mess;
> On victuals, so airy, I faintish should feel,
> I cannot consent to be lodged in a place
> Where there's nothing to eat and but little to steal.

The Indian's preference for cider to religion is the subject of another poem called *The Indian Convert,* published in the *American Museum* for 1789 (5. 206).   One of two Indian brothers has been converted to Christianity; the other, who still remains a heathen, notices the favors his brother receives from the whites, and questions him about the reasons for their kindness:

> 'How is it,' quoth he, 'the white folks are so friendly,
> To make you such presents, and treat you so kindly?'
> He answer'd, 'I give them a piece out of scripture,
> And now and then quote them a piece of a chapter;
> This pleases them well, and good cyder they give,
> If you do the same, the same you'll receive.'
> Quoth he to himself, 'So I will if am able,'
> Then getting some names by rote from the bible,

---

[48] First published in the *Time-Piece*, Dec. 11, 1797, under the title, *Thomas Swagum, an Oneida Indian, and a Missionary Parson.*   Cf. Pattee's edition of Freneau's *Poems,* 3. 189.

He went and sat himself down on the floor,
And said, 'Adam, Eve, Cain, the Devil, Job, Koar.'
He was ask'd, with surprise, what he meant by all this?
Quoth he, 'I mean cyder, why could not you guess?'

All such poems are of significance as they tend to show, in a humorous way, the Indian's stupidity in spiritual matters, and the ill-advised zeal of the missionary in attempting his conversion. While there were doubtless many who took the matter of the red man's salvation seriously, there was also a widespread tendency to represent the Indian as either very stupid or naïve, and thus to discredit the whole project.

The love-poems in which the Indian is the centre of interest, though not very numerous, are yet sufficient to show some of his other picturesque qualities. The noble savage, whom we have viewed sometimes in a heroic, sometimes in a pathetic posture, may also be conceived—at least by the poet's fancy—as a creature of varied sentiments, now perhaps tender and delicate, now again lofty or sublime. One of the earliest attempts to picture the Indian in love is associated with the visit of those celebrated chieftains who came to England in the time of Queen Anne. *The Four Indian Kings*,[49] as this piece was called, describes the ardent passion of one of these western monarchs for a very beautiful lady whom he had met in St. James' Park. One of his companions, whom he sends with a diamond ring, urges the fair one to pity her lover's despair—for upon her decision depends his life or death—but the lady is a firm Christian, and replies that not even 'crowns and royal dignity' can tempt her to wed a heathen king.

Of all Indian lovers it is poor, wronged Yarico who makes the greatest appeal to the poet's fancy. Her pathetic tale is recounted in a number of poems of varying length, all

---

[49] A broadside published in 1710. The rarity of this production justifies, we think, our reprinting it entire in an appendix, the text being taken from the copy in The John Carter Brown Library, Providence, R. I.

expressing much the same view.[50]   The element of universal appeal in her situation seems to have been her devotion to a faithless lover, who repaid her kindness with avarice and ingratitude.   Many of these poems merely relate in verse the story as told by Addison.   Others add various fanciful touches.   A very popular form was the epistle from Yarico to Inkle, in which the injured savage begins by rehearsing all the details of her attachment for the white man, and ends by upbraiding, reproaching, denouncing, and perhaps at the same time forgiving, the author of her misfortunes, the object of her love as well as of her hate.   Somewhat more original

---

[50] The following list of poems will give some indication of the popularity of this story.

The Story of Inkle and Yarico, Lond. Mag. 3 (1734). 257. Reprinted in the *Weekly Amusement* for Saturday, June 7, 1766.

The *Lond. Mag.* 5 (1736). 215 contains a poem, referring to this same work, entitled, *To the Author of an Epistle from Yarico to Inkle.*

Yarico's Epistle to Inkle, by John Winstanley, pp. 8-16 of his *Poems* (Dublin, 1751).

Yarico to Inkle, an Epistle, by Edward Jerningham (London, 1766).

Epistle from Inkle to Yarico, Lady's Magazine 13 (1782). 664.

A Poetical Version of the Much-admired Story of Inkle and Yarico, American Museum 11 (1791). 121.

Yarico to Inkle, ibid., p. 125.

An Epistle from Yarico to Inkle, together with their Characters as Related in the Spectator, by Isaac Story, Marblehead [Salem], 1792.

Inkle and Yarico, by Mr. C. Brown (London, 1799), a poem of some fifty-four pages, which the writer has not had opportunity to consult. Cf. *Crit. Rev.* 26. 348.

The story was treated in German by Christian F. Gellert, a translation of whose work appeared in the *Weekly Magazine, or Edinburgh Amusement* 14 (1771). 164-7.

A translation of Salomon Gesner's continuation of the story, in which Inkle repents, and is reunited to Yarico, appeared in the same issue of the *Weekly Magazine,* pp. 197-200.

I have not attempted to trace the story through the nineteenth century, but have found in the *Lady's Magazine* for 1802 several poetic epistles between the two lovers.

is the following slight lyric, in which Yarico laments the impending separation from her lover.[51]

> When night spreads her shadows around,
>   I will watch with delight on thy rest;
> I will soften thy bed on the ground,
>   And thy cheek shall be lodg'd on my breast.
>
> *Love* heeds not the storm nor the rain;
>   On *me* let their fury descend,
> This bosom shall never complain
>   While it shelters the life of a friend.
>
> O tell me what tears thee away?
>   To a *fair one,* ah! wouldst thou depart?
> Alas! to thy Yarico say
>   What maiden will love like this heart?
>
> Though resolv'd not my sorrows to hear;
>   Though resolv'd from a mourner to fly;
> The ocean shall bear thee a tear,
>   And the winds shall convey thee a sigh!

Several other Indian love-poems deserve passing mention at this point. In *The Complaint of Cascarilla,*[52] an Indian maiden expresses her grief for the loss of a lover who has fallen in war. Aside from its lyric beauty, this lament is also of interest for its delicate exotic coloring:

> The fairest cedar of the grove
> Arose less beauteous than my love;
> The pride of all our Indian youth,
> For valour, constancy, and truth.
>
> His eyes were bright as morning dew,
> His lips the Nepal's[53] crimsons hue;

---

[51] Published in *Gent. Mag.* 63 (1793). 560; also in the *Scots Magazine* for the same year, 55. 242.

[52] Published in the *American Museum* 9 (1788). 384; also in the *Massachusetts Magazine* 9 (1792). 327.

[53] The plant on which the cochineal is nourished; its blossoms are of a beautiful red.—Note of author.

His teeth, the silver plume so white
That wings the spotless bird[54] of night.

For me, th' unerring lance he threw,
For me the stedfast bow he drew;
Chac'd the fleet roe thro' mead and wood,
Or lur'd the tenants of the wood.

Mine was the spoil, the trophies mine,
The choicest skins my cot to line;
While for the youth a wreath I wove,
With flow'rs new gather'd from the grove,

But ah! those happy hours are fled;
I weep my dear Panama dead!
The clang of war his bosom fir'd,
He fought—was conquer'd—and expir'd,

Untomb'd—unshelter'd—lo! he lies:
No maid to close his faded eyes,
With flow'rs to deck his mournful bier,
Or greet his ashes with a tear!

There is a unique sort of picturesqueness, and a good deal of playful burlesque, in Joseph Smith's *Indian Eclogue*,[55] which represents a jilted lover standing on the banks of the Ohio, telling 'his sorrows to the gliding flood.' The chiefs, he says, would lead him to war, but he cares not for glory or honor, nor heeds any flame but that of love:

On me their praises and reproofs are lost,
No flame but love, but scorching love I boast,
The nimble Lawrah does my breast inspire,
Wakes every sense, and sets me all on fire;
Enraptur'd while I view her yellow neck,
As soft as bear-grease, and as beaver sleek.
From her grey eyes the living lightnings rush,
Like the fresh dew-drops glitt'ring thro' a bush.
But vain my songs re-echo through the shade,
Nor vows, nor tears, can move the haughty maid.

[54] The American owl, of a delicate white equal to snow.—Note of author.
[55] *Columbian Muse*, pp. 160-1.

Of all these poems, perhaps the most pleasing and graceful is the *Indian Love Song* contained in the *Gentleman's Magazine* for 1793 (63. 1049). The delicate lyric quality is in a way suggestive of Burns, and, if the sentiment and atmosphere suggest little that is peculiar to the American Indian, the beauty of the poem as a whole justifies the citation of it here as the best representation of the idealized lover.

It is interesting to note that the Indian lady celebrated in this piece is called *Imoinda,* after the heroine of Mrs. Behn's *Oroonoko.* Doubtless the writer had read this novel, and found in it the suggestion for his poem—a circumstance which would account for the purely conventional imagery, the lack of any allusions or descriptive touches that would not apply to the idealized savage of almost any clime:

My love is like yon golden ball,
    Nor shews so fair the hillock green;
Her voice is like the water-fall,
    And rich and comely is her mien.

See how her taper waist to meet,
    All bright her jetty ringlets flow;
Nor scuds the flying elk so fleet
    Nor bounds so light the mountain roe!

The pearly oister, from beneath
    The dashing wave, I'll steal for thee;
I'll deck my fair one with a wreath,
    Pluck'd from the spreading plantain-tree.

Sweet is the breath of opening flow'rs,
    Sweetly the birds disport in air;
But sweeter far are ev'ning bow'rs
    When Imoinda meets me there.

Pronounced idealization of the savage as the embodiment of natural goodness, living in a kind of primitive Arcadia, we find expressed in English poetry even as early as Dryden. In his *Conquest of Granada* occur the well-known lines:[56]

[56] Act I, sc. I.

> But know, that I alone am king of me.
> I am as free as nature first made man,
> Ere the base laws of servitude began,
> When wild in woods the noble savage ran.

The glorified state of nature which Dryden seems to place in some far-off, prehistoric time, is more specifically associated with the supposedly uncorrupted regions of the new world in an early eighteenth-century poem called, *Verses on the Prospect of Planting Arts and Learning in America*.[57] In his praise of primitive nature as the abode of those virtues which society has somehow lost, this writer anticipates by about a quarter of a century the expression of similar ideas in the writings of Rousseau:

> The Muse, disgusted at an age and clime
>   Barren of every glorious theme,
> In distant lands now waits a better time,
>   Producing subjects worthy fame:
>
> In happy climes, where from the genial sun
>   And virgin earth such scenes ensue,
> The force of art by nature seems outdone,
>   And fancied beauties by the true:
>
> In happy climes, the seat of innocence,
>   Where nature guides and virtue rules,
> Where men shall not impose for truth and sense
>   The pedantry of schools:
>
> There shall be sung another golden age,
>   The rise of empire and of arts,
> The good and great inspiring epic rage,
>   The wisest and noblest hearts.
>
> Not such as Europe breeds in her decay;
>   Such as she bred when fresh and young,
> When heavenly flame did animate her clay,
>   By future poets shall be sung.

[57] Included among the miscellaneous works of Bishop Berkeley. ed. Fraser (Oxford, 1901) 4. 365-6. Cf. the editor's note concerning date and authorship.

> Westward the course of empire takes its way;
> The first four acts already past,
> A fifth shall close the drama with the day;
> Time's noblest offspring is the last.

The notion of Virtue forsaking England to take up her abode in the new world seems to have appealed to many. Joseph Warton in *The Enthusiast* (1754) expresses a longing to follow in her train to these happy regions.[58]

> O who will bear me then to western climes,
> (Since Virtue leaves our wretched land) to fields
> Yet unpolluted with Iberian swords:
> The isles of Innocence, from mortal view
> Deeply retir'd, beneath a plantane's shade,
> Where Happiness and Quiet sit enthron'd
> With simple Indian swains, that I may hunt
> The boar and tiger through savannahs wild,
> Through fragrant deserts, and through citron groves.

An interesting contrast to this view of American emigration is brought out in Goldsmith's *Deserted Village*. Far from rejoicing in the westward course of empire, the rising civilization of the new world, Goldsmith paints in darkest colors the unhappy lot of those who must forsake sweet Auburn. The wildness of these distant lands he views with aversion, and makes the murderous savage[59] a part of the whole melancholy scene:

> To distant climes, a dreary scene,
> Where half the convex-world intrudes between,
> Through torrid tracts with fainting steps they go,
> Where wild Altama murmurs to their wo.

---

[58] 140-8.

[59] Goldsmith discusses various qualities of the Indian in his *Animated Nature* (London, 1774) 2. 229-230. Though he is inclined to view the Indian as an uncultivated savage possessing certain simple virtues, the picture which accompanies this account shows a good deal of idealization.

> Far different there from all that charm'd before,
> The various terrors of that horrid shore;
> Those blazing suns that dart a downward ray,
> And fiercely shed intolerable day;
> Those matted woods where birds forget to sing,
> But silent bats in drowsy clusters cling;
> Those poisonous fields with rank luxuriance crown'd,
> Where the dark scorpion gathers death around;
> Where at each step the stranger fears to wake
> The rattling terrors of the vengeful snake;
> Where crouching tigers wait their hapless prey,
> And savage men, more murd'rous still than they;
> While oft in whirls the mad tornado flies,
> Mingling the ravaged landscape with the skies.

The sad lot of the emigrant seems to have appealed strongly to Goldsmith's imagination, for in *The Traveller* he gives a similar picture of the ills awaiting those who cross the Atlantic—the tangled forest, the giddy tempest, and the brown Indian who marks the white man 'with murderous aim.'

Yet despite such strictures upon America as those of Goldsmith, many poets celebrate the greater happiness enjoyed by the man of nature. In the mid-eighteenth century, John Winstanley treats this theme in a poem called *The Happy Savage*.[60] With scarce a touch of exotic coloring or picturesque fancy, the poem, in a rather bare sort of way, pictures the contentment to be found in retirement from society, much after the manner in which Addison describes the primitive kind of happiness enjoyed by the African:[61]

> Happy the lonely savage! nor deceiv'd,
> Nor vex'd, nor griev'd, in ev'ry darksome cave,
> Under each verdant shade he takes repose,
> Sweet are his slumbers—of all human arts
> Happily ignorant, nor taught by wisdom,
> Numberless woes, nor polish'd into torment.

[60] First printed in *Gent. Mag.* 2 (1732). 718. Included in this author's poems, pp. 168-9 (Dublin, 1751):
[61] Cf. *Cato* i. 4. 63 ff.

Within the same decade as *The Happy Savage* appeared Gray's *Progress of Poesy*,[62] in one stanza of which he attempts to show the 'extensive influences of poetic genius over the remotest and most uncivilized nations: its connection with liberty, and the virtues that naturally attend on it.'[63] The Muse is represented as cheering not only the 'shivering native's dull abode' in the frozen north, but in the wild forests of South America as well:

> And oft, beneath the od'rous shade
> Of Chili's boundless forests laid,
> She deigns to hear the savage youth repeat,
> In loose numbers wildly sweet,
> Their feather-cinctur'd chiefs, and dusky loves.

This passage is of interest largely for its connection with Gray's much-talked-of romantic sympathies, and the notion which he shared with many others of his age that poetic inspiration was associated with the wildness and freedom of primitive peoples.[64]

In the latter part of the century the virtue of the uncorrupted savage is, as we have seen, brought out in a great variety of ways,[65] one of the most common being in the imaginary speeches of aged chieftains who dwell upon the

---

[62] Finished in 1754. Printed together with *The Bard*, in 1757.

[63] Annotation of the author.

[64] This view of poetic genius he develops more fully in *The Bard*. For a discussion of this whole subject cf. C. B. Tinker's *Nature's Simple Plan*, chap. 3. Cf. also Gray's letter to Brown, Feb. 17, 1763, in which he writes: 'Imagination dwelt many hundred years ago in all her pomp on the cold and barren mountains of Scotland. The truth (I believe) is that without any respect of climates she reigns in all nascent societies of men, where the necessities of life force every one to think and act much for himself.'—*The Letters of Thomas Gray*, ed. Tovey 3. 9.

[65] I am indebted to Professor F. E. Pierce for the reference to a German poem, *Der Wilde*, by J. G. Seume (Eng. tr. in Baskerville's *Poetry of Germany*, p. 145), in which the Indian's hospitality is painted in strong contrast to the incivility of the white man.

simplicity and innocence of their people before the coming of the whites. The vices and artificialities of civilization are also attacked in a poem of Francis Hawling's, called *A Discourse from King Tomo Chichy to his Nephew Prince Tonahohy.*[66] Besides giving his nephew a long discourse on his disapproval of the Europeans and their ways, Tomo Chichy urges him to shun learning and the arts, and be content to live according to the dictates of simple nature. Freneau also treats a somewhat similar theme, much more lightly and fancifully, however, in *The Indian Student, or, Force of Nature.* Shalum, the hero of this poem, is sent to Harvard College at the suggestion of a missionary; but books and lectures cannot take the place of his bow and arrows, nor the love of learning overcome his preference for hunting and fishing:

> No mystic wonders fired his mind;
> He sought to gain no learned degree,
> But only sense enough to find
> The squirrel in the hollow tree.
>
> The shady bank, the purling stream,
> The woody wild his heart possessed,
> The dewy lawn, his morning dream
> In fancy's gayest colours dressed.

Like some of the Indian converts we have encountered, this 'copper coloured boy' finds little to enjoy in his new surroundings: neither the mysteries of religion nor the subtleties of philosophy or science can yield the same contentment as his native woods, whither he at length decides to return:

> Let seraphs gain the bright abode,
> And heaven's sublimest manshions see—
> I only bow to Nature's God—
> The land of shades will do for me. . . .

---

[66] Included in *A Miscellany of Original Poems on Various Subjects,* by Mr. Francis Hawling (London, 1752), pp. 68-107.

> Where Nature's ancient forests grow,
> And mingled laurel never fades,
> My heart is fixed;—and I must go
> To die among my native shades.

The most ambitious of these attempts to idealize the North American Indians occurs in Mrs. Morton's *Ouabi; or, the Virtues of Nature,* a poem in four cantos published at Boston in 1790.[67] Despite its slender claim to remembrance for any outstanding literary merits, Mrs. Morton's verse tale is yet of considerable interest, partly for its attempt to secure native American atmosphere and picturesqueness, partly also for the dubious social moral implied in its conclusion, the changing about of husbands and wives, supposed to be one of the virtues of a people living by the dictates of uncorrupted nature. That the skeptical reader may not question her knowledge of the redskin and his ways, the conscientious Philenia seeks support for her statements by extended citations from the letters of William Penn, and other such sources of authority. The authoress also feels that some sort of explanation or apology is due for the seemingly incredible

---

[67] Mrs. Morton acknowledges that she founded her poem on the prose tale, *Azakia: A Canadian Story,* which appeared in *The American Museum* 6 (1789). 193-9. The story as it appears here, however, was taken from *The Universal Magazine* 62 (1783). 59-63. A French version of the story appeared in the *Spectateur du Nord* (Hamburg, August, 1798) ; and in the *Bibliothèque Britannique de Genève,* May, 1798, under the title, *Azakia and Celario.* For a study of this story in relation to Chateaubriand, cf. a study by F. Baldensperger and J. M. Caree, *Modern Language Review,* 8 (1913). 15-26. L. D. Loshe, in *The Early American Novel,* pp. 67-68, enters upon a discussion of this work in relation to early American fiction. We have already mentioned, in the preceding chapter, James Bacon's play founded on a review of Mrs. Morton's poem. As the writer states in his preface, his only change in the story 'is that of leaving Ouâbi in the arms of his youthful bride, rather than consign him to the cold embraces of the ghastly tyrant; which, as it offers no violence to the moral tendency of the work, will not, I trust, be deemed a deviation of much materiality.'

incident on which the whole story is founded—a European's forsaking society in order to experience the 'truth and god-like justice'[68] of the untutored Indians. 'I am aware,' she remarks in her introduction, 'it may be considered improbable, that an amiable and polished European should attach himself to the persons and manners of an uncivilized people; but there is now a living instance of a like propensity. A gentleman of fortune, born in America, and educated in all the refinements and luxuries of Great Britain, has lately attached himself to a female savage, in whom he finds every charm I have given my Azâkia; and in consequence of his inclination, has relinquished his own country and connections, incorporated himself into the society, and adopted the manners of the virtuous, though uncultivated Indian.'

At the opening of the story we find Celario, who had killed another youth in anger, an exile wandering through the forests of America. One day he hears the piercing cries of an Indian maiden, who, having become the captive of a Huron warrior, is begging her life of the remorseless savage. Celario rushes to the rescue of the unfortunate maiden, who proves to be Azâkia, wife of Ouâbi, the brave Illinois chieftain. Immediately he is struck with the lady's charms:[69]

> Her limbs were straighter than the mountain pine,
> Her hair far blacker than the raven's wing;
> Beauty had lent her form the waving line,
> Her breath gave fragrance to the balmy spring.
>
> Each bright perfection open'd on her face,
> Her flowing garment wanton'd in the breeze,
> Her slender feet the glitt'ring sandals grace,
> Her look was dignity, her movement ease.
>
> With splendid beads her braided tresses shone,
> Her bending waist a modest girdle bound,
> Her pearly teeth outvi'd the cygnet's down—
> She spoke—and music follow'd in the sound.

[68] P. 15.   [69] P. 11.

Then amidst yon Chiefs retire,
Seated round the sacred fire,
Waiting for the warrior-feast,
Let them hail thee as their guest.

Having never before seen a European, Azâkia regards Celario as a deity, and the report of his pistol as his thunder. Instead of playing the part of a deity, however, Celario immediately begins to make love. This gives opportunity to exhibit the superior chastity of the Indian women, who, as the writer states in her annotations, on receiving such attentions are supposed to reply, 'The friend that is before my eyes, prevents my seeing you.' Azâkia, therefore, repulses her would-be lover with the following delicate remonstrance :[70]

> See a graceful form arise!
> Now it fills my ravish'd eyes,
> Brighter than the morning star,
> 'T is Ouâbi, fam'd in war:
> Close before my bosom spread,
> O'er thy presence casts a shade,
> Full on him these eyes recline,
> And his person shuts out thine.

She then leads Celario, 'aw'd by her virtue,' to the Illinois camp, where 'constant truth, and blest Ouâbi reigns.'[71] The generous chieftain receives Celario as a brother, and listens with great concern while the white man describes all the vices of his countrymen which have driven him into this exile. When the Illinois next go forth to attack the Hurons, Celario, who has been adopted and clothed like an Indian, is seen among the other warriors.[72]

> Like white narcissus mid the tulip-bed,
> Or like a swan with peacocks on the plain.

In this enterprise Celario is wounded by an arrow, and carried back to enjoy the tender care of Azâkia. He struggles between reviving love and his duty to the friendly chief, but the wife of Ouâbi refuses all his advances. One day during Ouâbi's absence on a hunting trip, he urges his passion again, and the virtuous Azâkia answers :[73]

[70] P. 13.   [71] P. 13.   [72] P. 12.   [73] Pp. 23-24.

> Does the turtle learn to roam,
> When her mate has left his home?
> Will the bee forsake her hive?
> In the peopled wigwam thrive?
> Can Azâkia ever prove,
> Guardless of Ouâbi's love!

Soon Celario plans to leave his Indian friends, but Ouâbi presses him to remain with Azâkia while he is gone to war. In this second expedition against the Hurons, Ouâbi is taken captive, whereupon Azâkia, fearing his death, and warned, as she imagines, by his appearing to her in a dream, plans to join her husband by committing suicide. Celario persuades her to wait till he finds out if the great chieftain still lives. With a band of brave warriors he then sets out for the Huron country, arriving there just in time to find Ouâbi in the act of singing his death-song at the stake:[74]

> Rear'd midst the war-empurpled plain,
> What Illinois submits to pain!
> How can the glory darting fire
> The coward chill of death inspire!

> The sun a blazing heat bestows,
> The moon midst pensive evening glows,
> The stars in sparking beauty shine,
> And own their flaming source divine.

> Then let me hail th' immortal fire,
> And in the sacred flames expire;
> Nor yet those Huron hands restrain;
> This bosom scorns the throbs of pain.

> No griefs this warrior-soul can bow,
> No pangs contract this even brow;
> Not all your threats excite a fear,
> Nor all your force can start a tear.

[74] P. 37. This song was also printed in the *Scots Magazine* 55 (1793). 503.

> Think not with me my tribe decays,
> More glorious chiefs the hatchet raise;
> Not unreveng'd their sachem dies,
> Not unattended greets the skies.

After a daring rescue by Celario, Ouâbi, perceiving the attachment between the white man and his wife, instead of showing any jealousy, generously offers to give him Azâkia, while he takes in her place Zisma, the intended but unwelcome bride of Celario. But just as the wedding festivities are at their height, shrieks are heard, announcing that the great chief, Ouâbi, is dying. The only explanation for this sudden and unexpected calamity is the savage warrior's superior virtue, which is supposed to prevent his long surviving the humiliation and disgrace of having been a captive. This great nobility of soul also appears in the dying words of him 'whose life was virtue, and whose fate was pain':[75]

> To realms where godlike valour reigns,
> Exempt from ills, and freed from pains,
> Where this unconquer'd soul will shine,
> And all the victor's prize be mine,
> I go—nor vainly shed a tear,
> Ouâbi has no glory here;
> Unfit the Illinois to guide,
> No more dauntless warriors' pride—
> Since as a hapless captive led,
> Rack'd like a slave, he basely bled,
> No haughty Huron e'er shall boast,
> He deign'd to live, when fame was lost.[76]

[75] P. 49.
[76] P. 48.

CONCLUSION

To what conclusion, then, does our survey of American exoticism lead us? Doubtless the most fascinating of our many discoveries in the forgotten pages of historian and romancer is the elusive and even mysterious figure of the noble savage, now the good child of nature, projected against the background of polished society, now a creature of strangeness and wonder, emerging from the darker atmosphere of wildness and horror, with which the experience and the imagination of the European had alike associated him. Yet, despite the richness and variety of the material accumulated—highly significant, in its way, as an indication of the development of exotic sentiment in an 'age of prose and reason'—it is nevertheless necessary to be careful not to exaggerate the importance of a movement which is at most subordinate to the main currents of eighteenth-century thought, or force the evidence to point to some foregone conclusion, some ingenious theory, some novel and striking paradox, calculated to startle rather than convince judicious readers and critics.

For, after all, these many disconnected passages, casual allusions, and scattered productions, in which the Indian is in some way noticed, can hardly in themselves be said to constitute a literary or philosophic movement, although taken with the other impulses of the time—the 'return to nature,' the interest in everything wild, sentimental, or picturesque—they may easily be seen to fall within that large, loose, ill-defined, ill-understood current of thought and feeling, vaguely and often inaccurately characterized by the term romanticism. Hence, while it is seldom possible in any given genre—fiction, drama, or poetry—to trace a continuous and progressive growth of exotic sentiment throughout the century, it is nevertheless clear that there has been some sort of change between the year 1700, let us say, and the decades which mark the close of the century. To take an illustration from the drama, it might with much plausibility be maintained that Sheridan's conception of the Peruvian is as fanciful, extravagant, and essentially unreal as that of Dryden and Davenant, more that a century preceding. Yet, the relative frequency with which the Indian appears in all classes of literature between 1775 and 1800 tends to prove, what is perhaps sufficiently obvious, that the public taste had now come to embrace a number of subjects hitherto scarcely noticed, while literary invention had also in the unexplored forests of America found and appropriated to its own use new and peculiar objects of curiosity, mystery, and wonder.

If the fact that the accumulation of evidence cannot be so arranged as to show a steady and obvious progression from one extreme to another, is, from one point of view, disappointing, the same circumstance should nevertheless suggest, when we survey the century in the large, the extent, variety, and complexity of the whole exotic impulse. Were the interest in the natives of America confined to any one group, school, or coterie of writers, the problem of classifying their opinions would indeed be simple enough; but when we consider that the subject in its entirety extends over three centuries and spreads out over many lands, small matter of surprise it is that the variety of currents, cross currents, and counter currents sometimes seem to confuse the entire issue. Such conceptions of the savage as have one by one been considered are clearly the result of many influences, and, taken together, tend to show how much the whole subject was in the air, how many persons were attracted by its novelty and varied suggestiveness. That the Indian should in the eighteenth century have been viewed from so many sides—scientific, sentimental, philosophic—is but one of the many indications that the age which rejected authority and tradition sought to establish the naturalistic interpretation of life on the basis of as much knowledge as was then attainable.

Remarkable as are these philosophic abstractions evolved from speculation on the supposed state of nature, the student of *belles lettres* cannot fail to be impressed by that singular product of the purely literary imagination, the transformation of the sinister and forbidding savage into the idealized embodiment of picturesqueness, pathos, fortitude, and heroic sentiment.

APPENDIX.

THE FOUR INDIAN KINGS.

PART I.

HOW A BEAUTIFUL LADY CONQUERED ONE OF THE INDIAN KINGS.

Attend unto a true relation,
  Of four Indian Kings of late,
Who came to this Christian nation,
  To report their sorrows great,
Which by France they had sustained
  To the overthrow of trade;
That the seas might be regained,
  Who are come to beg our aid.

Having told their sad condition,
  To our good and gracious queen
With a humble low submission,
  Mixt with a courteous mien,
Noble they were all received
  In bold Britain's royal court.
Many lords and ladies grieved,
  At these Indian kings' report.
Now their message being ended,
  To the queen's great majesty;
They were further befriended
  Of the noble standers by.
With a glance of Britain's glory,
  Buildings, troops, and many things,
But now comes a pressing story,
  Love seiz'd one of these four Indian kings.
Thus, as it was then related,
  Walking forth to take the air,
In St. James's Park there waited
  Troops of handsome ladies fair,
Rich and gaudily attir'd,
  Rubies, jewels, diamond rings.

While he did his pain discover,
  Often sighing to the rest;
Like a broken hearted lover,
  Oft he smote upon his breast.
Breaking forth in lamentation,
  Oh, the pains that I endure!
The young ladies of this nation,
  They are more than mortal sure.
In his language he related,
  How her angel beauty bright,
His great heart had captivated,
  Ever since she appear'd in sight.
Tho' there are some fair and pretty
  Youthful, proper, straight, and tall,
In this Christian land and city,
  Yet she far excels them all,
Were I worthy of her favour,
  Which is much better than gold,
Then I might enjoy for ever,
  Charming blessings manifold.

But I fear she cannot love me,
  I must hope for no such thing:
That sweet saint is far above me,
  Although I am an Indian king.
Let me sign but my petition
  Unto that lady fair and clear:
Let her know my sad condition,
  How I languish under her.
If on me, after this trial,
  She will no eye of pity cast,
But return a flat denial,
  Friends I can but die at last.
If I fall by this distraction,
  Thro' a lady's cruelty;
It is some satisfaction
  That I do a martyr die.
Unto the goddess of great beauty,
  Brighter than the morning day:
Sure no greater piece of duty,
  No poor captive love can pay.

O this fatal burning fever,
  Gives me little hopes of life,
If so that I cannot have her
  For my love and lawful wife.
Bear to her this royal token,
  Tell her 't is my diamond ring;
Pray her that it mayn't be spoken,
  She'll destroy an Indian King.
Who is able to advance her
  In our fine America,
Let me soon receive an answer,
  From her hand without delay.
Every minute seems an hour,
  Every hour six. I'm sure;
Tell her it is in her power
  At this time to kill or cure.
Tell her that you see me ready
  To expire for her sake
And as she is a Christian lady,
  Sure she will some pity take.
I shall long for your returning
  From that pure unspotted cove,
All the while I do lie burning
  Wrapt in scorching flames of love.

Part II.

The lady's answer to the Indian King's request.

I will fly with your petition
  Unto that lady fair and clear,
For to tell your sad condition
  I will to her parents bear.
Show her how you do adore her,
  And lie bleeding for her sake;
Having laid the cause before her,
  She perhaps may pity take.
Ladies that are apt to glory
  In their youthful birth and state,
So hear I'll rehearse the story
  Of their being truely great.

So farewell, sir, for a season,
  I will soon return again:
If she's but endowed with reason,
  Labour is not spent in vain.
Having found her habitation,
  Which with diligence he sought,
Tho' renown'd in her station,
  She was to his presence brought.
Where he labour'd to discover
  How his lord and master lay,
Like a pensive wounded lover,
  By her charms the other day.
As a token of his honour,
  He has sent this ring of gold
Set with diamonds. Save the owner,
  For his griefs are manifold.
Life and death are both depending
  On what answer you can give,
Here he lies your charms commending
  Grant him love that he may live.
You may tell your lord and master,
  Said the charming lady fair,
Tho' I pity this disaster,
  Being catch'd in Cupid's snare
'Tis against all true discretion,
  To comply with what I scorn:
He's a Heathen by profession,
  I a Christian bred and born.
Was he king of many nations,
  Crowns and royal dignity,
And I born of mean relations,
  You may tell him that from me.

As long as I have life and breathing
  My true God I will adore,
Nor will ever wed a Heathen,
  For the richest Indian store.
I have had my education
  From my infant blooming youth,
In this Christian land and nation,
  Where the blessed word and truth
Is to be enjoy'd with pleasure,
  Amongst Christians mild and kind,

Which is more than all the treasure
  Can be had with Heathens wild.
Madam, let me be admitted
  Once to speak in his defence;
If he here then may be pity'd
  Breath not forth such violence.
He and all the rest were telling
  How well they lik'd this place;
And declared themselves right willing
  To receive the light of grace.
So then, lady, be not cruel,
  His unhappy state condole;
Quench the flame, abate the fuel,
  Spare his life, and save his soul.
Since it lies within your power
  Either to destroy or save,
Send him word this happy hour
  That you'll heal the wound you gave.
While the messenger he pleaded
  With this noble virtuous maid,
All the words then she minded
  Which his master he had said.
Then she spoke like one concerned,
  Tell your master this from me,
Let him, let him first be turned
  From his gross Idolatry.
If he will become a Christian,
  Live up to the truth reveal'd,
I will make him grant the question,
  Or before will never yield.
Altho' he was pleased to send me,
  His fine ring and diamond stone,
With this answer pray commend me
  To your master yet unknown.

INDEX